Designing Sustainable and Resilient Cities

This book explores the link between the Food-Water-Energy nexus and sustainability, and the extraordinary value that small tweaks to this nexus can achieve for more resilient cities and communities. Using data from Urban Living Labs in six participating cities (Eindhoven, Gdańsk, Miami, Southend-on-Sea, Taipei, and Uppsala) to co-define context-specific challenges, the results from each city are collated into an Integrated Decision Support System to guide and improve robust decision-making on future urban development.

The book presents contributions from CRUNCH, a transdisciplinary team of scholars and practitioners whose expertise spans urban climate modelling; food, water, and energy management; the design of resilient public space; collecting better urban data; and the development of smart city technology. Whilst previous works on the Food-Water-Energy nexus have focused on large, transnational cases, this book explores local ways to use the Food-Water-Energy nexus to improve urban resilience. It suggests tangible ways in which the cities and communities around us can become both more efficient and more climate resilient through small changes to their existing infrastructure.

Over half of the world's population lives in urban areas, and this is expected to increase to 68% by 2050. We urgently need to make our cities more resilient. This book provides a planning tool for decision-making and concludes with policy recommendations, making it relevant to a range of audiences including urbanists, environmentalists, architects, urban designers, and city planners, as well as students and scholars interested in alternative approaches to sustainability and resilience.

Prof. Alessandro Melis (RIBA, ARB, AoU) took over the role of Principal Investigator of CRUNCH in October 2018, and continued to lead the project until its completion in 2021. He is a Professor of Architecture, and the inaugural IDC Foundation Endowed Chair of New York Institute of Technology. Previously, he was a director of the Cluster for Sustainable Cities at the University of Portsmouth and, prior to this, the Head of Postgraduate Engagement at the School of Architecture and Planning, University of Auckland. Alessandro holds a Master's and a PhD in Architecture and Urban Design from the University of Florence.

Alessandro's specialist teaching, supervisory, and research interests are in the fields of climate-sensitive design, sustainable strategies for urban mutations, environmental policies, radical theories and criticism, resilience, and sustainable conservation. He is also a practising architect and is co-founder and design director of the studio

Heliopolis 21. Alessandro's projects, including the SR1938 Institute of the University of Pisa, Stella Maris Hospital, and the Auditorium of Sant'Anna, have been widely acknowledged as examples of excellence in sustainable design. In recognition of his contribution to architecture and design, in 2020 he was appointed Ambassador of Italian Design by Associazione Disegno Industriale and the Italian Ministry of Foreign Affairs. He was also the curator of the Italian National Pavilion at the 17th Venice Biennale of Architecture.

Dr. Julia Brown, a human geographer, is a Senior Lecturer in Environment and Development and Associate Head of Global Engagement in the School of the Environment, Geography, and Geosciences at the University of Portsmouth, UK. Joining UoP directly following the completion of her PhD at the Institute of Development Policy and Management (IDPM), University of Manchester, UK, Julia also holds a Master's of Research in Environment and Development and a Bachelor's of Science in Geography, both from the Department of Geography, University of Lancaster, UK.

Julia is a qualitative researcher, utilising semi-structured interviews and focus groups to undertake institutional analysis to understand the opportunities and barriers within the organisations charged with managing the environment and adoption of global best practice. Julia's research and consultancy has primarily focused on the field of water resource management in Sub-Saharan Africa and she is Co-I on the JPI Urban Europe (CRUNCH) project. For this book Julia collaborated with colleagues at Southend-on-Sea as it piloted the adoption of the Food-Water-Energy nexus. Collaborating with policymakers and practitioners lies at the heart of Julia's research, which sits at the academic-practitioner interface with a focus on realising policy and practice informing research.

Claire Coulter is a Teaching Fellow in the Operations and Systems Management Group in the Faculty of Business and Law at the University of Portsmouth, UK. She is currently working towards her PhD in Strategy, Enterprise and Innovation, exploring sustainable initiatives in the UK brewing industry. Prior to joining the University of Portsmouth, Claire spent ten years working as a managing editor and project manager in the academic publishing industry. She holds a Master's of Science in Project Management from the University of Portsmouth and a Master's of Studies and Bachelor's of Arts in Medieval and Modern Languages (German) from the University of Oxford.

Claire was the Project Coordinator for CRUNCH, responsible for the overall coordination of the project, as well as supporting the UK team with their research aims. Alongside her work on CRUNCH, Claire was also the Manager of the Portsmouth-based Cluster for Sustainable Cities and managed the expansion of the group to include partners from industry as well as academia. Claire's research uses semi-structured interviews and qualitative comparative analysis to understand the factors which support small urban food and drink businesses to make environmentally sustainable manufacturing decisions. She enjoys working with small businesses, encouraging SMEs to play an active role as partners within transdisciplinary projects, where their cutting-edge skills and expertise both challenge and complement traditional academic research.

Designing Sustainable and Resilient Cities

Small Interventions for Stronger Urban Food-Water-Energy Management

Edited by Alessandro Melis, Julia Brown, and Claire Coulter

NEW YORK AND LONDON

Cover image: AerialPerspective Works

First published 2023
by Routledge
605 Third Avenue, New York, NY 10158

and by Routledge
4 Park Square, Milton Park, Abingdon, Oxon, OX14 4RN

Routledge is an imprint of the Taylor & Francis Group, an informa business

© 2023 CRUNCH Project; selection and editorial matter, Alessandro Melis, Julia Brown, and Claire Coulter; individual chapters, the contributors

The right of Alessandro Melis, Julia Brown, and Claire Coulter to be identified as the authors of the editorial material, and of the authors for their individual chapters, has been asserted in accordance with sections 77 and 78 of the Copyright, Designs and Patents Act 1988.

The project Climate Resilient Urban Nexus CHoices (CRUNCH) was financially supported by the Belmont Forum and the framework of the Joint Programming Initiative Urban Europe, with support from the European Union's Horizon 2020 Research and Innovation Programme under grant agreement No. 730254.

All rights reserved. No part of this book may be reprinted or reproduced or utilised in any form or by any electronic, mechanical, or other means, now known or hereafter invented, including photocopying and recording, or in any information storage or retrieval system, without permission in writing from the publishers.

Trademark notice: Product or corporate names may be trademarks or registered trademarks, and are used only for identification and explanation without intent to infringe.

Library of Congress Cataloging-in-Publication Data
Names: Melis, Alessandro, editor. | Brown, Julia Catherine, editor. | Coulter, Claire (Project coordinator), editor.
Title: Designing sustainable and resilient cities: small interventions for stronger urban food-water-energy management / edited by Alessandro Melis, Julia Brown and Claire Coulter.
Description: New York, NY: Routledge, 2022. | Includes bibliographical references and index.
Identifiers: LCCN 2021058550 (print) | LCCN 2021058551 (ebook) | ISBN 9780367631987 (hardback) | ISBN 9780367631970 (paperback) | ISBN 9781003112495 (ebook)
Subjects: LCSH: Sustainable urban development. | City planning—Environmental aspects.
Classification: LCC HT241 .D4698 2022 (print) | LCC HT241 (ebook) | DDC 307.1/416—dc23/eng/20220103
LC record available at https://lccn.loc.gov/2021058550
LC ebook record available at https://lccn.loc.gov/2021058551

ISBN: 978-0-367-63198-7 (hbk)
ISBN: 978-0-367-63197-0 (pbk)
ISBN: 978-1-003-11249-5 (ebk)

DOI: 10.4324/9781003112495

Typeset in Bembo Std
by Apex CoVantage, LLC

Contents

CRUNCH contributors	xi
Preface	xv
Steffen Lehmann	
Introduction	1
Julia Brown, Claire Coulter, and Alessandro Melis	
PART I: Urban Living Laboratories	7
1.0 Introducing the CRUNCH Urban Living Labs	9
Claire Coulter	
1.1 Eindhoven: Brainport Smart District: A circular economy experiment	10
Maryam Ghodsvali, Gamze Dane, and Bauke de Vries	
1.2 Gdańsk: Urban Initiative Laboratory	12
Joanna Bach-Głowińska, Karolina Krośnicka, Jacek Łubiński, and Joanna Tobolewicz	
1.3 Miami: Data-driven planning and scenario tools	16
Thomas Spiegelhalter	
1.4 Southend-on-Sea: Green infrastructure for climate resilience	19
Claire Coulter	

1.5 Taipei: Sustainable management for wastescapes: A Food-Water-Energy nexus experiment — 21

Mei-Hua Yuan, Pei-Te Chiueh, Yu-Sen Chang, Hsin-hsin Tung, Chang-Ping Yu, Hwong-wen Ma, and Shang-Lien Lo

1.6 Uppsala: Groundwater management in the neighbourhood of Rosendal — 24

Vera van Zoest, Edith Ngai, Shashank Shekher Tripathi, and Archit Suryawanshi

PART II: Food-Water-Energy nexus findings — 26

2. The urban living lab as an adaptive governance mechanism for the transdisciplinary Food-Water-Energy nexus: Lessons learned from six local contexts — 27

Maryam Ghodsvali, Gamze Dane, and Bauke de Vries

3. Urban greening snakes and ladders: A case study of the practical realities of implementing Food-Water-Energy nexus projects in Southend-on-Sea, UK — 59

Heather Rumble and Julia Brown

4. Capacity: Transforming challenges into opportunities — 87

Joanna Bach-Głowińska, Jacek Łubiński, and Joanna Tobolewicz

5. Data and knowledge supporting decision-making for the urban Food-Water-Energy nexus — 97

Mei-Hua Yuan, Joanna Bach-Głowińska, Pei-Te Chiueh, Yu-Sen Chang, Hsin-hsin Tung, Chang-Ping Yu, Hwong-wen Ma, Jacek Łubiński, and Shang-Lien Lo

6. Development of an integrated decision support system (IDSS) — 119

Vera van Zoest, Edith Ngai, Shashank Shekher Tripathi, and Archit Suryawanshi

7. Genetic Food-Water-Energy nexus design research for Miami's Greater Islands: Climate Resilient Urban Nexus CHoices (CRUNCH) – scripting and coding AI-MLs — 139

Thomas Spiegelhalter, Levente Juhász, and Srikanth Namuduri

8. The role of Digital Twins in the CRUNCH project   159
Chris Cooper and Claire Coulter

Conclusion   181
Julia Brown, Claire Coulter, and Alessandro Melis

Index   191

CRUNCH contributors

Joanna Bach-Głowińska is an Adjunct in the Department of Urban Design and Regional Planning at the Gdańsk University of Technology, leading the Urban Initiative Laboratory focused on Smart Cities. Her recent research concentrates on the Patterns of Creativity – the implementation of the algorithm model that she created for cities on Creativity Actions Probability.

Julia Brown is a qualitative human geographer and Senior Lecturer in environment and development in the Department of Geography at the University of Portsmouth, with a particular focus on sustainable rural water resource management in Sub-Saharan Africa.

Yu-Sen Chang is Professor for Horticulture and Landscape Architecture, National Taiwan University, and Director of the Urban Agriculture Research Center, which works across urban greening, urban farming, and human health and wellbeing.

Pei-Te Chiueh is Professor of Graduate Institute of Environmental Engineering, National Taiwan University. Her research interests lie in quantifying the impact of multi-scale environmental challenges and waste recovery technologies.

Chris Cooper is CTO of KnowNow Information, and an expert in Smarter Cities. He is an award-winning innovator and transport geek, with a background in large-scale enterprise architecture, and systems design and operations.

Claire Coulter is a Teaching Fellow in project management at the University of Portsmouth. She is the Project Coordinator for CRUNCH, and her research explores strategies for encouraging environmentally sustainable behaviour in urban SMEs.

Gamze Dane is an Assistant Professor at the Urban Systems and Real Estate Unit of Eindhoven University of Technology. Her expertise is on urban planning, geographical information systems, urban informatics, and human-environment interactions.

Maryam Ghodsvali is a PhD candidate in the Built Environment Department, Eindhoven University of Technology. Her main research foci are co-design initiatives and the design and implementation of transdisciplinary decision-making processes via digital tools.

Levente Juhász is a Florida International University GIS Center Researcher and works on the CRUNCH IDSS-app. He held visiting positions in Italy and Austria and worked before as a data scientist for geospatial start-ups. He has expertise in geospatial big data analysis and modelling, spatial statistics, computation, and advanced web technologies.

Karolina Krośnicka is an Associate Professor at the Department of Urban Design and Regional Planning, Faculty of Architecture, Gdańsk University of Technology. Her current research interests concentrate on the theory of urban dynamics, port-city spatial relations, spatial planning of coastal regions, and redevelopment of post-industrial areas.

Steffen Lehmann is a tenured full Professor of Architecture and former Director of schools of architecture, including the UNLV School of Architecture in Las Vegas. Previously, Steffen was the chair-holder of the UNESCO Chair for Sustainable Urban Development for the Asia-Pacific Region, a professor at the University of Portsmouth, and is the founding PI and creator of the CRUNCH research project.

Shang-Lien Lo is a Distinguished Professor at the Graduate Institute of Environmental Engineering, National Taiwan University. His research interests include water and wastewater treatment; microwave-induced technologies; environmental nanomaterials reduction and recycling of heavy metal-containing sludge; soil and groundwater pollution control; and sustainable development indictors.

Jacek Łubiński is a Professor of Mechanical Engineering at the Gdańsk University of Technology. His research interests include machine design, mechanical design, tribology and tribometrology, tribometer development, mechanical engineering experiment design, forensic engineering, mechanical failure analysis, 3D printing, polymer technology, CAD, FEM, electronics in mechanical applications, and vice versa.

Hwong-wen Ma teaches at the Graduate Institute of Environmental Engineering, National Taiwan University. His research focuses on the development of integrated environmental assessment methods for depicting transition paths to sustainability.

Alessandro Melis is an Italian architect and the curator of the Italian National Pavilion at the 17th Venice Biennale. He is also a professor of architecture, and the inaugural IDC Foundation endowed chair of the New York Institute of Technology.

Srikanth Namuduri was a Florida International University senior data scientist working on the Food-Water-Energy (FWE) nexus for the City of Miami, South Miami, and Miami Beach. He brings several years of experience in data analysis, machine learning, deep learning, the Internet of Things, and Systems Engineering.

Edith Ngai is an Associate Professor in the Department of Electrical and Electronic Engineering, The University of Hong Kong. Before that, she was an Associate Professor at Uppsala University, Sweden. Her research interests include Internet of Things, mobile computing, machine learning, and data analytics for smart cities.

Heather Rumble is a Senior Lecturer in the School of the Environment, Geography and Geosciences at the University of Portsmouth. She is an urban ecologist, specialising in green infrastructure and urban greenspaces.

Thomas Spiegelhalter is a global expert on Sustainability and is the Co-Director of the Structures and Environmental Technologies Lab at Florida International University-Architecture. He has conducted awarded research in Europe, Asia, Africa and the Americas on numerous carbon-neutral realisations projects, and large-scale sustainability master planning.

Archit Suryawanshi, Uppsala University, was a project assistant in the Uppsala CRUNCH team, aiding with the development of the Integrated Decision Support System, in particular the back-end and deployment of the web portal on the UU cloud.

CRUNCH contributors

Joanna Tobolewicz is the former Plenipotentiary of the Mayor of Gdańsk for Energy. She has been involved in creating Gdańsk's energy policy, exploring ways to reduce greenhouse gas emissions and pollution and increase the uptake of renewable energy sources, as well as other projects in smart cities in the area of smart solutions in municipal energy.

Shashank Shekher Tripathi was a project assistant in the Uppsala CRUNCH team, assisting with the development of the Integrated Decision Support System, in particular the front-end of the web portal.

Hsin-hsin Tung is a Professor in the Graduate Institute of Environmental Engineering at National Taiwan University. Her research interests include disinfection and disinfection byproducts, biological water and wastewater treatment, microbial ecology, and microbial source tracking.

Bauke de Vries is professor for Information Systems in the Built Environment, and scientific board member of the Smart Cities programme at the Eindhoven University of Technology. Bauke's areas of expertise are systems engineering, city information modelling, and process modelling. Recently, he has been deeply involved in Smart Cities research and development.

Chang-Ping Yu is a Professor in the Graduate Institute of Environmental Engineering at National Taiwan University. His research focuses on environmental biotechnology for wastewater treatment, bioremediation, biodegradation of emerging contaminants, microbial fuel cells, microalgae, anaerobic digestion, and membrane bioreactors.

Mei-Hua Yuan is an Assistant Research Fellow at the research center for environmental changes, ACADEMIA SINICA. She continues to have a strong interest in the sustainability of coupled human-natural systems grounded in empirical evidence and topics like ecosystem services assessment, ecological economics, and Food-Water-Energy nexus.

Vera van Zoest is a postdoctoral researcher at the Information Technology department of Uppsala University, Sweden. She has a background in spatial planning, geo-information science, and spatio-temporal statistical modelling of environmental variables in smart cities.

Preface

How the urban nexus will make your city more resource efficient

Steffen Lehmann

The way that cities are conceived, planned and managed does not always recognise the interconnections between the different systems they run on. But this must change if we are to address future challenges. The Food-Water-Energy nexus is an opportunity to make cities more resource efficient.

Great cities are not always practical or efficient; they can be romantic, grandiose, multi-layered and poetic places. However, in the light of climate change, population growth, resource depletion, and political insecurity, they must also increasingly become resource-efficient and resilient spaces if they are to have a future in our rapidly changing world.

Cities can be compared to a greedy living organism. They require constant sustenance in the form of resources such as water or energy, and they produce waste, which needs to be carefully managed if it is not to cause health and environmental issues.

For example, traditional methods of producing our food require considerable amounts of both water and energy, which may not be used for other purposes, resulting in water and power shortages and producing waste and pollution. As the global population exceeds 7.5 billion, an increasing number of cities around the world are looking for new ways of thinking and solutions to solve the growing challenges of food supply, water and energy management.

The visible structure of any city is laid out by its pattern of streets, boulevards, parklands, and building blocks, and its network of public spaces, waterfronts, gardens, squares, and infrastructural systems. But much of the infrastructure remains invisible (both actually and metaphorically), underground and out of date.

Preface

Our increasing demand for food, water and energy often exceeds the capabilities of any one city, region, or government. A collaborative approach is required to meet these demands and develop better integrated approaches to food, water and energy management.

A 'nexus' is a focal point that bundles together a series of connections and links, such as a system of urban infrastructure. Cities have often been called 'systems of systems', and we are starting to have a better understanding of the ways in which the sectors within a city are interdependent and interconnected.

This is called urban nexus thinking, and we believe that using this will help cities to better understand the interrelated and complex systems where energy, water, food and waste systems intersect.

The CRUNCH (Climate Resilient Urban Nexus CHoices) project takes food, water and energy as one complex system, leading to increased knowledge and discoveries that cannot emerge when these areas are investigated separately in 'silos'.

The CRUNCH project aimed to help cities solve the increasing challenges of food, water and energy management by using an integrated approach to facilitate decision-making, and by learning from city to city. The project aimed to identify and leverage untapped resource potential revealed through the interdependencies between food, water, and energy, resulting in the potential for increased resource efficiency.

CRUNCH's potential nexus solutions include urban food production with renewable energy systems through biomass (anaerobic digestion using organic waste) – that is, holding, cleaning and draining water naturally through an integrative and systemic ecological approach combined with sustainable storage solutions and urban drainage (reducing flood risk).

After looking at case studies in six very different participating cities – Southend-on-Sea, Miami, Taipei, Eindhoven, Gdańsk and Uppsala – the innovative and practical element of the project was the development of a new Integrated Decision Support System (IDSS) and visualisation models (please refer to diagram below) which will help planners make more informed decisions for the sustainable future of cities.

It uses expert and lay knowledge in waste, food, water and energy management and urban planning, mobility, architecture, and governance, which we believe will increase resource efficiency by over 10 per cent. In real-life terms, this means for the residents of these cities that there is less waste generation, better air quality, and lower CO_2 emissions, resulting in an enhanced quality of life for all.

After accounting for trade-offs, the synergies and benefits would widely outweigh the effort to reconfigure, renew or retrofit the existing infrastructural systems. Taking a nexus approach and basing decisions on the IDSS will, initial research indicates, result in considerable potential savings which can be invested in social and health programmes, which will make cities healthier and happier spaces to live and work.

There are numerous reasons to increase the resource efficiency of cities and to reduce the environmental impact on natural resources in a world with growing populations and consumption. One reason is resource productivity, which also improves the competitiveness of cities, as higher resource efficiency is likely to deliver environmental, economic and resource benefits.

As indicated, it may also result in considerable positive social and health outcomes. The researchers suggest that if one can scale up this way of thinking and approach for city planning, it could lead to new ways to meet the resource challenges of the

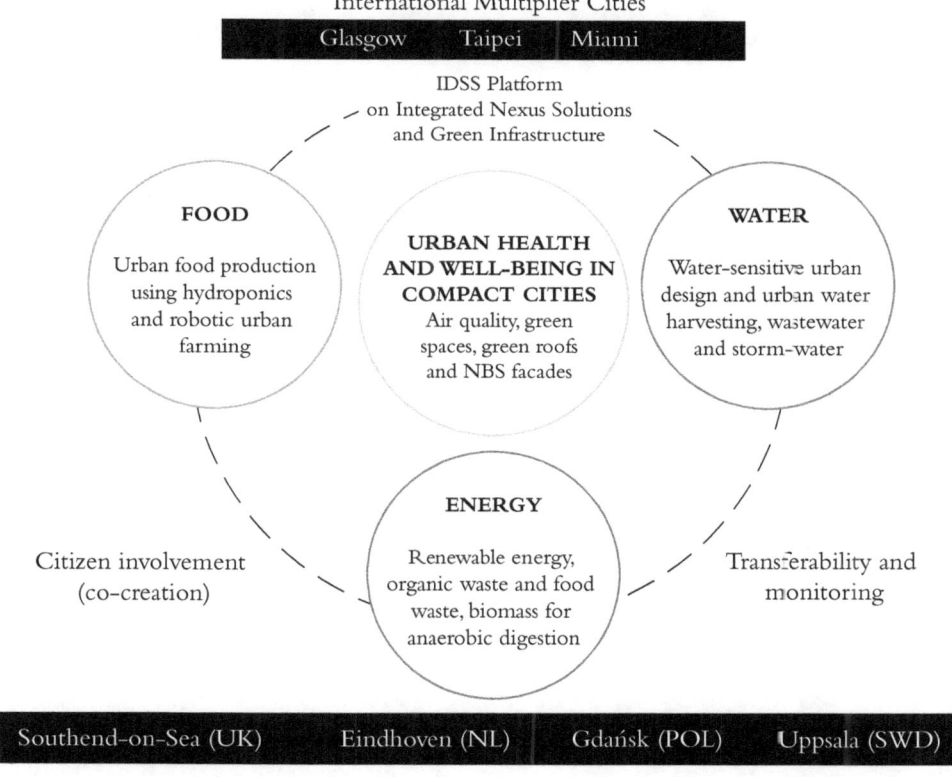

Figure 0.1: Case studies in six participating cities – Southend-on-Sea, Miami, Taipei, Eindhoven, Gdańsk and Uppsala are examined (Lehmann, 2017)

Preface

future. It also presents a practical way to operationalise sustainable development by helping to decouple resource use from economic growth.

Rethinking infrastructural systems will be one of the major urban challenges for the coming decades. The urban nexus is still an emerging concept, requiring more testing in cities, which the CRUNCH project has begun to do.

Dr. Steffen Lehmann, Professor of Architecture at the
University of Nevada, Las Vegas
He was the initiator of the CRUNCH project in 2016

Introduction

Julia Brown, Claire Coulter, and Alessandro Melis

Over half of the world's population lives in urban areas, and this is expected to increase to 68% by 2050. Urbanisation, the changing pattern of human residence from rural to urban areas, combined with global population growth, could add another 2.5 billion people to urban areas by 2050 (UN DESA, 2018). This growing concentration of people within cities, along with changing lifestyle preferences, means that urban areas are placing increasing demands on ecosystems to provide for their water, food (accounting for 70% of freshwater withdrawals) and energy needs (FAO, 2014). At the same time, many cities are experiencing problems of environmental degradation and resource scarcity, and more broadly, our cities are facing increased pressure from the effects of climate change. Changing weather patterns and increased temperatures are already influencing our cities, contributing towards drought, flooding, fatal heatwaves and an increase in natural disasters such as hurricanes (Hunt & Watkiss, 2011; Bulkeley, 2012; While & Whitehead, 2013). The UN stresses that we must focus on sustainable urbanisation that appreciates and balances the three pillars of sustainable development – economic, social and environmental – whilst also being inclusive and equitable (UN DESA, 2018).

The central argument of this collection is the urgent need to make our cities more resilient and flexible to meet the sustainability challenges of the future, as well as to develop viable and healthy places in which to work and live. As 2020 has shown, we should never be confident of predicting what these challenges are going to be in advance. In terms of climate change resilience, the Food-Water-Energy (FWE) nexus is one of the approaches that has been advocated. Food-Water-Energy interactions are, today, of fundamental interest for the political and scientific community, as well as society in general, and will be, even more so, in the coming decades.

In recognition of the fragmented status of research and expertise on the Food-Water-Energy nexus, as well as the dearth of attributable impacts of research on policy, the Belmont Forum and Joint Programming Initiative Urban Europe established the international transdisciplinary initiative Sustainable Urbanisation Global Initiative (SUGI) in 2017 to develop new and impactful innovative solutions to nexus challenges. The CRUNCH project was one of 15 beneficiaries of SUGI funding and specifically aimed to influence the strategic choices of decision makers.

The Climate Resilient Urban Nexus CHoices (CRUNCH) project (2018–2021) was designed to test the contribution that nexus thinking could make towards strengthening urban resilience. To do this, Urban Living Labs (ULLs) – fixed sites with opportunities to experiment and learn from real-time innovations (Marvin et al., 2018) – were established in six participating cities – Eindhoven (the Netherlands), Gdańsk (Poland), Uppsala (Sweden), Southend-on-Sea (UK), Miami (USA) and Taipei (Taiwan) – to co-define context-specific challenges. The results from each city were collated into an Integrated Decision Support System, to guide and improve robust decision-making on future urban development. The choice of locations and contexts supports the call of Marvin et al. (2018) to have more ULLs in diverse national and international settings, with the aim of transdisciplinary international knowledge exchange.

CRUNCH also aimed to demonstrate how the FWE nexus can strengthen urban metabolism and resilience through the creation of an interconnected knowledge platform with intersectoral indicators, an Integrated Decision Support System (IDSS), to be used as a support tool and an assessment framework, to guide the decision-making process, regardless of the scale and location of the intervention. The aspiration is, in fact, to ensure an integrated approach to facilitate decision-making and learning from city to city.

The difference in scale and objectives of the six urban living labs in the partner cities, even within the nexus objectives, has strengthened the need for versatile and transferable tools for decision-making and strategic processes. The ambition to solve the growing urban challenges surrounding the coordinated management of food, water and energy could therefore be transferable to other strategic and ecological objectives, through the integration of the indicators used for the IDSS platform.

The six case study cities that underpin the project range in size from 170,000 inhabitants to 2.7 million and cover three continents. Consequently, this book aims to appeal to a global audience, with take-home lessons for cities on a range of different scales. The different locations and climate challenges faced by each of the case

Introduction

study cities fed into the IDSS, allowing other cities worldwide to find a range of FWE nexus solutions which are applicable to them.

This book presents contributions from CRUNCH, a transdisciplinary team of scholars and practitioners whose expertise spans urban climate modelling; food, water and energy management; the design of resilient public space; collecting better urban data; and the development of smart city technology. Whilst previous works on the Food-Water-Energy nexus have focused on large, transnational cases, CRUNCH explores local ways to use the Food-Water-Energy nexus to improve urban resilience. It suggests tangible ways in which the cities and communities around us can become both more efficient and more climate resilient through small changes to their existing infrastructure.

The structure of book

This book is structured in two parts. Part I provides short descriptions of each of the six cities and the Urban Living Lab (ULLs) sites, providing a context for the interventions that were then piloted.

Part II focuses on the nexus findings from the interdisciplinary teams, with the first four chapters in this section providing reflections on the experiences of ULLs and yielding useful lessons for practitioners. These four chapters also help progress academic discussions on the nexus approach, resilience and ULLs.

Chapter 2, by the Eindhoven team (Maryam Ghodsvali, Gamze Dane, Bauke de Vries), focuses on urban communities, which are described as being the end users of urban developments and services. The Eindhoven ULL was co-designed by the case study community, a small, relatively homogenous group of end users. The central argument of the chapter is the need for clarity over how ULLs may usefully be integrated within the structures of local government. Learning outcomes from the chapter include the challenges of engaging end users in nexus thinking and of integrating them into local government structures. The chapter also usefully draws upon the experiences from other ULLs on engagements and establishing holistic approaches and transdisciplinary teams. The research and stakeholder engagement across the ULLs by the Eindhoven researchers was instrumental in the development of the IDSS, discussed in the Uppsala chapter.

In Chapter 3, "Urban greening snakes and ladders: A case study of the practical realities of implementing Food-Water-Energy nexus projects in Southend-on-Sea, UK", Heather Rumble and Julia Brown focus on the practical realities of implementing nexus urban greening projects in a UK coastal commuter city. The chapter details the challenge of trying to match the CRUNCH project goals to a funded project with an infrastructure budget, and the difficulties of aligning timescales and focus. CRUNCH was able to align to SoS's Cool Towns project, which developed, with input from the CRUNCH UK team, a proposal for the installation of raised Zero Mass Water panels that convert air into water which could then be used to irrigate edibles, whilst also providing shaded areas to help combat urban heat stress. The SoS project was one of the few ULLs that attempted to integrate all three FWE elements into a single pilot. The project still faced barriers, which the chapter details. To contextualise the findings, the authors conducted expert interviews with practitioners in the UK, Netherlands and Germany in order to provide a set of conclusions that will be of use to practitioners and academics; notably, the importance of communication to overcome silos within local government, financing and maintenance budgets, and the value of slow incremental approaches, what the authors term 'greening by stealth'.

Whilst all the partners were impacted by Covid, the city of Gdańsk was still reeling from the public assignation of their major site in January 2019. Chapter 4, written by Joanna Bach-Głowińska, Jacek Łubiński and Joanna Tobolewicz, provides an overview of the initial development of their ULL, 'Nexus Square', in a business park before the project faced the twin challenges of the aftermath of the assignation and then Covid 19. During the pandemic, the ULL was commandeered and repurposed as a diagnostic laboratory, and the team saw their project derailed. However, what this chapter demonstrates is how the team was able to transform these challenges into potential learning opportunities. The project highlights the need for more consideration over upscaling of projects and the need for greater stakeholder inclusion. These are lessons that are broadly applicable to all FWE projects.

In Chapter 5, "Data and knowledge supporting decision-making for the urban Food-Water-Energy nexus", our Taipei colleagues (Mei-Hua Yuan, Pei-Te Chiueh, Yu-Sen Chang, Hsin-hsin Tung, Chang-Ping Yu, Hwong-wen Ma, and Shang-Lien Lo), with input from the Gdańsk team (Joanna Bach-Głowińska and Jacek Łubiński), have written a bridging chapter between the proceeding ULL-focused chapters and the resulting data and knowledge which fed into the development of the IDSS that will help to support decision-making at governmental level. The Taipei chapter makes the case, already raised in the previous chapters, for an inclusive approach to city planning: urban environmental problems are no longer the exclusive realm of experts, they need the participation of different stakeholder groups. There is a recognition that to facilitate more inclusive planning a platform is needed to bring together different sectors to utilise and integrate nexus approaches into city plans. The chapter argues that ULLs can assist planners to evaluate the fit of solutions to specific challenges in a structured manner through the identification of indicators and testing scenarios across time. From a comprehensive literature review, the Taipei team developed a framework comprising three categories (research and development; testing and implementation and, finally, knowledge and communication), which is usefully presented as a model which used CRUNCH partner cities to ensure the framework was applicable to a range of cities.

The book then provides, in the remaining three more technically orientated chapters, before the concluding chapter, an overview of the development process of the CRUNCH IDSS.

The Uppsala team (Vera van Zoest, Edith Ngai, Shashank Shekher Tripathi, Archit Suryawanshi) led the CRUNCH work package to develop the IDSS; the successful launch of which is the major contribution of the project. The CRUNCH IDSS represents a unique attempt to unite the FWE nexus into a single decision support tool for city planners, with the benefit of transferability: as new ULLs can be subsequently added to further strengthen the broader applicability of the IDSS. Chapter 6, "Development of an Integrated Decision Support System (IDSS)", details how the Uppsala team were able to draw upon data from the six ULLS to help the development of the IDSS. The chapter walks the reader through the development stages of the IDSS: the model base for FWE followed by the input parameters for the model. The chapter then explores the user interface, which allows the user to interact with the model. The model allows planners to envisage self-sufficiency conditions in terms of food, water and energy, with a climate scenario calculated for 2030.

While Miami has been the beneficiary of funding to mitigate against the effects of climate change, Thomas Spiegelhalter, Levente Juhász, and Srikanth Namuduri, the authors of Chapter 7 "Genetic Food-Water-Energy nexus design research for Miami's Greater Islands: Climate Resilient Urban Nexus CHoices (CRUNCH) – scripting and coding AI-MLs", argue that Miami's sustainability master plans are not yet carbon neutral: the Miami team promotes carbon neutrality as the route to urban resilience in the face of sea level rise. The Miami ULL is virtual in that it utilises different city-wide carbon scenarios to develop an IDSS app – a digital geomap-based platform designed for a wide variety of users to appreciate the possible flooding inundation outcomes on the city between 2018 and 2100. The chapter details the development of the IDSS app, its application and types of data used, and the user interface.

The third more technically orientated chapter, Chapter 8 "The Role of Digital Twins in the CRUNCH project", has been written by a CRUNCH practitioner partner, Chris Cooper of KnowNow Information, and Claire Coulter. It is forward-looking and discusses the importance of Digital Twins and standards for interoperability and ease of knowledge transfer. The chapter not only outlines the growing role that Digital Twins are playing in urban development projects but also the vital role of developing and adhering to standards and standard operating principles in order to maximise the value of the data that underpins our Digital Twins. It reminds us that data is not only valuable at the point of making a key decision, but through good management our historical data from projects such as the ULLs can help to show what worked and what didn't, and help to inform and shape decisions that take place well beyond the end of our project's lifetime.

The final chapter summarises the key learning outcomes from the different chapters and the CRUNCH project, and the impact of the project going forward to promoting the agenda of urban resilience through nexus approaches.

References

Bulkeley, H. (2012). *Cities and climate change*. Routledge: London. https://doi.org/10.4324/9780203077207

FAO. (2014). The Water-Energy-Food Nexus. A new approach in support of food security and sustainable agriculture. *Rome The Food and Agricultural Organisation of the United Nations*. http://www.fao.org/3/bl496e/bl496e.pdf

Hunt, A., & Watkiss, P. (2011). Climate change impacts and adaptation in cities: A review of the literature. *Climatic Change, 104*, 13–49. https://doi.org/10.1007/s10584-010-9975-6

Marvin, S., Bulkeley, H., Mai, L., McCormick, K., & Voytenko Palgan, Y. (2018). *Urban Living Labs: Experimenting with city futures*. Routledge: London.

Sukhwani, V., Shaw, R., Kumer Mitra, B., & Yan, W. (2019). Optimizing Food-Energy-Water (FEW) nexus to foster collective resilience in urban-rural systems. *Progress in Disaster Science, 8*, 10012. https://doi.org/10.1016/j.pdisas.2019.100005

UN. (2018). Revision of World Urbanization Prospects. *Population Division of the UN Department of Economic and Social Affairs*. https://population.un.org.wup/Publications/Files/WUP2018-KeyFacts.pdf

While, A., & Whitehead, M. (2013). Cities, urbanisation and climate change. *Urban Studies, 50*(7), 1325–1331. https://doi.org/10.1177/0042098013480963

PART I
URBAN LIVING LABORATORIES

Chapter 1.0

Introducing the CRUNCH Urban Living Labs

Claire Coulter

Although climate change is affecting every community, around the world different cities are facing their own unique climate-driven challenges. These challenges may be driven by location (e.g. coastal, on a river, inland), by access to resources (e.g. changes in food harvests, access to water), or by other social, political or economic factors. Despite the differences in the challenges facing each city, under the surface, the links between food, water and energy are an important constant, and trade-offs connected to food shortages, a lack of water, and insufficient energy resources underpin many of the most significant issues facing urban municipalities worldwide.

Six cities were partners in the CRUNCH project, each hosting an Urban Living Lab (ULL) – a location within the city to use as a test bed for piloting climate-resilient strategies – taking advantage of the Food-Water-Energy (FWE) nexus. One of the key aims for CRUNCH was to co-define context-specific challenges for each of the ULLs in the participating cities. In the section which follows, each of the six urban sites is described, outlining the specific climate challenges faced by that particular location and the strategies implemented to mitigate against them.

The six sites not only vary in their geographic location but also in their size, their scope, and ultimately their success. The data collected from each site was vital for constructing the CRUNCH Integrated Decision Support System, which we hope provides a model for urban planners and other interested parties in working out the potential for making similar interventions in their own cities. More than this, however, we hope that the practical lessons learnt from our shared experience of implementing six different ULLs in a very short (and volatile) period will help others who wish to experiment and improve the urban resilience of their own communities.

DOI: 10.4324/9781003112495-3

Chapter 1.1

Eindhoven: Brainport Smart District

A circular economy experiment

Maryam Ghodsvali, Gamze Dane, and Bauke de Vries

For several years, Eindhoven, located in the south Netherlands, has been facing severe climate-related issues, including flooding, heat stress, air pollution, and a decrease in biodiversity. Such critical issues for the city have been exacerbated by climate change and rapid population growth. The rapid population growth in recent years has also led to the disruption of balanced natural resource consumption, which has had detrimental consequences for the urban environment and quality of life. For the City, maintaining such human-nature integration, with the demanding challenges that come with it, depends heavily on human activities.

Since 2010, Eindhoven has furthered the cause of socio-ecological integrity through a political restructuring direction that organises respective actors to work cooperatively. In practice, with a vision of integrated blue (water), green (flora), and grey (built environment) infrastructure, Eindhoven has mobilised the creative power of quintuple helix parties, including government industry, academia, citizens, and nature all together. Citizens have been challenged to discuss the ecological problems within their district and organise the exchanges with potential suppliers providing solutions to the problem posed. Such a governance approach is an essential vehicle for achieving the desired cross-sectoral and transdisciplinary synergies among humans and nature.

Brainport Smart District (BSD), an adaptive urban ambition, has been designed to realise Eindhoven's desired development policy. The ambition is to realise a sustainable, circular, and socially cohesive neighbourhood that benefits from joint food production, water management, energy generation, joint digital data management, and revolutionary transport systems. It will be an attractive living environment where self-sufficiency, organic development, and co-creation with end-users are paramount, and man's collaboration with nature and its resources are combined with technology. BSD's distinctive character is the application of the latest technologies and knowledge. Over the next ten years, 1,500 new houses and 12 hectares of business park will be built in BSD based on the needs of people living and working in the area.

Regarding the joint food, water, and energy management, the starting point was mapping the demand of the future residents of Brainport Smart District. Therefore, BSD has made an initial estimate of water, food, and energy consumption. It is crucial for BSD to design a system with low energy demand and minimisation of the use of raw materials. As soon as the demand for raw materials has been limited as much as possible, it is time to look at the exchange of residual flows. For example, if a building or sewer produces residual heat, it would be ideal for storing that heat and using it on site. It is especially important to take into account locally available resources (such as rainwater or heat from local water bodies) and raw materials. Once the possibilities for synergy have been exhausted, it is time to look at how the remaining demand can be met with clean, renewable, and otherwise environmentally friendly sources. Local resources are preferable, as their impact is usually smaller, and efficiency is higher. It is also important to collect feedback on how the system works so that neighbourhoods can function optimally. This iterative feedback system includes measuring performance and having a transparent information network to keep the system running properly and efficiently.

Chapter 1.2

Gdańsk

Urban Initiative Laboratory

Joanna Bach-Głowińska, Karolina Krośnicka, Jacek Łubiński, and Joanna Tobolewicz

Gdańsk is Poland's principal seaport, situated on the southern edge of the Gdańsk Bay on the Baltic Sea. The city is the capital and largest city of the Pomeranian Voivodeship. Gdańsk, in a conurbation with the city of Gdynia and the resort town of Sopot, and suburban communities, jointly forms Poland's fourth largest metropolitan area, with a population approaching 1.4 million. The CRUNCH project aims to upgrade the Smart City concept in Gdańsk by introducing the Food-Water-Energy nexus to a city. In contrast to traditional innovation experiments aimed at testing and demonstration, Living Labs focus on broad stakeholder involvement, co-creation, and strategic learning to achieve systemic change (Van den Bosch, 2010) and better anticipation of constraints on upscaling and inclusion (Dijk et al., 2019). Therefore, the Urban Initiative Laboratory (UIL) in Gdańsk was set up via the CRUNCH project agreement between the City of Gdańsk and academia, Gdańsk University of Technology (GUT), with the aim of introducing this more institutionalised form of Living Labs into urban governance structures (Bylund, 2020). All three pillars of the ULL (business, city, and research) were included as leading stakeholders in the UIL processes in Gdańsk when the third partner, Oliva Business Centre, joined the CRUNCH project. The Gdańsk UIL set up experiments focusing on the key Urban Living Laboratory (ULL) domains – i.e. a variety of city policy procedures and mix of functionalities and interdependences across dimensions – to search for data indicators, establish assessment tools, and describe good practices.

The ULL FWE Nexus CBD Multimodal Node was the first ULL domain in the CRUNCH project which conducted tests on the regional scale to study the process of activating and facilitating urban stakeholders. The ULL began through the choice of a crucial urban point in the Gdańsk metropolis which was best for generating fresh ideas and new concepts, in order to strengthen the development on its crossroads. The Gdańsk Development Plan 2016 (Studium, p. 206) introduced a new Infinity Loop Model based on three major functional nodes (Gdynia Port, Gdańsk Port, and the Airport). The paradigm shift of Gdańsk's development evolved from the bipolar Gdańsk-Gdynia model to the one based on Tri Nodes. The Infinity Loop follows the lines of the transport system routes: the new light-rail system in the Upper Terrace and the major transport links between Gdańsk city centre and the port in the eastern part of the city. The dynamic development in-between the nodes at the heart of the Infinity Loop is well established in the blooming Central Business District in Oliwa. Therefore, the Macro ULL FWE Nexus CBD was chosen to be at this location. The idea of the CBD Multimodal Node emerged during several ULLs dedicated to urban concepts for the stimulation of synergetic development at this focal point of the Gdańsk metropolis. Students at the Faculty of Architecture, GUT (vol. 2018/2019), dealt with master plans and strategies for the FWE Nexus CBD Multimodal Node. The UIL works focused on the Macro ULL FWE Nexus CBD Multimodal, which led to the ULL procedure amendments, the adaptation of ULL definitions, and setting the aims, milestones, and the stakeholders' group changes according to the ULL phases. The main results were presented at the first ULL CBD Multimodal Stakeholders' meeting. The main ULL FWE Nexus CBD Multimodal outcome is the CBD master plan, prepared jointly by the project's academic partner (Gdańsk University of Technology) and business partner (Oliva Business Centre).

The next CRUNCH domain was the Gdańsk ULL FWE Nexus Neighbourhood. A hybrid position at the boundaries of local administration, research and society proved beneficial for increasing public awareness of how to adapt to climate change in Gdańsk. The ULL FWE Nexus Neighbourhood was a proposed greenfield transit-oriented neighbourhood at Gdańsk Airport Station. Students at the Faculty of Architecture, GUT (vol. 2019/2020), developed the master plan for a low-carbon residential neighbourhood. The master plan was focused on adaptation to climate change, the circular economy, and low-emissions targeted at zero waste. The project emphasised public awareness of how to adapt to climate change in Gdańsk, presenting smart solutions aimed at self-sufficiency on a FWE Nexus urban scale. The main result of the ULL FWE Nexus Neighbourhood was its input into the Integrated Support Decision System Platform in the CRUNCH project. The main

ULL FWE Nexus Neighbourhood outcome is the master plan in three scenarios of development.

The pathways towards the Micro ULL FWE Nexus Square were established together by academics, city experts, business partners, and international experts as stakeholders. The several thematic Urban Living Labs undertaken within carefully selected groups had created chances for user friendly innovations. As far as the solutions are concerned, they have not been tested under real-life conditions in the city of Gdańsk, because they have been postponed to a time after the Covid-19 pandemic. The FWE Nexus Square prototype will tackle, on a microscale, urban challenges related to food waste and the effective use and reusage of water, and demonstrate how to make energy resources (incl. solar and wind) combined with reused water (i.e. rainwater) sufficient for running the FWE Nexus in place as soon as the pandemic is over. A flexible approach is planned, with modular design, allowing for the easy interchange of media management systems to compare, study and optimise the flow and use of energy and water. The integrated multi-channel monitoring system will allow for the detailed tracking of individual use of media by devices on board. Despite the coronavirus, the theoretical concept of the FWE Nexus Square happened to be the starting point for the concepts that led to various patent applications: the Co-modal Local Node and Non-invasive Measurement System, in the form of open licences under the commonality agreements between the city of Gdańsk and Gdańsk University of Technology. The Non-invasive Measurement System is about to be tested in the Laboratory Tribology and Bearing Technology (Faculty of Mechanical Engineering and Ocean Technology) at GUT, which remains in continued operation despite the coronavirus. The laboratory was selected for its multi-functionality, as the space available is divided into two parts, each occupying one of the two floors in the building. The ground floor is dedicated to scientific research work and the upper floor houses teaching rooms for small student groups. The two floors share same entrance and the general plan of the building is a semi-open space.

The Gdańsk experience addressed, first, how knowledge is co-produced between research, business, and city experts. A strong motivation to act together is a necessity for adapting the city for climate change, and solidarity is the key word here. Secondly, the Urban Initiative Laboratory practised the issues of co-creation in order to improve the prototype with local communities. The stimulation of social and end-user innovation resulted in finding solutions together. Urban Living Labs focused on the FWE nexus serve as an educational platform for how saturation of the urban environment with technology influences the life of humans and the environment. Thirdly, changes in the planning system (especially in procurement) are proposed, to make the innovation solutions more visible in public spaces. Finally, the systemic approach was achieved by providing a universal set of indicators, and solutions which were filed for patent applications.

References

Dijk, M., da Schio, N., Diethart, M., Hoflehner, T. et al. (2019). How to anticipate constraints on upscaling inclusive Living Lab experiments, SmarterLabs project, JPI Urban Europe 2019.

Studium uwarunkowań i kierunków zagospodarowania przestrzennego miasta Gdańska. https://www.gdansk.pl/studium/obowiazujace-studium-suikzp,a,113625

Van den Bosch, S. (2010). Transition experiments: Exploring societal changes towards sustainability [Erasmus University Rotterdam].

Chapter 1.3

Miami

Data-driven planning and scenario tools

Thomas Spiegelhalter

ULL City of Miami Beach, Zip Codes 33109, 33139, 33140, 33141
   Population: 88,885 (Estimate: 2019). Area: City 39.41 km², Land 19.90 km², Water 19.51 km², 62.37%, Elevation 90–180 cm
ULL City of South Miami, Zip Codes 33143, 33155
   Population: 11,911 (Estimate: 2019). Area: City 5.98 km², Land 5.87 km², Water 0.11 km², 0%, Elevation 90–300 cm
The selected ULL areas for the cities of South Miami and Miami Beach are mostly influenced by the tropical monsoon climate based on the Köppen Climate Classification (Weatherbase; World Map of Köppen-Geiger Climate Classification). The city's low sea level elevations, coastal and island locations, position just above the Tropic of Cancer, and proximity to the Gulf Stream shape its climatic dynamics. Average winter high temperatures, from December to March, range from 24.7–26.8 °C. The wet season begins sometime in June, ending in mid-October. During this period, temperatures range from 29–35 °C, with increased heat island impacts due to climate change. These extremes are accompanied by high humidity, though the heat is often relieved in the afternoon by thunderstorms or by changing sea breezes that develop off the Atlantic Ocean or are caused by the nearby Everglade swamps. Much of the year's 1,572 mm of rainfall occurs during this period. Dew points in the warm months range from 22.2 °C in June to 23.2 °C in August (NowData). Hurricane season with tornadoes officially runs from June 1 through November 30, although hurricanes can develop beyond those dates. Around more than 40% of Miami homes are built upon floodplains and are in flood-risk zones (ibid). Miami and the Greater

Islands is one of the major US coastal cities most affected by Climate Change ("Irma spared America"; Cusick, 2020). Global sea level rise, which in Miami will be 80 cm by 2060, will increase storm surges up to 6 meters, cause more intense flooding, and threaten the city's drinking water supply (Impact on South Florida, n.d.; Rami, Keyes, & Kingdon, 2020). Real estate prices in Miami already reflect the increase in real estate prices at a higher elevation within the city than real estate at a lower height (Luscombe, 2020).

The Miami CRUNCH ULL addresses the FWE nexus (food, water, renewable energy) for demography, infrastructure and properties, facilities, land use, and the pandemic. It aims to support local decision and policymakers, and practitioners and civil society organisations, by translating the key findings of an in-depth review of literature, knowledge and research evidence on the FWE nexus into the analysis and generative design of the ULL with the IDSS platform (Spiegelhalter & Levente). The IDSS includes creating AI-ML-GIS-BIM-Python-Green-Blue-Infraworks data-driven planning and scenario tools for the IDSS; identifying a data baseline and Digital Twin for the city's needs; and testing and optimising the models using different carbon-positive and resilient scenarios from now to 2100. Working across scales, policy questions, and innovative urban planning and design methods, the research focuses on working with communities and municipalities, enabling the conceptualisation and visualisation for the FWE nexus projects.

References

Cusick, D. (2020, 4 February). Miami is the 'most vulnerable' coastal city worldwide. *Scientific American*. https://www.scientificamerican.com/article/miami-is-the-most-vulnerable-coastal-city-worldwide/. Retrieved 6 January 2021.

"Impact on South Florida" (n.d). Miamidade.gov. http://www.miamidade.gov/environment/climate-change-impact.asp. Retrieved 6 January 2021.

"Irma spared America, but still had a big effect on it" (2017, 15 September). *The Economist*. https://www.economist.com/united-states/2017/09/14/irma-spared-america-but-still-had-a-big-effect-on-it. Retrieved 6 January 2021.

Luscombe, R. (2020, 21 April). Will Florida be lost forever to the climate crisis? https://www.theguardian.com/environment/2020/apr/21/florida-climate-crisis-sea-level-habitat-loss. *The Guardian*. Retrieved January 6, 2021.

NowData. https://w2.weather.gov/climate/xmacis.php?wfo=mfl. Retrieved 6 January 2021.

Raimi, D., Keyes, A., & Kingdon, C. (2020, 30 January). Florida climate outlook: Assessing physical and economic impacts through 2040. *Resources for the Future.* https://www.rff.org/publications/reports/florida-climate-outlook/. Retrieved 6 January 2021.

Weatherbase. http://www.weatherbase.com/weather/weather-summary.php3?s=20227&cityname=Miami%2C+Florida%2C+United+States+of+America&units=. Retrieved 6 January 2021.

World Map of Köppen-Geiger Climate Classification. http://koeppen-geiger.vu-wien.ac.at/pdf/kottek_et_al_2006_A4.pdf. Retrieved 6 January 2021.

Chapter 1.4

Southend-on-Sea

Green infrastructure for climate resilience

Claire Coulter

Southend is located 40 miles east of London on the north side of the Thames Estuary. It is one of the most densely populated urban areas in the East of England (pop. 179,800 people) and home to the 'driest place in the UK' (Great Wakering). As a seaside resort with over 6 million visitors per year, Southend needs to identify how it can respond to climate change and implement solutions to benefit public health for both residents and visitors. To address the future climate impacts of flooding, drought, and heat stress in the local area, Southend Borough Council would like to deploy more green infrastructure across its urban landscape, and this will become a major feature of the Council's next Sustainability Strategy moving forwards. The proposed ULL site near the High Street is fully paved, with little greenery, and has high footfall, with at least 9,000 users visiting the High Street area daily, for a mixture of work and leisure purposes.

The green infrastructure project aims to make use of vegetation to reduce flooding and improve urban cooling and air quality. It will contribute towards a decrease in the energy being used for cooling purposes and improve air quality in the area. It is hoped that it will also encourage pedestrians and cyclists to use the space, which is located close to a major railway station, and thus encourage the uptake of sustainable, fossil-fuel-free methods of transport. There is also potential for the plants to incorporate edible crops such as fruit trees and herbs, as part of the greening project. Local restaurants along the High Street could also be encouraged to grow their own herbs and salad vegetables as part of their contribution towards a greener environment.

DOI: 10.4324/9781003112495-7

As part of its commitment to a more sustainable future, Southend is part of three ongoing Interreg projects:

Cool Towns is looking to deploy different heat resilience measures, including green infrastructures such as tree planters, tree pits, and water capturing features (e.g. rills) as a means of cooling and supplying air hydration. It is also looking at installing canopy shading solutions and providing public drinking water features to tackle the human health impact of heat stress.
SPONGE2020 is delivering sustainable urban drainage measures, like swales, rain gardens and rills, through a participative adaptation approach.
NSCiti2S will invest in green infrastructures in a residential regeneration scheme (e.g. green roofs, permeable paving, and rain gardens) to inform their case for green infrastructure investment.

CRUNCH has been working alongside these projects to explore how the Food-Water-Energy nexus can be integrated moving forwards. Initially, it was planned for the CRUNCH ULL in Southend to adopt both qualitative and quantitative methods, with sensors along the High Street collecting data on air quality, temperature, and plant wellbeing. Visual complexity analysis was to be used to explore how people use the streetscape, and interviews were to be conducted with different groups of street users to assess how they perceive and use the public space along the High Street. However, due to a combination of planning and maintenance issues, as well as the effects of the Covid-19 pandemic, the data collection was unable to proceed as planned.

Instead, the CRUNCH ULL has centred around the installation of hydropanels, which use sunlight and air to create water from the atmosphere. Although initially designed to provide drinking water, the plan was to also use these panels in Southend to provide water for irrigation, mitigating against some of the barriers associated with the ongoing maintenance of green infrastructure. Due to delays caused by Covid-19, the installation of these panels is still ongoing at the time of writing, but it is hoped that they will be able to demonstrate a practical, small-scale way of utilising the Food-Water-Energy nexus in a busy urban environment.

Chapter 1.5

Taipei: Sustainable management for wastescapes

A Food-Water-Energy nexus experiment

Mei-Hua Yuan, Pei-Te Chiueh, Yu-Sen Chang, Hsin-hsin Tung, Chang-Ping Yu, Hwong-wen Ma, and Shang-Lien Lo

Increased natural resource consumption and related waste production are rapidly leading to great social and environmental challenges and the formation of landscapes of waste. These wastescapes are particularly vulnerable to the uncertainties of climate change and population growth, and their problems are further exacerbated by limitations of food, energy and fresh water at the local level.

With 2.6 million inhabitants and a total area of 271 km², Taipei City's density is 5th worldwide. Each year, approximately 1 million tons of municipal solid waste is collected from citizens and deposited in landfills. Fudeken Landfill was the first and largest household waste site in Taipei City and was operated by the Taipei City government. More than 8 million m³ of garbage in total was dumped there between 1985 and 2002, after which a major landfill recovery project was implemented. The landfill site was reopened as the Fudeken Environmental Restoration Park, focusing on wastescape management and restoring ecosystems of the once-beautiful area. Currently, Fudeken Park has been chosen as an environmental education site, requiring its transformation into an ecological space. The challenge is how to transform the site for environmental education and make it a place where nature and humanity co-exist harmoniously; the project proposes a new area for environmental education activities and support for food, energy and water quality.

In 2018, the National Taiwan University research team initiated a three-stage process. The first stage, which began in 2018, was researching synergies and trade-offs between food, energy and water production. The functional linkages, synergies

DOI: 10.4324/9781003112495-8

and trade-off analyses between energy generated by methane and leachate were explored. Researchers made a deep and robust survey to understand the landfill site, particularly from food, energy and water perspectives. They also put together wide-ranging questionnaires and conducted a series of intensive walking interviews with local residents, in addition to site observations to explore possible nature-based solutions. The second stage, which began in 2019, was to evaluate potential solutions by citizens and technicians. Academics were invited to share their knowledge and experience in the field to introduce design concepts and techniques, together with environmental solutions. More than one hundred individuals (government, citizens, engineers, experts, elected representatives, students) were involved in two workshops. The third stage, which began in 2020, is establishing a symbolic locality of innovation, focusing on the construction and performance assessment of the proposed solutions. This includes onsite construction processes, installation for

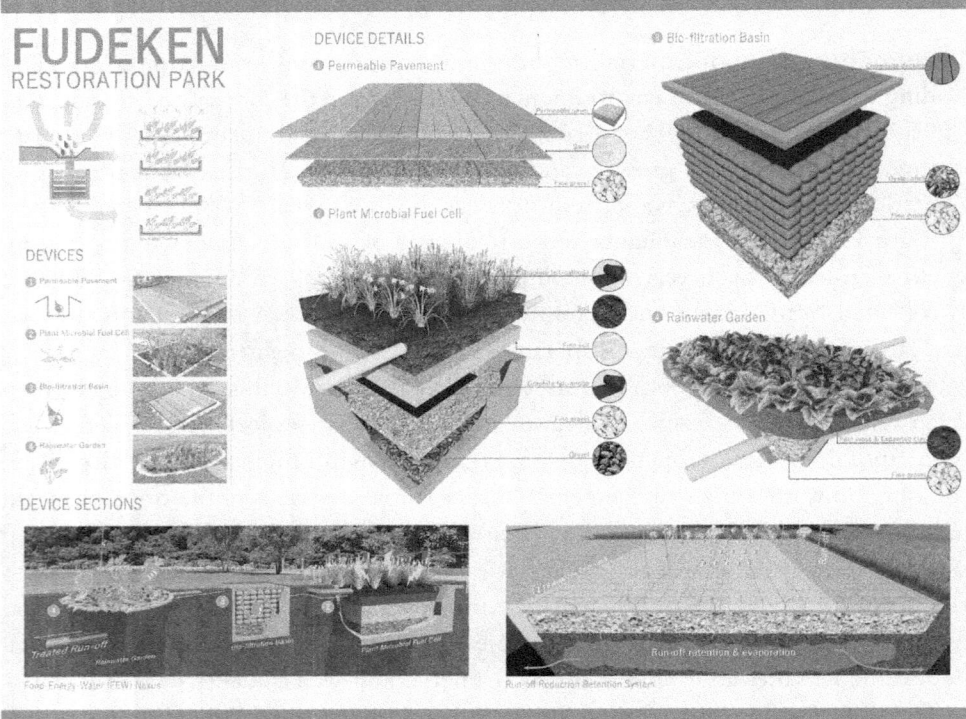

Figure 1.1: Overview of a living lab cocreation environment on informing future landfill design and governance practices

monitoring, and post-construction training for local people in how to operate and maintain the facilities. This stage also includes presenting the final outcome in 2D drawings and physical 3D models for environmental education use.

The design of the first pilot zone provides an opportunity to tackle nature-based solutions (see Figure 1.1). It plays a major role in urban mobility (e.g. pollutant removal, runoff reduction, water recycling, electricity generation, edible plant cultivation, and recreational landscapes, etc.). Four main designs were considered based on co-design processes among stakeholders and were characterised by the merging of each solution. These include (1) permeable pavement; (2) plant microbial fuel cell; (3) bio-filtration basin and (4) rain garden.

The project initiated a consultative process, inviting significant organisations to a workshop. Then the detailed nature-based solution was co-designed with experts from National Taiwan University and the municipal authorities. Interviews and a questionnaire survey were employed to elicit stakeholder discourses on risks and their solutions. Experts from National Taiwan University provided four technical option packages, each within a given budget. Following a series of steps, the range of public perspectives was synthesised into a final agreement. By integrating the management and governance of environmental resources across a range of sectors and scales, long-neglected interlinkages between food, energy and water in a landfill site are becoming visible.

Chapter 1.6

Uppsala

Groundwater management in the neighbourhood of Rosendal

Vera van Zoest, Edith Ngai, Shashank Shekher Tripathi, and Archit Suryawanshi

The municipality of Uppsala is the fourth largest municipality in Sweden in terms of population size, with around 230,000 inhabitants. A large part of the population in the city of Uppsala consists of students. Uppsala University is the oldest university in Scandinavia and has attracted many researchers and students since its foundation in 1477. Ever since, the city has been growing rapidly. This has led to an increased pressure on the real estate market, and Uppsala is looking for space to expand.

The neighbourhood of Rosendal is a newly built neighbourhood intended to facilitate the growth of the city and the increase in population. The vision for Rosendal includes 3,500 houses and apartments as well as schools, shops, and facilities. Apartments range in size and price, with the aim to create a diverse neighbourhood. The buildings all look different, creating variation and dynamics in the area. The setup of the neighbourhood invites people to meet and connect.

Although Rosendal looks like a relatively normal neighbourhood from the outside, it is dealing with unique challenges that are hidden below the surface. In a shortage of space around Uppsala, Rosendal had to be built right on top of a water conservation area. Ground water is the main source of drinking water for the city, which makes it important to keep it clean and safe – especially when climate change leads to more drought in the summers with a potential shortage of water for both irrigation and tap water use. The key challenge is how to keep the ground water clean when building Rosendal on top of the water conservative area.

Uppsala: Groundwater management

Below the surface, Rosendal looks a lot different from most regular neighbourhoods. An impermeable layer protects the ground water reservoir from rain water leaking in from the surface, which could potentially be contaminated by dust and oil from the roads. Infiltration layers that lead the water to a surface pond have been carefully designed based on different types of sand and stones. Sensors in the rainwater sewage system measure the amount of contamination in the water.

To further avoid the amount of contamination in the rain water, cars are not allowed to drive through the neighbourhood. A mobility house at the entrance of the neighbourhood provides parking spaces for the residents and visitors as well as shared cars and bikes. Besides that, fast and easily accessible public transport connects the different parts of the neighbourhood.

Through these innovations, Rosendal serves as a testbed for future expansions of the city on water protection areas. The sensor readings of the water quality are carefully tracked to keep an eye on the quality of the drinking water in the city. Meanwhile, Rosendal provides a modern and quiet living area. The absence of cars makes it safer for people to walk and children to play, and the squares provide tranquillity and a place to meet. Taking Rosendal as an example, it is expected that more neighbourhoods will arise in a similar fashion around Uppsala.

Figure 1.2: The Talltorget square in Rosendal
Source: Tengbom arkitekter & WSP arkitekter.

PART II
FOOD-WATER-ENERGY NEXUS FINDINGS

Chapter 2

The urban living lab as an adaptive governance mechanism for the transdisciplinary Food-Water-Energy nexus

Lessons learned from six local contexts

Maryam Ghodsvali*, Gamze Dane, and Bauke de Vries

1. Introduction

As many cities worldwide try to restore the balance in trade-offs between the food, water, and energy sectors (i.e. the FWE nexus), it has gradually been discerned that, beyond the adoption of new technologies and infrastructure, changes are required in how practices and policies shift (Gorddard et al., 2016; Colloff et al., 2019). Projections prove that the upward global trend in urbanisation combined with the overall growth of the world's population could boost human demand for FWE in excess of nature's regeneration capacity. By 2030, humans will require 50% more food, 30% more water, and 50% more energy (Cairns, Wilsdon, & O'Donovan, 2017) at a rate of 100% faster than their regeneration by nature (European Commission, 2017). Human behaviour regarding resource consumption is of central importance in ecosystems' integrity and the implementation of integrated nexus solutions for the FWE sectors (Ghodsvali, Krishnamurthy, & de Vries, 2019). However, urban communities will not modify their consumption behaviour while gaps exist regarding the awareness of the severity of the issue and the role of stakeholders at human scales (Yan & Roggema, 2019).

*Corresponding author.

In response to these challenges, a new governance mechanism that shifts policies and practices towards communication, experimentation, and learning is emerging in the form of the Urban Living Lab (ULL). ULLs constitute a form of innovative governance mechanism whereby stakeholders that are in a value chain co-create ideas, plans, and service propositions and experiment with solutions to urban sustainability challenges in a real-life environment (Bulkeley et al., 2016). The co-creation process, with its reliance on iterative consultation, suggests stakeholder involvement at multiple stages throughout the FWE nexus process (Davis & Andrew, 2017). The experimentation process, consisting of various participatory approaches, establishes new forms of collaboration among stakeholders, guides urban policies, and navigates the dynamics of urban transformation (Nevens et al., 2013; Frantzeskaki et al., 2018). For cities trying to maintain an ecological balance, ULLs appeal as an open form of collective urban experimentation towards transformative improvements.

However, policymakers and other FWE nexus actors are struggling with the implementation of ULLs and are seeking guidance on their further development (de Kraker, Scholl, & van Wanroij, 2016). This operational weakness is mainly due to a lack of evidence-based guidelines concerning how a ULL can best be organised and integrated into the local governance structure of nexus-emphasised cities. This practical shortcoming calls for a critical reflection on the experience of FWE nexus projects in implementing ULLs, to help guide others towards an effective route into collaborative innovations that meet local socio-ecological challenges.

This study aims to frame the understanding of how ULLs are being operationalised in urban governance for the nexus linking food, water, and energy in cities. After a thorough review of the literature on the characteristics of ULLs and their recent contribution to the transdisciplinary FWE nexus (section 2), we selected six local case studies of nexus ULLs for further analysis (sub-section 3.1). The empirical cases are part of an ongoing FWE-nexus ULL project called Climate Resilient Urban Nexus CHoices (CRUNCH), which aims to create an interconnected knowledge platform in support of the increasing challenges of food, water, and energy management. The selection of multiple case studies is supposed to broaden the potential rigor of the study by improving the validity and robustness of the results (Yin, 2009). We assessed key operational characteristics of the selected ULLs and the likelihood of advancing their performance in terms of the transdisciplinary FWE nexus. Our findings lay down guiding principles for the development of ULLs for the practical challenges of the transdisciplinary FWE nexus (sub-section 3.2 and section 4).

2. The ULL through the lens of the transdisciplinary FWE nexus

The essence of the transdisciplinary FWE nexus is about building capacity to inclusively gain more from less, in the context of the natural food, water, and energy sectors (Scott, Kurian, & Wescoat, 2015; Ghodsvali, Krishnamurthy, & de Vries, 2019). Acting upon this concept requires *cooperative interactions, localised interventions, a resilient alliance, efficient resolutions*, and *adaptive capacity* (Ghodsvali, Krishnamurthy, & de Vries, 2019). The ULL approach is a way to put these theoretical propositions into practice (Baccarne et al., 2016; Ghodsvali, Dane, & de Vries, 2022).

From the transdisciplinary FWE nexus perspective, ULLs perform beyond simply promoting learning and innovation. They undergo a structured process in which a wide range of nexus actors (i.e. civil society, academia, government, and industry), through implementing a combination of diverse participatory methodologies (e.g. co-creation workshops and focus groups), give shape to socio-ecological interventions and govern development resolutions in real time (Bulkeley et al., 2016; Ghodsvali, Dane, & de Vries, 2022).

Empirical research on the transdisciplinary FWE nexus underlined four key peculiarities shared by ULLs (see, e.g., Almirall, Lee, & Wareham, 2012; Mulder, 2012; Nesti, 2017). First, ULLs are founded on a network of relationships among their *actors and users* inspired by the quintuple helix model – i.e. collective interaction and exchange of knowledge between the political system, civil society, the natural environment, the economic system, and the education system (Carayannis, Barth, & Campbell, 2012). Along with the transdisciplinary nature of nexus practices, ULLs forge an effective public-private-people partnership, placing people at the very centre of the innovation process (Molinari, 2011). This relational structure in turn facilitates *cooperative interactions* as part of the transdisciplinary nexus requirements through which different actors, organisations, and ecosystems are able to collaborate.

Second, ULLs enable the adoption of *co-creation approaches* for socio-ecological problems that are designed, prototyped, evaluated, and refined with participants in real-world settings (Pierson & Lievens, 2005). Through comprising of co-creation, a form of collaborative innovation, ULLs represent a remarkable shift from passive user engagement to a more active approach based on the dominant paradigm of iterative consultation and participatory knowledge production. They develop a knowledge-driven society, thereby potentially leveraging the knowledge circulating in the urban environment (Baccarne et al., 2016; Cardullo, Kitchin, & Di Feliciantonio, 2018). From the transdisciplinary FWE nexus perspective, the ULL approach, including experimentation and learning, explores the possibility of directing societal behaviour change and optimising the overall ecological impact of a ULL's development (Davis & Andrew, 2017; Lund, 2018). More specifically, it contributes towards the requirement of the transdisciplinary FWE nexus to characterise paradigms of *localised interventions* based on the collaborative knowledge of society.

Third, at the core of ULLs lies the concept of collective responsibility, from which stakeholders can form the basis for a concerted *governance structure* (Halbe et al., 2015; Voytenko et al., 2016). The basic idea is that instead of delegating responsibilities to specific stakeholders, such as politicians or certain businesses, ULLs make an effort to remain inclusive to all different stakeholders and to foster joint innovations (Chesbrough, 2003; Nesti, 2018). Within ULLs, participants are encouraged to brainstorm and discuss ideas for which the operational knowledge is diffused across society, and in turn practical solutions to FWE nexus challenges are offered by governments, scholars, and industrial coordinators together with communities. Hence a *resilient alliance*, in terms of concerted action across multiple actors (i.e. the FWE nexus quintuple helix system), is promoted through a continuous process of knowledge diffusion and the division of responsibilities. This concept of a coordination role is significant for a ULL to be effective within the transdisciplinary FWE nexus process, since it underpins the ability of ULLs to build the *adaptive capacity* of the nexus social system to meet mutual challenges. It facilitates explicit learning among nexus participants and allows for the refinement of developmental visions and how to better align them with the needs of the end-users (Voytenko et al., 2016).

Fourth, ULLs are characterised by their concern for *socio-technical system design* utilising Information and Communication Technologies (ICT) (Nesti, 2017). Active collaboration with citizens often necessitates generating new content, instant sharing with others, and testing the outcomes of decisions. ICT provides great opportunities for active collaboration, since it enables interactions at all times with lower costs of connection, and facilitates the transformation of thorough knowledge (Meijer, 2012). Communities utilising ICT for inclusive and active collaborations benefit from empowerment and social progress. From a transdisciplinary FWE nexus perspective, ICT infrastructure supports ULLs with social progress through enabling mutual interactions, a continuous exchange of knowledge, and the transformation of expert knowledge into information that is comprehensible to all participants. This interlinked socio-technical systems design in turn particularly contributes to the nexus' goal for an *efficient resolution* of socio-ecological transformations which meet environmental changes with social progress.

Notwithstanding commonalities, there are apparent differences in the way that ULLs have been implemented in the practice of the transdisciplinary FWE nexus. The urban contexts of FWE nexus practices vary in their social, institutional, and environmental aspects, and the ULL approach is implemented differently in accordance with this (Ghodsvali, Krishnamurthy, & de Vries, 2019). Transdisciplinary FWE nexus practices need to modify the ULL approach with regard to context-based specifications and complexities. Research often depicts practical experiences as versatile guidelines which development operations can learn from and, if applicable, can adapt. Hence cities need to obtain adequate evidence in order to draw up operational guidelines for adopting the ULL approach in the context of the transdisciplinary FWE nexus.

This study aimed to collect sufficient evidence of the use of ULLs in transdisciplinary FWE nexus actions across the world, in order to provide cities with empirical knowledge and operational guidelines. In doing so, we first developed a framework of the key components of a ULL for operationalising the transdisciplinary FWE nexus (sub-section 2.1). The components are derived from the above-described peculiarities shared by ULLs in the practice of the transdisciplinary FWE nexus (i.e. actors and users, co-creation approaches, governance structure, and socio-technical system design). The framework developed proposes relevant variables through which cities can characterise, appraise, and test a ULL's performance in terms of the transdisciplinary FWE nexus. Next, in order to draw out further nexus developments on practical experiences, this study investigated the performance of six nexus ULLs citing the proposed framework. The understanding of various ways through which nexus ULLs are implemented in different socio-political contexts with varying ecological complexities can guide cities towards an adaptive governance mechanism for more inclusive environmental management protocols.

2.1. Key operational components for employing ULLs in the transdisciplinary FWE nexus

This sub-section addresses the defining characteristics of the ULL approach in operationalising the transdisciplinary FWE nexus. Drawing conclusions from the insights from theoretical and empirical research (section 2), four key operational components for implementing the ULL approach in the transdisciplinary FWE nexus can be identified: actors and users, co-creation approaches, governance structure, and socio-technical system design (Figure 2.1). Each of these is comprehensively explored below.

- **Actors and users** provide the ULL's community with their specific wealth of knowledge and expertise, assisting in boundary-spanning knowledge transfer results (Bergvall-Kåreborn et al., 2009). The actors, whose participation in a nexus ULL's activities is required, are at a minimum: end-users of the FWE sectors; in many cases citizens, knowledge institutes, private actors (e.g. companies, industry, and businesses), and public actors (e.g. governments and public organisations). These actors, in addition to their need for active and continuous participation in ULL activities, need to have the power to influence the process (Prahalad & Ramaswamy, 2004). The balance of power among all ULL actors enables their active partnership in innovations and development.
- **Co-creation approaches** represent methodologies and tools aimed at experimentation and learning (e.g. workshops, design thinking, and group discussions) that emerge as best practices within a ULL's processes (Mulder, 2012). To qualify as co-creation, a transdisciplinary FWE nexus process that is highly dependent on stakeholder engagement needs the targeted actors and users of the ULL to be involved in all sorts of development phases and activities. In addition to being asked for their opinions, actors within nexus ULLs should have power in decision-making processes (Steen & van Bueren, 2017). The development mechanism of ULLs is iterative, which implies that after being created and designed the prototypes of solutions to FWE nexus challenges are validated and tested by stakeholders. The evaluation and refinement gathered from these phases are employed in further developments and improvements.
- The **governance structure** stands for a collaboration setting that handles the way in which ULLs are organised on different operational or strategic levels in their FWE nexus activities (Molinari & Schumacher, 2011). The strategic level addresses several issues, such as the way in which ULL actors and users are involved concerning their responsibility and influence, the ownership of the ULL, and the way in which the management structure handles the delicate balance between leading and controlling. The operational level comprises aspects such as a road map to empirical practices, progress monitoring, and the way that

The urban living lab

development strategies are validated and refined. It is crucial for nexus ULLs that ultimate responsibility for decisions and strategies lies with all of its actors. For this to happen, governance models and the allocation of resources are of vital importance.
- Finally, the **socio-technical system design** component outlines the role of technology in facilitating new ways of co-creating innovations among ULL actors. A ULL is a context-based experience which is complicated to replicate in exactly the same way elsewhere. A combination of the ICT-based collaborative context, open innovation platforms, user-centred development methods, and public–private–people partnerships proposes potentially transformational effects on socio-ecological systems (Molinari, 2011).

The framework developed not only signifies the most crucial components of a ULL in operationalising the transdisciplinary FWE nexus but also enables the determining of bridges between existing nexus ULLs. The multiplicity of aspects explained by this framework drives the design and development of future nexus ULLs to learn from each other, benchmark the validation of actors' attitudes, adopt best practices, and interconnect similar ULLs in environment and approach.

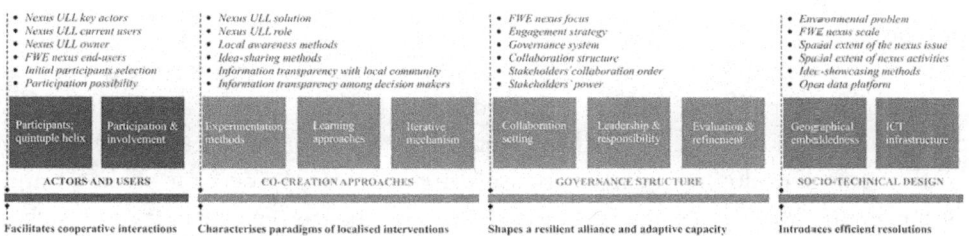

Figure 2.1: The assessment framework for defining characteristics of Urban Living Labs (ULLs) in operationalising the transdisciplinary Food-Water-Energy (FWE) nexus

Actors and users, co-creation approaches, governance structure, and socio-technical system design are the four key components that significantly contribute to practical innovations in the transdisciplinary FWE nexus. Each component, relying on multiple factors (coloured text boxes), contributes towards a specific requirement for operationalising the transdisciplinary FWE nexus concept in a real-life environment (linked via dashed lines). Nexus ULLs foster social, administrative, and technological innovations through supporting community-focused/led participation, running various sorts of experimental and learning methods, governing active involvements and shared responsibilities, and identifying a distinct spatial form of governance associated with desired digital platforms that support nexus ULL activities. This framework offers a set of categorical variables (bullet points) based on an online survey that was conducted for the assessment of the characteristics of the selected ULLs in this study.

Source: Adapted from Molinari (2011); Nevens et al. (2013); Baccarne et al. (2016); Voytenko et al. (2016); Steen & Van Bueren (2017); Chronéer, Ståhlbröst, & Habibipour (2019); Ghodsvali, Krishnamurthy, & de Vries (2019).

Hence, a real-life-practices assessment was conducted for a set of selected FWE nexus ULLs investigating the components defined in Figure 2.1. (Given that this study, due to time and resources availability limitation, involved a small number of ULL actors for data collection, the framework should also be further validated on a larger scale.)

3. ULLs in the practice of the transdisciplinary FWE nexus: insights from six local experiences

3.1. Case selection and research methods

This research employed a qualitative multiple case-study method to obtain empirical evidence of six nexus-emphasised cities, namely Miami Beach, USA; Southend-on-Sea, UK; Eindhoven region, the Netherlands; Gdańsk, Poland; Uppsala, Sweden; and Taipei, Taiwan, for organising and integrating the ULL approach into their local governance structure. The case selection criteria required that the ULLs must have links to the FWE nexus, innovate in a real-life environment, engage multiple stakeholders including people, and emphasise the role of actors and users in innovation. Moreover, the chosen cases reflect the diversity in FWE nexus ULLs, as they were driven by diverse types of actors. Figure 2.2 presents an overview of the cases in general.

It can be seen from the data in Figure 2.2 that many variations on FWE nexus themes can be put into practice. Carbon neutrality and circularity are instances of the studied nexus ULLs themes linked to the concept of the transdisciplinary FWE nexus. Developing a carbon-neutral city, on closer inspection of the Miami Beach nexus ULL, refers to nature-based, coastal blue-green infrastructures that support a mix of renewable energy-harnessing and storage systems, organic food waste for biomass, hydroponics, and wastewater treatment strategies. Moreover, the circularity in Brainport Smart District (BSD) in Helmond – i.e. the Eindhoven region ULL – will be realised in conjunction with collaboration between humans and nature and its resources combined with existing and future technology. In BSD, smart technologies for mobility, a strong social foundation, and clean energy generation (organic urban agriculture, and a circular water system for becoming hydrologically neutral) are the means to support circularity and, in turn, the transdisciplinary FWE nexus.

The urban living lab

Urban Living Lab	Geographical location	Main theme	Operational scale	Running time
Miami	Miami, USA	Carbon neutrality	City level	2017–present
Southend High Street	Southend-on-Sea, UK	Green infrastructure	Street level	2018–present
Brainport Smart District	Eindhoven, the Netherlands	Circularity	District level	2018–present
Olivia Business Centre	Gdańsk, Poland	Local microclimate	Building level	2010–present
Rosendal	Uppsala, Sweden	Socio-eco-techno integration	District level	2016–present
Fudeken Envi. Restoration Park	Taipei, Taiwan	Ecosystems integrity	Neighbourhood level	2016–present

Figure 2.2: An overview of the selected ULLs operating in the practice of the transdisciplinary FWE nexus process

Data collection

Research data on the characteristics of the selected nexus ULLs were collected through an online survey and an in-person focus group discussion. Thirty stakeholders in the case studies, including governmental authorities, scholars, industrial coordinators, technical specialists, and users provided research information. Participant selection was based on the purposive sampling technique in order to reliably characterise and criticise the selected nexus ULLs from the perspective of their key, well-informed actors. To ensure confidentiality, the identities of participants have been withheld. During the data collection, the participants were first asked to complete an online survey (Appendix A: Table A.1) and then to participate in a face-to-face focus group discussion.

Through the online survey, we explored the association between the actors which a nexus ULL may involve, mechanisms that best support their interactions, and the technical infrastructure that may facilitate a consensus of opinions on nexus solutions. Multiple categorical variables, following the proposed framework (Figure 2.1), formed survey questions encompassing 25 scaling and multiple-choice questions. The contribution of the research participants to the survey resulted in a set of qualitative data.

Through the face-to-face focus group discussion, we linked the likely challenges of practical nexus experiences to the variant ULL approaches and environments across the case studies. In the face-to-face group discussion, the research participants were first asked to define the core problem that their ULL faces in implementing the transdisciplinary FWE nexus in practice, and then to elaborate on the immediate and secondary causes and effects of the problem raised. This manner of issue mapping – i.e. problem tree – guides the activities for the effective development of the nexus ULLs concerning context specifications and the available capabilities of the political, social, ecological, economic, and education systems. Afterwards, the qualitative data collected were cross-checked with the participants to verify the key findings.

Data analysis

For analysing the data collected, this study followed a multi-phased, analytical process, including Multiple Correspondence Analysis (MCA) for the survey data, and the Logical Framework Approach (LFA) for the group discussion data.

MCA is a multivariate statistical technique designed to explore underlying structures in a categorical dataset and is a particularly useful method for dealing with survey data (Abdi & Valentin, 2007). The general strategy of MCA is to look for the principal dimension explaining the variability of individuals (i.e. survey respondents), and to closely examine the links between variables (i.e. categorical variables forming the survey questions, see Figure 2.1). Given that the data collected for this research is categorical, and we aim to analyse it for discovering variabilities of the selected nexus ULLs, the MCA technique should prove useful to this research. Having J variables (i.e. the categorical variables that form our survey questions) each comprising of K categories (i.e. the response options to the questions), and I individuals (i.e. the 30 survey respondents in this study), MCA generates a Complete Disjunctive Table (CDT). The CDT represents individuals as rows and categories as columns, with binary values illustrating whether each category belongs to each individual or not (Zárraga & Goitisolo, 2011). Relying on the CDT, MCA creates a low-dimensional point cloud to explore relations between individuals and categories. The MCA dimensions separate individuals based on the categories that differentiate them extremely from the average. MCA uses the frequency distribution to distribute all of the categories across each of the computed dimensions, with categories with the lowest distance being considered those with the highest degree of similarity in the corresponding dimension (Rodriguez-Sabate et al., 2017). In MCA, the individuals are located in a *K-J* dimensional space, which gets bigger and bigger as the number of categories per variable increases. Therefore, even if the variables are firmly linked, the maximal percentage of inertia there can be in a given dimension (i.e. the percentage of each dimension's contribution towards defining the main subject of the analysis) is $J/(K-J)*100$, which for this study is 14%. Based on the inertia value and Cronbach's alpha greater than 0.7, a measure of dimensions' reliability (Field, 2013), this study extracted the first two MCA dimensions yielding a total variance of 13.5% to interpret the results (see Appendix A: Table A.2). Interpreting the MCA point cloud, individuals with a significant number of categories in common are located close to the origin of the point cloud, and those of which have rare common categories are located at the periphery of the point cloud. This interpretation applies to the categories as well. Rare categories are located away from the point cloud origin. Accordingly, the MCA technique enables the detection of relationships among the ULLs' actors, approaches, governance structures, and socio-technical design factors. Subsequently, the MCA result investigates the possibilities of adopting the ULL approach and the best way in which it can be organised for the transdisciplinary FWE nexus. In this study, the MCA method was performed using the "FactoMineR" package R.

LFA is a systematic and participatory technique of mapping out core problems, as well as their contributing causes–effects and means–ends relationships. This technique supports ULL actors to set clear and achievable goals, and strategies for the best ways to attain them. An open brainstorming session is the first step in employing this participatory technique. In consultation with participants, employing visual methods, namely flipcharts or colour cards, a core problem and a hierarchy of its immediate and secondary causes and effects (i.e. the problem tree) are established. These arrangements can be useful in building a community's awareness of a nexus problem, the way that they contribute to the problem, and how the problem affects their living conditions. The second step is to reformulate the negative situations of the problem tree into positive solutions, presenting means–ends relationships (i.e. the objective tree). It is of central importance that all ULL actors are involved in the discussions, giving their feedback. The objective tree created provides an outline of the desired future situation, including effective means by which ends can be achieved. After creating the desired future situation, the third step is to form possible interventions. This step requires a balance to deal with different stakeholder interests. Through a group discussion session, this research analysed six problem trees, each created by representative actors of the selected nexus ULLs. Subsequently, it developed a Logical Framework Matrix (LFM) as the main result of the LFA technique for possible operational guidelines for the nexus ULLs.

3.2. Current status of the CRUNCH ULLs in operationalising the transdisciplinary FWE nexus

This research aims at obtaining two main pieces of information about the nexus ULLs examined: 1) the defining operational characteristics of a FWE nexus ULL, and 2) the likelihood of advanced implementation levels of the transdisciplinary FWE nexus employing the ULL approach.

3.2.1. The defining operational characteristics of the FWE nexus ULL

The MCA determined the defining characteristics upon which the nexus ULL approach has been employed in the different studied socio-ecological contexts. From the MCA dimensions obtained, there were clear differentiating values among the FWE nexus cases studied in employing the ULL approach (Appendix A: Table A.2 and Figure 2.3). The variables stakeholder power, idea-showcasing methods, and local awareness methods, which presented similar discrimination measures in both dimensions, contribute significantly to the variant performance of the selected nexus ULLs.

On closer inspection of the power balance among the stakeholders of the nexus ULLs studied, there are various kinds of operational commonality. A top-down governance system enabling collaboration among key nexus stakeholders is the defining operational commonality across the studied nexus ULLs (Figure 2.3, A). In Taipei, local government, in cooperation with academics, has significant power over the decisions that affect nexus-related actions in Futekeng Rehabilitation Park (FRP). Likewise, the Olivia Business Centre (OBC) ULL in Poland operates under the great power of the municipality and academics. In both the FRP and OBC

ULLs, the ultimate responsibility for nexus-based decisions lies with the public actors. People and local communities are solely considered as end-users of services that the ULL sites offer and are not automatically involved in the process of the ULL's development.

In comparison, BSD ULL of Helmond, Eindhoven region and Uppsala were the more promising of the six nexus ULLs in terms of a public-private-people partnership. The BSD ULL in Helmond, Eindhoven region and the Södra District (SD) ULL in Uppsala possess various characteristics of an effective FWE nexus ULL working towards transdisciplinarity. Although they have different approaches in co-creating the scope of the nexus ULL and setting up the technical communication infrastructure, their main merit is the level of openness for cooperative interactions. By broadening the collaboration to the entire community (who are either directly or indirectly influenced by nexus-related problems, decisions, and development plans), the BSD and SD ULLs ascertained how transdisciplinarity boosts the effectiveness of FWE nexus practices. They both engage stakeholders from multiple disciplines, though by adopting different techniques and infrastructure. Opting for an ad-hoc infrastructure, as in BSD, stakeholders feel less restricted in testing out innovations that are linked to the thematic focus of the ULL. It is of vital importance that new ideas and solutions can be created and shared amongst every stakeholder when joining the ULL initiative. If SD had a mixed set of experimentation and learning tools, the possibility for seizing new opportunities for innovative ideas would have been higher.

Despite all the nexus ULLs studied having various commonalities in practice, Miami and Southend-on-Sea formed a distinct group. This difference may be due to the missing links in their value chains and the unequal contribution of stakeholders. For instance, the Southend Central Highstreet (SCH) ULL in Southend-on-Sea focused on green infrastructure though there was no thematic expert involved in executive decisions. This gap brought about missed opportunities for building more innovative services in that domain. A good variety of stakeholders is what Southend-on-Sea missed while setting up its nexus ULL. Regarding Miami Beach (MB), a clear narrowed-down thematic focus will lead to complementary motives for collaboration within the ULL, which, in turn, will benefit the community aspect and creation of new partnerships. Carbon neutrality includes various thematic focuses (e.g. renewable energy, hydroponics, wastewater treatment) that perform more accurately and comprehensively at the micro level.

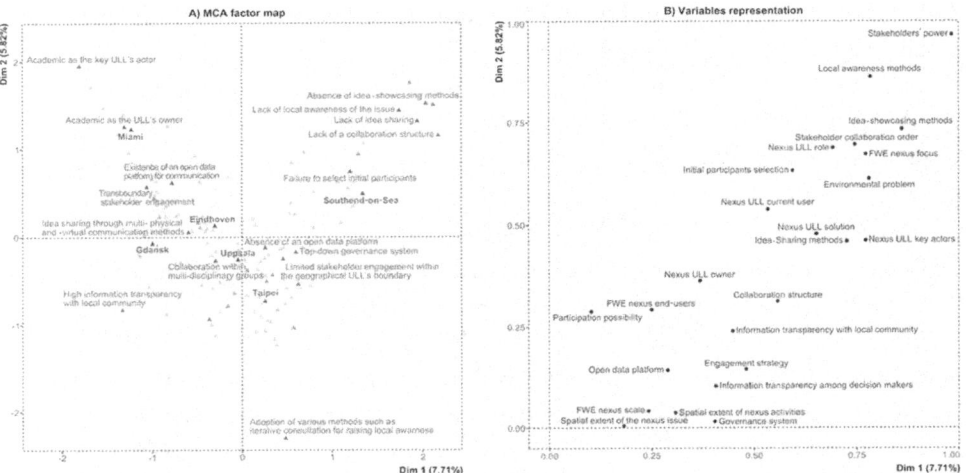

Figure 2.3: Multiple Correspondence Analysis (MCA) plots showing A) how differently the ULLs studied operate in terms of the transdisciplinary FWE nexus, and B) what variables significantly contribute towards the effective operation of the transdisciplinary FWE nexus across the nexus ULLs examined

In plot (A), red triangles, along with their descriptive statements, represent MCA categories with the largest contribution in characterising the ULLs examined, which are visualised in green. The distance between two triangles shows how different or similar they are. The closer the categories are located to each other, the more similar their categorisation pattern. The centre of the plot represents the average characteristics of the nexus ULLs examined. Unique categorisation patterns result in a triangle's location being further away from the centre. Therefore, categories that are located close to the centre represent the most common characteristics of the nexus ULLs studied. Plot (B) illustrates MCA variables (given in Figure 2.1) along the two extracted principal dimensions. The further a variable is placed from the centre point of the plot, the greater the contribution it has for understanding the distinguishing characteristics of the nexus ULLs studied.

The balance of stakeholder power and responsibilities is what the nexus ULLs studied should emphasise most while developing their FWE nexus strategies (Figure 2.3, B), although each should consider other conditions that need to exist for advanced performance (see sub-section 3.2.2 and Figure 2.4).

3.2.2. The likelihood of advancing the FWE nexus ULL implementation

The LFA, based on the structures of the problem and objective trees, identified logical linkages between the strategic intent of the ULLs studied for operationalising the transdisciplinary FWE nexus and the prerequisite activities and conditions for such development. The findings from the group discussion session (i.e. problem trees, see Appendix B: Figure B.1), identifying negative aspects of the current nexus ULL situations, established positive achievements that can contribute towards eliminating the problems which were subsequently used for the projects' strategy description in the Logical Framework Matrix (LFM). The LFM contains three items of information in this research: *project strategies* elaborating the strategic intent and alignment of each nexus ULL project, *success measures* appraising the performance and signs of the nexus ULL projects' improvement, and *assumptions* highlighting potential risks to functional prerequisites. Figure 2.4 provides the sequential steps leading to the LFM development, which describes activities to be undertaken in order to reduce the impacts of barriers to the transdisciplinary FWE nexus through the ULL approach.

The structures of the problem trees show how the barriers identified impact the realisation of transdisciplinarity in FWE nexus projects. Lack of community capacity and governance practices have directly affected people's inability to participate in FWE nexus projects. In addition, a lack of professional and technical competence in transdisciplinary engagement and the absence of adequate security caused the affected people to be unwilling to participate. Furthermore, scientific and technical knowledge issues limit the opportunity for nexus end-users and other indirectly affected people to participate in the development of the project, since the nexus ULLs have been mostly founded on thorough expertise and ICT-based communication infrastructure. Therefore, inability, unwillingness, and a limited opportunity to participate can be considered as the main reasons for the lack of community participation in FWE nexus ULLs, and accordingly, the failure of the transdisciplinarity perspective.

Following the establishment of a means-ends relationship among a nexus ULL's objectives, it becomes clear that to realise the transdisciplinary FWE nexus in practice, the affected community needs to be enabled to participate. For this to happen, the structure of the nexus community needs to be re-established, community ownership of the ULL ownership should be encouraged, and management for transition support, as well as social accountability opportunities, must be provided. From our findings, a multimodal communication platform, relying on a common language supporting real-time collaboration in both physical and virtual spheres, is the potential benefit of the ULL approach for FWE nexus practices, in order to overcome a disconnection between the general public and the concerns of politicians.

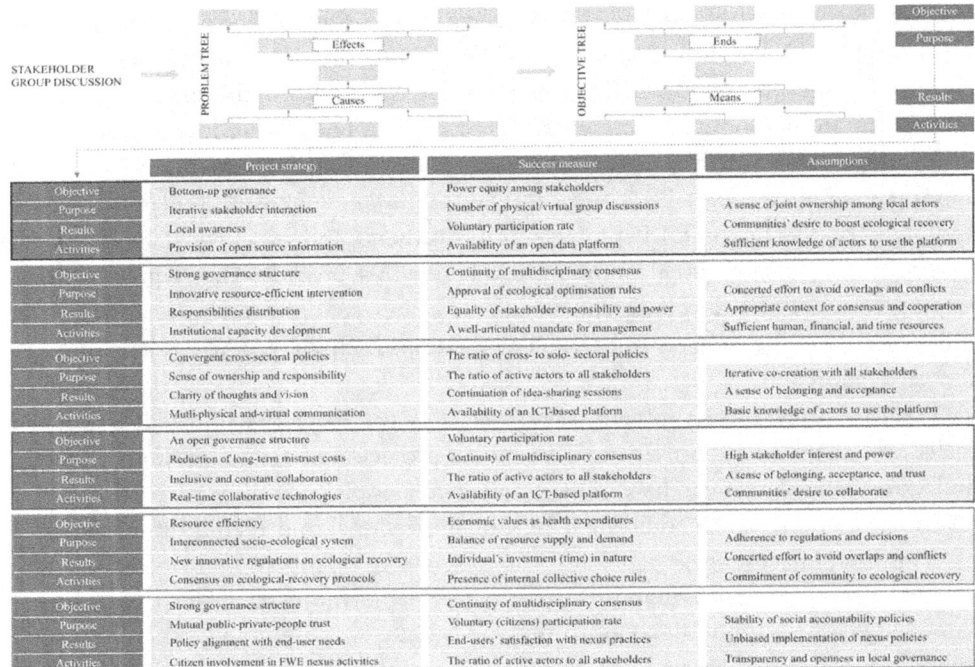

Figure 2.4: The Logical Framework Matrix (LFM) of the CRUNCH nexus ULLs

LFM is the placement of activities into an ordered hierarchy of purposes and results, systematically culminating in the principal objective each project has. "Activities" refers to tasks and resources that along with the existence of some other conditions (i.e. "assumptions") bring about some noticeable "results". The "results", referring to potential deliverables of activities along with associated assumptions, lead to the project "purpose". The project "purpose", referring to expected project changes along with the existence of some other conditions, fulfils the project's "Objective". In general, the objective, purpose, result, and activities target the strategic intent of the project and answer the question of *what the project is trying to accomplish and how*. This matrix gives the nexus ULLs coherence across the various aspects of their main problem at hand and serves as a guideline for a nexus ULL's governance structure and activities. The logical framework analysis has been done for all of the six selected nexus ULLs in this study, distinguished by coloured outlines in the matrix. The colours are assigned to the case studies as in Figure 2.1. The LFM presented was developed based on the defining characteristics of the nexus ULLs presented in Figure 2.1 and Figure 2.2 and on the problem trees that were developed (see Appendix B: Figure B.1).

4. Knowledge requirements for implementing transdisciplinary FWE nexus ULLs

FWE nexus stakeholders require a platform and structure to communicate, negotiate, and integrate their perspectives. Such a structure is complicated to develop and manage, since the FWE nexus challenges extend over multiple scales and dimensions. The ecological dimension of the FWE nexus is closely interwoven with the social, political, and economic dimensions. Consequently, FWE nexus projects are surrounded by various uncertainties and involve several interdependent stakeholders, often with diverging interests and perspectives on the actual nature of the problem as well as on possible ways to solve it. To acquire knowledge relevant to the management of such complex challenges, scientists need a structure of integrated approaches that involves multiple perspectives and various types of expertise (de Kraker, Kroeze, & Kirschner, 2011). Participatory modelling in nexus ULL applications is a structured process conducted with stakeholders to evaluate the social, ecological, and economic dimensions of the complex FWE nexus problem and the impacts of policy choices.

Investigations into the role of ICT-based participatory modelling methods and tools suggest that they are advantageous for the multiplicity of spatial and temporal scales of environmental challenges, the complexity of interactions between the social and ecological systems, and the uncertainties around stakeholders' understanding of the system and its related challenges (de Kraker, Kroeze, & Kirschner, 2011). A higher degree of local stakeholder involvement in the development of participatory models can raise the effectiveness of the process in the form of transdisciplinary tools, although this is resource- and time- intensive, and complicated to scale up.

A range of factors are of vital importance in identifying actionable policy options and instruments for engaging the transdisciplinary FWE nexus concept, ULL approach, and computer-supported participatory platform. Regarding the strategy for such engagement in the socio-ecological transition, the nexus ULLs examined in this research have experienced multiple obstacles, including lack of transparency and complexity of participatory tools, which often made direct stakeholder interactions impossible, with a low degree of user-friendliness and a lack of support for aligning feasible policy options with stakeholders' interests (either spatially or temporally) (Figure 2.3). To surmount these obstacles, the use of participatory-supported models should be made using innovative geographical, semi-quantitative methods and tools that translate conceptual models to stakeholder perspectives and to simulation models. In addition, the tools and methods should be flexible in terms of the diversity of stakeholder interests and values; in other words, in terms of the alignment of different goal definitions. Moreover, the models should be more efficient in terms of iterative stakeholder interactions, which are often restricted due to limited time availability.

Various innovative tools and methods are offered to help with the likely instrumental obstacles to a governance mechanism with people at the very centre of the process; they are potentially applicable to the ULL approach for the transdisciplinary FWE nexus (Ghodsvali, Krishnamurthy, & de Vries, 2019). Instances include multi-player gaming experiments in a face-to-face or virtual reality setting (Mochizuki, Magnuszewski, & Linnerooth-Bayer, 2018; Agusdinata & Lukosch, 2019), creating interfaces between participants and computer models through participatory scenario development for exploration through alternative future storylines (Johnson & Karlberg, 2017; Colloff et al., 2019), and participatory geographic information systems potentially open to the multi-dimensional visualisation of ecological changes for interactive decision-support experiences (Karpouzoglou, Pereira, & Doshi, 2017; Kraftl et al., 2019).

An intensive participatory modelling approach may consequently increase the effectiveness and efficiency of the ULL approach in supporting an adaptive governance mechanism for the transdisciplinary FWE nexus. The following statements explore how the strategy of such an engagement between the transdisciplinary FWE nexus concept, the ULL approach, and a computer-supported participatory platform promotes requisites for a sustainable socio-ecological transition (see Figure 2.1). The use of participatory modelling methods and tools, specific to contextual complexities, supports:

- **Sociability to facilitate cooperative interactions**
  Through the FWE nexus projects, direct and indirect stakeholders should regularly collaborate in order to cope with the uncertain challenges of socio-ecological transitions. Working as a team can support participants in learning from each other and exchanging useful information. Thus, the structure of nexus social networks and the capacity of individuals to interact with each other are of primary importance in constructing knowledge. In addition, a greater number of stakeholders of potential benefit for progressing opportunities as it maximises corrections and improvements, although it also raises additional concerns over the management of a more extensive collaboration. Virtual collaboration, along with face-to-face discussion, serves as a practical solution to extensive nexus collaborations. As an advantage, virtual collaboration operates across space, time, and organisational boundaries. Moreover, virtual collaboration overcomes the likely emotional states within face-to-face meetings and minimises the risk of impeding the negotiation process.

- **Knowledge co-production to characterise paradigms of localised interventions**
  In FWE nexus projects where all stakeholders have to collaborate as a team on new socio-ecological solutions, every stakeholder should have a chance to propose their experiences and democratically take the initiative. It means an all-together-decision-making that is a requisite for the transdisciplinary FWE nexus. Such decisions entail potential risks associated with the uncertainties of stakeholder engagement, consensus, and the future, which can be part of the creative process. Exploration of new ideas and experimentation with new solutions through participatory modelling tools involving local stakeholders may potentially contribute to a reduction in the nexus transdisciplinarity attendant risks.

- **Corporate governance to shape a resilient alliance and adaptive capacity**
  Accountability, fairness, transparency, assurance, leadership, and stakeholder management are of primary importance in empowering a community for ecological-conservation purposes. The contextual design embedded in the participatory-supported ULL mechanisms attaches great importance to power dynamics in multi-stakeholder nexus processes (Ghodsvali, Krishnamurthy, & de Vries, 2019). The contextual inquiry captures detailed information about how stakeholders affected by a nexus project interact with the environment in their normal life. In addition to the support for participatory modelling methods in distributing an equitable balance of power, it supports nexus stakeholders to understand others' interests, and in turn adjusts and prioritises their ideas and tasks.

- **Socio-eco-techno integration to introduce efficient resolutions** Exploring innovative ideas, experimenting with different future scenarios, and learning adaptable responses to ecological changes are the collection of participatory-supported ULL mechanisms through which FWE nexus resolutions are controlled and operated. Best practice is to seek this through the integration of computer-supported participatory techniques into socio-ecological concerns. Although experiments vary significantly in objective and scale, they always rely on an iterative procedure and logical exploration. FWE nexus experimentation provides insight into cause and effect relationships by indicating which outcome occurs when a specific factor is manipulated. Experimenting with social innovation, including new technology, strategies, ideas, and institutions, enhances the capacity of social and ecological systems to help steer away from multiple FWE resource thresholds. The trial-and-error logic promotes the need of FWE nexus projects to experiment through iterative consultation and the subsequent mutual understanding among participants. Moreover, experimentation may provide nexus actors with a sense of joint ownership and raise opportunities for accountability.

By integrating the above-described potential benefits of participatory modelling methods into the nexus ULL approach, FWE nexus projects might be able to end up with new context-specified solutions and operational concepts.

5. Concluding remarks

A ULL can potentially support the accomplishment of the transdisciplinary FWE nexus if there is a well-balanced social-ecological-technological integration. From the literature and existing empirical evidence, there appear to be many requisites for making the ULL approach more effective and efficient as an adaptive governance mechanism for the transdisciplinary FWE nexus. However, a critical evaluation of these requisites and the best way to satisfy them has not been conducted so far, and no operational guidelines are available on how to adopt the ULL approach to effectively and efficiently support the transdisciplinary FWE nexus, emphasising inclusive, active, and direct stakeholder engagement. This knowledge gap requires thorough studies of the interactions between the ULL approach and the varying related participatory settings and the transdisciplinary process in the FWE nexus. Thus far, evaluations of participatory techniques in nexus ULLs have been characterised by limited attention to socio-technical design and the development of innovation processes (e.g. Molinari & Schumacher, 2011). We suggest that such evaluations could greatly benefit from the fields of corporate governance, sociability, knowledge co-production, and, in particular, from the rapidly expanding area of ICT-supported participatory modelling methods and tools. Studies show how the insights from ICT-supported participatory modelling are supportive in designing collaboration support tools, facilitating negotiation and learning processes, building consensus, and evaluating the effectiveness of jointly made decisions. We expect, therefore, that integrating the fields of participatory modelling via ICT tools, the ULL approach, and the FWE nexus will considerably advance our capabilities in accomplishing the concept of transdisciplinarity for more sustainable environmental and natural resource management.

Acknowledgements

This work was supported by the Netherlands Organization for Scientific Research (NWO) in the framework of the Joint Programming Initiative Urban Europe, with support from the European Union's Horizon 2020 Research and Innovation Program under grant agreement No 730254.

References

Abdi, H., & Valentin, D. (2007). Multiple correspondence analysis. In N. J. Salkind (Ed.), *Encyclopedia of Measurement and Statistics*. Thousand Oaks, CA: SAGE Publications.

Agusdinata, D. B., & Lukosch, H. (2019). Supporting interventions to reduce household greenhouse gas emissions: A transdisciplinary role-playing game development. *Simulation & Gaming*, 50(3), 359–376. https://doi.org/10.1177/1046878119848135

Almirall, E., Lee, M., & Wareham, J. (2012). Mapping living labs in the landscape of innovation methodologies. *Technology Innovation Management Review*, 2(9), 12–18. https://doi.org/10.22215/timreview/603

Baccarne, B., Logghe, S., Schuurman, D., & De Marez, L. (2016). Governing quintuple helix innovation: Urban living labs and socio-ecological entrepreneurship. *Technology Innovation Management Review*, 6(3), 22–30. https://doi.org/10.22215/timreview/972

Bergvall-Kåreborn, B., Ihlström Eriksson, C., Ståhlbröst, A., & Svensson, J. (2009). A milieu for innovation – Defining living labs. In *Proceedings of the 2nd ISPIM innovation symposium: Simulating recovery – the Role of innovation management*. New York City, USA, 6–9 December 2009. Retrieved from http://urn.kb.se/resolve?urn=urn:nbn:se:ltu:diva-31540

Bulkeley, H., Coenen, L., Frantzeskaki, N. et al. (2016). Urban living labs: Governing urban sustainability transitions. *Current Opinion in Environmental Sustainability*, 22, 13–17. https://doi.org/10.1016/j.cosust.2017.02.003

Cairns, R., Wilsdon, J., & O'Donovan, C. (2017). *Sustainability in turbulent times: Lessons from The Nexus Network for supporting transdisciplinary research*. The Nexus Network. Retrieved from http://www.thenexusnetwork.org/wp-content/uploads/2017/03/sustainability-in-turbulent-times.pdf

Carayannis, E. G., Barth, T. D., & Campbell, D. F. (2012). The Quintuple Helix innovation model: Global warming as a challenge and driver for innovation. *Journal of Innovation and Entrepreneurship*, 1(1), 2. https://doi.org/10.1186/2192-5372-1-2

Cardullo, P., Kitchin, R., & Di Feliciantonio, C. (2018). Living labs and vacancy in the neoliberal city. *Cities, 73*, 44–50. https://doi.org/10.1016/j.cities.2017.10.008

Chesbrough, H. W. (2003). *Open innovation: The new imperative for creating and profiting from technology*. Boston, MA: Harvard Business School Press.

Chronéer, D., Ståhlbröst, A., & Habibipour, A. (2019). Urban living labs: Towards an integrated understanding of their key components. *Technology Innovation Management Review, 9*(3), 50–62. https://doi.org/10.22215/timreview/1224

Colloff, M. J., Doody, T. M., Overton, I. C. et al. (2019). Re-framing the decision context over trade-offs among ecosystem services and wellbeing in a major river basin where water resources are highly contested. *Sustainability Science, 14*(3), 713–731. https://doi.org/10.1007/s11625-018-0630-x

Davis, A., & Andrew, J. (2017). Co-creating urban environments to engage citizens in a low-carbon future. *Procedia Engineering, 180*, 651–657. https://doi.org/10.1016/j.proeng.2017.04.224

de Kraker, J., Kroeze, C., & Kirschner, P. (2011). Computer models as social learning tools in participatory integrated assessment. *International Journal of Agricultural Sustainability, 9*(2), 297–309. https://doi.org/10.1080/14735903.2011.582356

de Kraker, J., Scholl, C., & van Wanroij, T. (2016). Urban labs – A new approach in the governance of sustainable urban development. In *Sustainable Development Research at ICIS: Taking stock and looking ahead* (pp. 335–346). Datawyse / Universitaire Pers Maastricht.

European Commission. (2017). Global demand for resources | Knowledge for policy. Retrieved February 21, 2020, from https://ec.europa.eu/knowledge4policy/foresight/topic/aggravating-resource-scarcity/global-demand-resources-materials_en

Field, A. (2013). *Discovering Statistics Using IBM SPSS Statistics* (Fourth, Vol. 53). (M. Carmichael, Ed.). Los Angeles: SAGE.

Frantzeskaki, N., van Steenbergen, F., & Stedman, R. C. (2018). Sense of place and experimentation in urban sustainability transitions: The resilience lab in Carnisse, Rotterdam, The Netherlands. *Sustainability Science, 13*(4), 1045–1059. https://doi.org/10.1007/s11625-018-0562-5

Ghodsvali, M., Dane, G., & de Vries, B. (2022). The nexus social-ecological system framework (NexSESF): A conceptual and empirical examination of transdisciplinary food-water-energy nexus. *Environmental Science & Policy, 130*(July 2021), 16–24.

Ghodsvali, M., Krishnamurthy, S., & de Vries, B. (2019). Review of transdisciplinary approaches to food-water-energy nexus: A guide towards sustainable development. *Environmental Science & Policy, 101*, 266–278. https://doi.org/10.1016/j.envsci.2019.09.003

Gorddard, R., Colloff, M. J., Wise, R. M. et al. (2016). Values, rules and knowledge: Adaptation as change in the decision context. *Environmental Science & Policy, 57*, 60–69. https://doi.org/10.1016/j.envsci.2015.12.004

Halbe, J., Pahl-Wostl, C., Lange, M. A., & Velonis, C. (2015). Governance of transitions towards sustainable development – the water-energy-food nexus in Cyprus. *Water International, 40*(5–6), 877–894. https://doi.org/10.1080/02508060.2015.1070328

Johnson, O. W., & Karlberg, L. (2017). Co-exploring the water-energy-food nexus: Facilitating dialogue through participatory scenario building. *Frontiers in Environmental Science, 5*(May), 1–12. https://doi.org/10.3389/fenvs.2017.00024

Karpouzoglou, T., Pereira, L. M., & Doshi, S. (2017). Bridging ICTs with governance capabilities for food-energy-water sustainability. In *Food, Energy and Water Sustainability* (pp. 222–238). Routledge. https://doi.org/10.9774/GLEAF.9781315696522_13

Kraftl, P., Balastieri, J. A. P., Campos, A. E. M. et al. (2019). (Re)thinking (re)connection: Young people, "natures" and the water-energy-food nexus in São Paulo State, Brazil. *Transactions of the Institute of British Geographers, 44*(2), 299–314. https://doi.org/10.1111/tran.12277

Lund, D. H. (2018). Co-creation in urban governance: From inclusion to innovation. *Scandinavian Journal of Public Administration, 22*(2).

Meijer, A. (2012). Co-production in an information age: Individual and community engagement supported by new media. *VOLUNTAS: International Journal of Voluntary and Nonprofit Organizations, 23*(4), 1156–1172. https://doi.org/10.1007/s11266-012-9311-z

Mochizuki, J., Magnuszewski, P., & Linnerooth-Bayer, J. (2018). Games for aiding stakeholder deliberation on nexus policy issues. In S. Hülsmann, & R. Ardakanian (Eds.), *Managing Water, Soil and Waste Resources to Achieve Sustainable Development Goals* (pp. 93–124). Cham: Springer International Publishing. https://doi.org/10.1007/978-3-319-75163-4_5

Molinari, F. (2011). Living labs as multi-stakeholder platforms for the egovernance of innovation. In *Proceedings of the 5th International Conference on Theory and Practice* of *Electronic Governance – ICEGOV '11* (p. 131). New York, NY: ACM Press. https://doi.org/10.1145/2072069.2072092

Molinari, F., & Schumacher, J. (2011). *Best practices database for living labs: Overview of the living lab approach*. Retrieved from https://api.semanticscholar.org/Corpus ID:44119161

Mulder, I. (2012). Living labbing the Rotterdam Way: Co-creation as an enabler for urban innovation. *Technology Innovation Management Review, 2*(9), 39–43. https://doi.org/10.22215/timreview/607

Nesti, G. (2017). Living labs: A new tool for co-production? In A. Bisello, D. Vettorato, R. Stephens, & P. Elisei (Eds.), *Smart and Sustainable Planning for Cities and Regions* (pp. 267–281). Cham: Springer International Publishing. https://doi.org/10.1007/978-3-319-44899-2_16

Nesti, G. (2018). Co-production for innovation: The urban living lab experience. *Policy and Society, 37*(3), 310–325. https://doi.org/10.1080/14494035.2017.1374692

Nevens, F., Frantzeskaki, N., Gorissen, L., & Loorbach, D. (2013). Urban transition labs: Co-creating transformative action for sustainable cities. *Journal of Cleaner Production, 50*, 111–122. https://doi.org/10.1016/j.jclepro.2012.12.001

Pierson, J., & Lievens, B. (2005). Configuring living labs for a 'thick' understanding of innovation. *Ethnographic Praxis in Industry Conference Proceedings (EPIC)*, (1), 114–127. https://doi.org/10.1111/j.1559-8918.2005.tb00012.x

Prahalad, C. K., & Ramaswamy, V. (2004). Co-creation experiences: The next practice in value creation. *Journal of Interactive Marketing, 18*(3), 5–14. https://doi.org/10.1002/dir.20015

Rodriguez-Sabate, C., Morales, I., Sanchez, A., & Rodriguez, M. (2017). The multiple correspondence analysis method and brain functional connectivity: Its application to the study of the non-linear relationships of motor cortex and basal ganglia. *Frontiers in Neuroscience, 11*(JUN). https://doi.org/10.3389/fnins.2017.00345

Scott, C. A., Kurian, M., & Wescoat, J. L. (2015). The water-energy-food nexus: Enhancing adaptive capacity to complex global challenges. In M. Kurian, & R. Ardakanian (Eds.), *Governing the Nexus* (pp. 15–38). Cham: Springer International Publishing. https://doi.org/10.1007/978-3-319-05747-7_2

Steen, K., & van Bueren, E. (2017). The defining characteristics of urban living labs. *Technology Innovation Management Review, 7*(7), 21–33.

Voytenko, Y., McCormick, K., Evans, J., & Schliwa, G. (2016). Urban living labs for sustainability and low carbon cities in Europe: Towards a research agenda. *Journal of Cleaner Production*, *123*, 45–54. https://doi.org/10.1016/j.jclepro.2015.08.053

Yan, W., & Roggema, R. (2019). Developing a design-led approach for the food-energy-water nexus in cities. *Urban Planning*, *4*(1), 123. https://doi.org/10.17645/up.v4i1.1739

Yin, R. K. (2009). *Case Study Research: Design and Methods* (4th ed.). SAGE Publications.

Zárraga, A., & Goitisolo, B. (2011). Correspondence analysis of surveys with multiple response questions. In S. Ingrassia, R. Rocci, & M. Vichi (Eds.), *New Perspectives in Statistical Modeling and Data Analysis* (pp. 505–513). Berlin, Heidelberg: Springer. https://doi.org/10.1007/978-3-642-11363-5_57

Appendix A. Methodological details

Table A.1: Questions of the online survey conducted on the design, processes, and practices of the selected ULLs

1- What are the environmental problems your city deals with?

€ Densification € Biodiversity loss € Pollution € Heat stress € Water scarcity € Flooding € Lax food security € Other:

2- What is the focus of the nexus project in your city? (one or more choice)

€ Strategic planning € Policy interventions € Analytical approach € Development actions € Other:

Please explain your choice in detail.

3- What is the scale of the nexus project in your city?

€ City scale € Neighborhood scale € Building scale

4- What is the relevance of the designed Urban Living Lab in relation to the aim of the nexus project in your city?

€ Studying existing governance structure and processes € Assessing existing state of the challenges in your city € Increasing co-creation and participation € Testing the usefulness of the ULL approach € Other:

5- What are the solutions that proposed ULL explores?

€ Repurposing existing areas € Densification of existing urban areas € Development of innovative solutions on green/blue infrastructure

€ Creation of mixed-use areas € Increasing awareness through participation € Other:

Please explain your choice in detail.

6- To what degree following stakeholders are involved in the proposed ULL?

	1 (Low)	2	3	4	5 (High)
Academic/University					
Municipality					
Industry/Professional					
Local community					

7- Who are defined as current users in the proposed location of the ULL?

8- Who are defined as end-users in the nexus project of your city?

€ Existing group of users € Future users € Proxy (through a representative)

9- Who are the key actors in the proposed ULL?

€ Governmental actors € Industry € Financial actors € Local community € Academic € Other:

10- Please select the collaboration order of stakeholders within proposed ULL.

	Government	Industry	Academic	Local community	Financial actors
1 (First) – 5 (Last)					

11- Does the issue go beyond the administrative borders of your city/municipality?

€ Yes € No € Maybe

12- At which level of administrative boundary are the nexus activities of the proposed ULL managed?

€ National € Regional € Local

13- How was the ULL's engagement strategy identified geographically?

€ Within the ULL area € Beyond the ULL area

If "beyond the ULL area", please identify the extent.

(*Continued*)

Table A.1: (Continued)

14- What is the governance system of the proposed ULL?

€ Top-down   € Bottom-up   € Top-down and bottom-up

15- How was the selection of initial participants from the community made?

| € Open to everyone (self-selection) | € Stakeholder representative | € Demographically representative | € Specific individuals | € Other: |

16- Is it possible for all community members to participate in the ULL?

€ Yes, within the ULL boundary   € Yes, from outside the ULL boundary   € No

17- How do different actors collaborate in the ULL?

| € Working individually | € Within multi-disciplinary groups | € In groups of similar backgrounds | € Other |

18- How does the ULL approach raise local awareness about the nexus concerns?

| € Information sharing | € Consultation | € Collaboration | € Empowerment | € Other: |

19- How do the ULL actors share ideas?

| € One-way physical communication (e.g., post) | € One-way virtual communication (e.g., media, advertising) | € Two-way physical communication (e.g., workshops, booths) | € Two-way virtual communication (e.g., apps, remote attendance) | € Multi-model sharing (combination of physical and virtual methods) |

20- Is there an open data platform that all different actors of the ULL have access to?

€ Yes   € No

If yes, please add the link.

21- How transparent is the knowledge sharing within the proposed ULL?

                            1 (Low)   2   3   4   5 (High)

Between decision makers and local community

Between decision makers

22- Please identify methods used to showcase ideas between decision makers and community through the proposed ULL.

☐ Gamification ☐ 3D model ☐ Rendering and images ☐ Discussing examples of current studies ☐ Other:

23- Who is the owner of the proposed ULL in your city?

☐ Local government ☐ The Municipality ☐ Industry ☐ Local community ☐ Other:

24- Please identify policy barriers your city faces that prevent the integrated resource management in your city?

Please explain your answer.

25- How aligned are current political interests to the interest of local community in the context of nexus challenges in your city?

Please explain your answer.

Table A.2: MCA dimensions discrimination measures

Categorical variables	*MCA dimensions*	
	Dimension 1	Dimension 2
Stakeholders' power	0.983	0.966
Idea-showcasing methods	0.861	0.734
Local awareness methods	0.791	0.862
Nexus ULL key actors	0.783	0.462
Environmental problem	0.780	0.613
FWE nexus focus	0.772	0.672
Stakeholder collaboration order	0.746	0.696
Idea-sharing methods	0.726	0.460
Nexus ULL role	0.693	0.688
Nexus ULL solution	0.652	0.478
Initial participants selection	0.594	0.632
Collaboration structure	0.558	0.313

(*Continued*)

Table A.2: (Continued)

Categorical variables	MCA dimensions	
	Dimension 1	Dimension 2
Nexus ULL current user	0.534	0.538
Information transparency with local community	0.448	0.240
Information transparency among decision makers	0.406	0.104
Governance system	0.404	0.016
Nexus ULL owner	0.368	0.364
Spatial extent of nexus activities	0.308	0.033
Open data platform	0.289	0.143
FWE nexus end-users	0.250	0.293
FWE nexus scale	0.243	0.028
Spatial extent of the nexus issue	0.182	0.005
Participation possibility	0.102	0.288
Active total	12.955	9.773
Percentage of variance	7.712	5.817

Appendix B. Analytical details

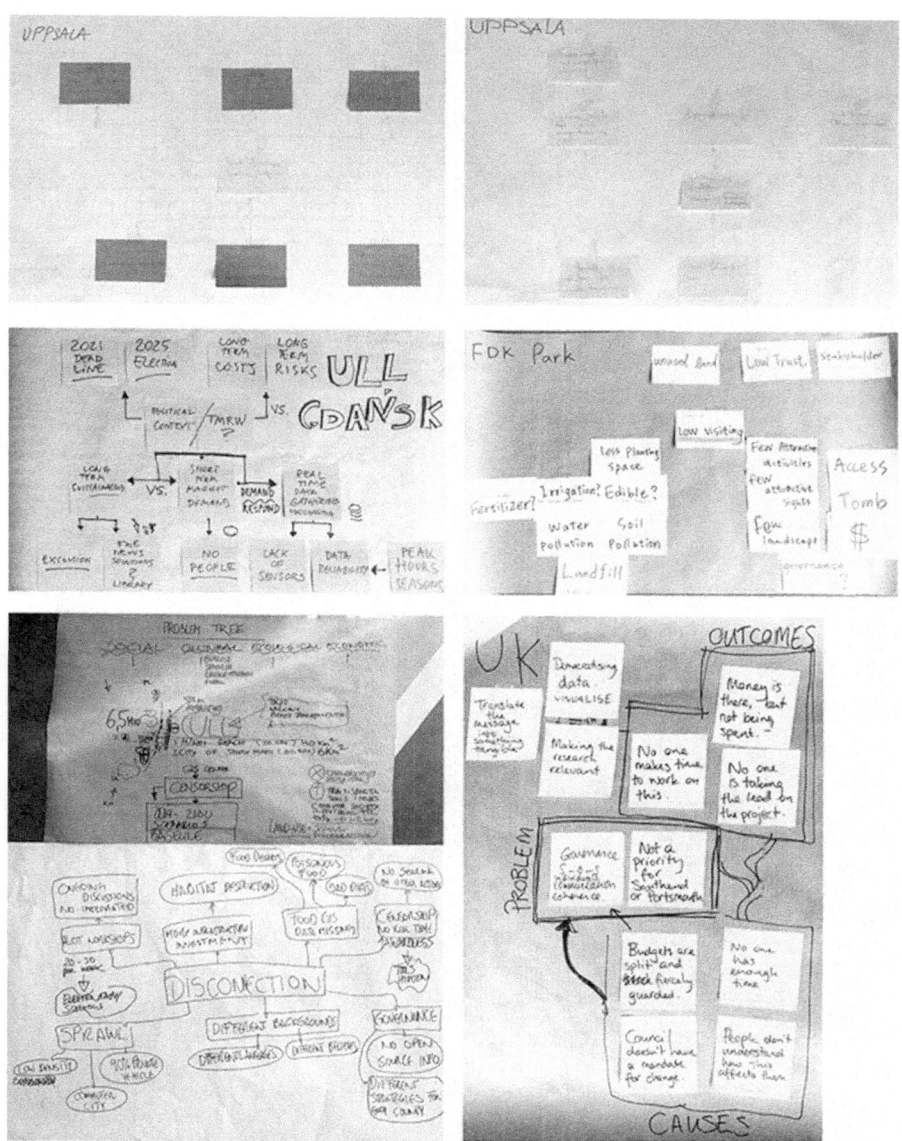

Figure B.1: Problem trees of the nexus ULLs selected for this research

Teams of multiple stakeholders from each ULL, through a focus group discussion, debated the main problem of their nexus ULL and defined its associated causes and effects. The problem trees were analysed for a logical strategic guideline (see Figure 2.4).

Chapter 3

Urban greening snakes and ladders

A case study of the practical realities of implementing Food-Water-Energy nexus projects in Southend-on-Sea, UK

Heather Rumble and Julia Brown

1. Introduction

As the CRUNCH project launched in April 2018, Southend-on-Sea (SoS) presented as an exciting location to test innovative nature-based nexus solutions. The proposed Urban Living Lab (ULL) location was part of the urban regeneration plan for the town centre, specifically the High Street and its immediate environ, which funnels 6 million visitors to the seafront esplanade and world-famous leisure pier every year. In order to address future climate impacts – of flooding, drought and heat stress in the Borough – Southend Borough Council (SBC) recognised it needed to deploy more urban greenery across its landscape to benefit public health for both residents and visitors. Many of the aforementioned challenges, notably flooding and heat stress, in the proposed ULL were exacerbated by urban design. As with many similarly sized urban areas across the UK, Southend saw its town centre redeveloped in the 1960s, with original historical buildings replaced with more functional mid-century architecture. The form of urban development, with widespread use of impermeable surfaces and reliance on grey infrastructure and minimal greening, has radically transformed the urban landscape, interrupting the natural hydrological cycle, which thus contributes to flash flooding and summer heat stress. SBC commissioned a consultative future scoping project, Vision 2050, that provides a clear road map for

DOI: 10.4324/9781003112495-12

the council to align its programming. In the scoping, participating residents raised concerns over the condition of the High Street – the quality of roads and pavements – and had aspirations for the town centre and its public spaces to be "clean, attractive and thriving". The consultative process highlighted strong support for environmental issues and a clear commitment to "reimagining our High Street" was made.[1]

The connection between the form of urban design and the ameliorating impact of urban greening was championed within the council by the self-financing Energy and Sustainability team, who had successfully secured EU Interreg funding, matched by the council, for three urban greening (UG) projects to kick-start the transformation of the High Street and surrounding side streets. The CRUNCH project ULL was originally conceived to sit alongside these urban regeneration plans for the town centre, which had funding for new UG infrastructure and, importantly, a team – Energy and Sustainability – who were committed to incorporating Food-Water-Energy nexus approaches into their designs

While the ingredients were in place to test the potential of nexus approaches within an UG agenda, as we moved to the practical reality of implementation, the project hit the planning, policy, and political buffers. This chapter will explore why, despite the weight of evidence that supports the introduction of UG to overcome many urban challenges, its implementation has been slow. By focusing on a second-tier city in the UK, rather than a large administrative capital, we can illuminate the challenges that urban areas face in matching up public aspirations for clean and attractive green with specific implementation barriers. We suggest that larger urban spaces, such as the UK's 12 'core' cities (e.g. Manchester and Glasgow), are on a different trajectory: their lessons may not always translate to smaller towns and cities, where, in reality, the majority of our populations live.[2] The academic literature on identifying barriers and presenting potential solutions is still in its infancy, and we hope to contribute to this growing and important field with this chapter, which is organised as follows. We provide a short review of the evidence in support of UG followed by a summary of barriers identified in the literature, which are often not place-specific. We then present the case study of the UG snakes and ladders experienced by SBC, which we will broaden into a discussion on the themes that emerged from our case study, drawing upon 6 expert interviews with practitioners in the UK, Netherlands, and Germany, in order to contextualise the findings more broadly. We also develop some potential solutions to barriers that are relevant to similar sized urban areas.

2. The case for urban greening

The benefits that cities gain from installing urban greenery (whether in the guise of green infrastructure or nature-based solutions – NBS) are now well documented, with Sustainable Drainage Systems (SuDS), air pollution mitigation, reduction of the urban heat island (UHI) and human health and wellbeing all well researched.

In terms of SuDS, the vast amount of soil sealing in cities, through the use of tarmac and concrete, means that water is unable to percolate into the groundwater, resulting in flash flooding and, over time, the over-extraction of aquifers. It is now commonly acknowledged that reducing soil-sealing by including areas of greenery rather than paving, as well as installing larger-scale vegetation, such as trees and green roofs, makes a valuable contribution to city drainage systems (Scalenghe & Ajmone-Marsan, 2009). They can provide physically (Ellis, 2013) and cost effective (Jaffe, 2010; Ossa-Moreno, Smith, & Mijic, 2017; Vincent et al., 2017) solutions to the problem when planned correctly.

Urban greenery also effectively ameliorates rising city temperatures caused by the UHI. Plants are effective at cooling their immediate environment through evapotranspiration (Peters, Hiller, & McFadden, 2011), shading (Akbari, Pomerantz, & Taha, 2001), and by attenuating solar radiation (Tooke et al., 2011). When planted in sufficient numbers – for example, in well-designed parks – Park Cool Islands may be formed, achieving temperature reductions of up to 5 °C (Brown et al., 2015). Well-designed UG projects such as Lyon's Rue Garibaldi, France, reduces summer temperatures by up to 8 °C (Trees and Design Action Group, 2016) by smartly integrating green and grey infrastructure.

Air pollution is also seen as a major threat to human health, for which UG could play an important part in ameliorating. Poor air quality in the UK was responsible for 29,000 premature deaths in 2008, shortening lifespans by up to 11 years (COMEAP, 2010). UG can significantly contribute to urban infrastructures to alleviate this (Baró et al., 2014). Trees, in particular, have a large surface area onto which particulate matter may adhere, removing it from the air; on a city-wide scale, the installation of trees can have a significant positive impact on reducing this harmful particulate matter. In the London iTree survey (Rogers et al., 2015), it was estimated that almost 1,700 tonnes of air pollutants a year were removed by trees, saving £68m worth of associated costs, including costs for healthcare.

Urbanites are at increased risk of mental health issues than rural populations (Evans et al., 2020), and UG has also been shown to combat this. Kaplan and

Kaplan's (1989) Attention Restoration Theory has now been repeated many times, demonstrating that viewing "natural attention grabbers" – such as the ocean, trees, and clouds – reduces the build-up of stress fatigue (Lee et al., 2015). Ulrich's (1984) study demonstrating that nature also has salutogenic benefits, with mental and physical health patients recovering faster from illness when confronted with more natural environments, has also now been repeated many times. In addition, those that perceive themselves to live in areas with high-quality greenspace on average experience lower cortisol levels than those that do not (Thompson, Aspinall, & Roe, 2014).

UG benefits city dwellers in many other ways: it has been shown that people spend more money in greener high streets (Wolf, 2005). The enhanced biodiversity associated with UG also provides additional ecosystem services, such as pest and disease reduction, increased pollination and seed dispersal, water filtration, and carbon sequestration.

While there is now excellent evidence that UG in cities is beneficial, there is mounting evidence that the lack of wildlife in our cities is causing a global environmental crisis. Most people live in cities (United Nations, 2018), an environment that is also depauperate in wildlife, limiting their experiences with nature. For example, Balmford et al. (2002) demonstrated that children in the UK can name more Pokémon than they can native species. Urbanites' paucity of knowledge about nature poses a serious challenge for championing nature outside of cities, where it provides us with vital life support systems such as providing our food, energy and oxygen, sequestering carbon, and reducing flooding (Constanza et al., 2014); the value gained from these ecosystem services are thought to exceed global GDP by at least 2x (ibid.). Thus, experiencing nature in cities through UG is essential to enable people to understand the wider benefits that nature provides.

3. Barriers to urban greening

Despite the large body of evidence in support of UG (section 2), its implementation has still been extremely slow (Byrne & Yang, 2009; Johns, 2019; Matthews, Lo, & Byrne, 2015). Governments, local authorities, and other interest groups all cite the inclusion of UG in cities as a priority (e.g. Mayor of London/London Assembly, 2016; Portsmouth City Council, 2019; Toronto, Johns, 2019). Public support for UG has been high throughout this period (Byrne & Yang, 2009; Matthews et al., 2015). Yet outside major 'core' cities, such as London, Sheffield, and Manchester in the UK, there is still a paucity of green infrastructure, while sales of astroturf have reportedly increased (Wallop, 2020), and cities continue to be dominated by impermeable surfaces (Ellis, 2013). Less traditional UG, such as green roofs and living walls, for which reliable technologies have now been well established in the developed world for over two decades, are still a rarity in most urban settings. This chapter seeks to address this call by Johns (2019) to understand why cities have been so slow to adopt UG.

There is an emerging body of research into barriers faced when implementing UG projects. An analysis of this literature draws out commonly mentioned barriers that can be broadly placed into seven categories: first, the *biophysical character and morphology of urban spaces*. Current land use, its ownership, and the resultant space available for greening is thought to have considerable bearing on UG uptake and in some instances pose an insurmountable barrier to its implementation (Matthews, Lo, & Byrne, 2015; Johns, 2019).

Economics and the dearth of funding is the second key barrier to the installation of GI; in the UK, local councils, who are a significant land manager in cities, have had their budgets cut by an average of ⅔ since 2010 (LGA, 2018), leaving UG as a luxury item. Matthews, Lo and Byrne (2015) report on the perception that UG is expensive vis-à-vis grey infrastructure; Johns (2019) reports that cities in the USA are still spending more on grey than green infrastructure. In reality, as with grey infrastructure, the costs of UG can vary greatly depending on scale and design; UG can be far more cost effective than grey infrastructure in many instances.

The literature suggests that there are significant issues that go beyond economics, and Matthews et al. (2015) suggest that barriers relating to political-institutional and socio-cultural concerns have had less attention paid to them. Our third category thus relates to *politics and the strength of political support* for the greening agenda in practice, alongside active engagement with climate mitigation (ibid.). Issues over the quality of leadership at the city-level are also raised by Johns (2019) and Winz Trowsdale, and Brierley (2014). It appears that while there is support at these upper levels for UG in the abstract, this often does not translate into the support that is needed for projects to be implemented, and a sense of urgency over climate mitigation is missing. Following on from this is the recognition that the very institutions and organisations charged with implementing the greening agenda are themselves a major blockage to its realisation: they represent the fourth category. Specifically, *a lack of leadership, collaboration, and communication between different municipal departments*, who effectively work in silos, is commonly mentioned (Cettner et al., 2013; Roe & Mell, 2013; Winz, Trowsdale, & Brierley,

2014; Matthews, Lo, & Byrne, 2015; Johns, 2019). Institutional inertia reinforces path dependency, and a reluctance to innovate is the consequence (Lennon, 2014; Matthews, Lo, & Byrne, 2015; O'Donnell, Lamond, & Thorne, 2017; Johns, 2019). *A lack of knowledge of and expertise in UG* within local authorities (LAs) as well as amongst citizens is also hampering its uptake (Johns, 2019; Roy et al., 2008); this is the fifth category.

Our sixth barrier is *confusion over terminology*, namely the conflation of the terms green infrastructure (GI), nature-based solutions (NBS), and UG, and the promotion of its multifunctional benefits, which may be contributing to the previous barrier over knowledge of UG and progress in its adoption. Matthews et al. (2015) suggest that this ambiguity leads to confusion and stymies progress because it hampers effective communication between silos and stakeholders. Our final identified barrier to progressing the greening agenda in a range of contexts is the *legal and planning system* (Byrne & Yang, 2009; Lennon, 2014; Winz, Trowsdale, & Brierley, 2014; Matthews, Lo, & Byrne, 2015; Johns, 2019), which, it is argued, has not adapted to enable UG projects to be implemented. As a result, we often try to fit UG into current legal and planning systems, which are not fit for purpose.

We suggest that barriers are likely to be complex and context dependent, which is why we advocate in-depth case studies to understand the place specific barriers. Taking a qualitative approach, we review one LA's struggle to introduce UG within the city of SoS as a way to demonstrate the real barriers that LAs face when trying to integrate nature into cities and in so doing contribute to this important field of inquiry.

4. Methods

The data for the case study comprises the outcome of regular dialogue and update meetings with SBC project promoters as well as additional desk-based research of publicly available information. The role of the CRUNCH team was to provide practical advice over nexus solutions and their incorporation into UG. In order to contextualise the greening efforts in SoS, we interviewed 6 expert practitioners across the UK and Europe. These were: a German-based freelance landscape planner; Glasgow city planner; Eindhoven city policymaker; UK-based academic-practitioner; and two members of the SBC Energy and Sustainability team. Interviews were conducted in accordance with the University of Portsmouth's ethical procedures.

5. Case study of Southend-on-Sea

5.1 Introduction to Southend-on-Sea

As outlined in the introduction, SoS was selected as the UK ULL for the CRUNCH project because, while it has a unique set of attributes, it shares many commonalities with other UK seaside towns and second-tier cities. Lying on the north side of the Thames Estuary, and 40 miles east of central London, SoS is home to the driest place in the UK, Great Wakering, and it is also a seaside resort with over 6 million visitors a year. While 81% of residents in SoS are classed as economically active, it has pockets of deprivation, with 10% of the population living in workless households (nomis.web.co.uk). In the 2011 census, 90% identified their ethnic origin as being white British, and as of March 2020, almost 20% of the population were classed as retired (the UK average is 13%). SoS also has some of the most densely populated wards outside of central London, with an average of 39 people per hectare (southend.gov.uk; nomis.web.co.uk). SBC became a unitary authority in 1998, with responsibility for all functions.

The CRUNCH ULL covers a 0.5 km2 area that encompasses the city centre neighbourhood, with an estimated population of 4,700. It is described by the EU SUNRISE project[3] as being a "dynamic neighbourhood" comprising diverse residential demographics, with businesses situated close to the two railway stations (p. 34). Encompassing some of SoS's most deprived wards, with up to 30% classed as economically inactive, the area has been targeted for regeneration. The SUNRISE project notes a divide between the original, less affluent, older residents and those who have moved into the regenerated parts who tend to be younger and more affluent (p. 35). SBC employees note that the impact of austerity and the financial crisis of 2008 has caused a noticeable decline in the High Street, which is common to many high streets in the UK (Millington & Ntounis, 2017). As the SUNRISE project notes, in order to encourage more people into city centres and to support businesses across Europe, the "streetscape and public spaces must be improved to support the overall offer" (p. 36). In this vein, the Energy and Sustainability team at SBC were created to drive the UG and climate adaptation innovations related to these aims.

5.2 A story of UG snakes and ladders

The SBC self-financed Energy and Sustainability team realised that without new funding streams the team and their agenda was at risk. European Union Interreg funding provided a win-win opportunity to secure and grow the team and provide funds for new GI innovations in the target regeneration area. The team successfully secured three ongoing Interreg projects that also addressed urban heating and flooding and whose timing and topic related to the remit of CRUNCH:

1. **Cool Towns** sought to deploy heat reduction measures such as tree planters, tree pits, and water-capturing features (e.g. rills) as a means of cooling and supplying air hydration. It also sought to install canopy shading solutions and provide public drinking water features to tackle the human health impact of heat stress.
2. **SPONGE2020** implements SuDS measures, like swales, rain gardens, and rills, through a participative adaptation approach to identify at-risk locations.
3. **Nature Smart Cities (NSCiti2S)** invests in GI (e.g. green roofs, permeable paving, and rain gardens), in a residential regeneration scheme. It also provides capacity-building around the business cases for GI investment.[4]

In addition, SBC has successfully received other funding that also addresses identified sustainability issues in central SoS, including those that have the potential to incorporate nexus UG into their designs. TRIPS, funded under the UK National Productivity Infrastructure Fund, seeks to improve the connectivity in central SoS and revamp public spaces by improving surfacing and providing additional seating and planting where practical. SUNRISE[5], funded by the EU, focuses on central SoS, gathering suggestions and ideas for improvement from those who live within the neighbourhood. Emerging from the participatory process in early 2019 was the aspiration for 'a softer feel to the existing streetscape . . . the area is dominated too much by hard landscaping and needs to be broken up by trees and planting' (p. 99). The SUNRISE project did not provide specific recommendations over the form this greening could take or highlight any potential barriers (p. 98), but the importance of the SUNRISE consultation along with the scoping or the Vision 2050 document is that there appears to be support for UG from SoS residents (though greening and 'softening' may mean different things to different people).

With these concurrent funded projects coalescing around the city centre and the proposed CRUNCH ULL, optimism prevailed that SoS had the potential to transform its urban landscape through nexus UG solutions. An important learning point of the project has been the hugely complex funding arrangements in place and the fact that timescales rarely neatly coincide. From the foregoing, it is apparent that SBC has a lot of concurrent projects that need to be managed – while they are addressing particular issues, there is potential for overlap, and they are not, in reality, part of a coordinated master plan. Importantly, they all have different funding arrangements and timescales, some of which are not funded well enough or are not of long enough duration to be achieved in isolation. Therefore, in order to progress the three match-funded Interreg projects, the Energy and Sustainability team needed to 'piggyback' onto other funded projects with bigger budgets for infrastructure and/or with longer timescales for completion. For example, with regards to the Cool Towns project, the Project Manager admits: "the budget is not huge", and it needed to "find a larger scale project to tag along to" (4/8/2020). Identifying the most eligible project to contribute to in terms of remit, scope, and implementation timescale, recognising the often- protracted nature of council approvals, took time and persistence by the Cool Towns Project Manager. Ultimately, Cool Towns was matched with the TRIPS project in the spring of 2019 (a year into CRUNCH), which put the focus on the High Street and pier. This is one of Southend's busiest public areas, with a high footfall of at least 9,000 daily users (residents, workers and tourists). The earlier SUNRISE project had provided the impetus for the project, proposing greenery on the High Street to soften the area.

Not only is this mismatch between the time taken to implement projects and the timescales of European funding a challenge for delivering innovation in LAs, but it poses further challenges for advisory and monitoring projects such as CRUNCH. The CRUNCH project faced the same challenge as the three SoS Interreg projects, in that the short timescale (April 2018–2021) meant that it needed to align to a project that was able to be completed by the end of 2021, namely one of the match-funded Interreg projects being implemented by the Energy and Sustainability team. Initial discussions focused on linking CRUNCH to the Sponge project and looking at the potential amelioration of fatbergs by the fast-food restaurants in SoS using nexus solutions. However, it was finally agreed that as Cool Towns had successfully linked to the TRIPS (and so was likely to be implemented in the timeframe), this should become the focus for the CRUNCH project. The CRUNCH team, in effect, had to wait until this matching took place in May 2019 before making progress with how to integrate the Food-Water-Energy nexus into UG designs in a meaningful way.

The initial Cool Towns-TRIPS-CRUNCH hybrid plans were to test and demonstrate how UG, including Food-Water-Energy nexus solutions, could be integrated into the streetscape to promote urban cooling, reduce heat stress and air conditioning costs/energy use, and improve air quality along the High Street, and discussions took place in the summer of 2019. The potential for planting edible crops such as fruit trees and herbs, thus integrating nexus ideas, was also discussed as a way to increase engagement with the general public. In line with the TRIPS remit, it was also hoped that greening would entice pedestrians and cyclists to use the space, which is located close to a major railway station, and thus encourage the uptake of fossil-fuel-free transport.

Proposals to plant trees in the High Street hit a blockage when a survey indicated the presence of ground utilities and pipework which could not be disturbed, meaning the team were not able to progress with infrastructure such as tree pits. Green roofs and walls were also proposed but identifying who the landowners of buildings in the project area were, in order to gain permission for any infrastructure that may abut their property, was proving to be another obstacle. Further, scepticism over green walls and green roofs was detected in the SoS Parks team, who often referred to failed examples from 20 years ago; this posed a major challenge because the Parks team were an essential partner in providing the future maintenance of any greenery installed. Finally, planters were proposed as a solution to the utilities and landowner issues, but concerns over maintenance and on-going watering were again raised by the Parks team; the CRUNCH team suggested the utilisation of the community to aid with this, but this idea was not taken forward. Thus, considerable time and thought went into collaborating with planners to determine what was possible. Mindful of project timescales, the CRUNCH and Cool Towns teams had to downscale their ambitions in order to make any progress.

Discussions continued through the summer of 2019, and the focus of Cool Towns became the installation of Zero Mass Water (ZMW) technology and a green wall within the civic centre, where there were no issues over land ownership. ZMW comprises a series of solar panels that convert air into drinking quality water (see Figure 3.1), and it was proposed to site two in prominent locations: the pier (a listed building) – seen as a "high profile opportunity for Cool Towns" – and also a new housing development. The focus was on providing drinking water and some shading to provide cool public spaces in the height of summer, to tackle issues of thermal discomfort. With two of the three nexus areas (water and energy) covered by this technology, the CRUNCH team sought ways to develop this project into something that could further integrate nexus thinking, determining that ZMW was a potential solution to the concerns raised by the Parks team about maintaining planters, as such technology is able to provide a self-watering system. Furthermore, the idea of including edibles within the planters was revisited as the planters could be used to grow herbs and thus showcase the Food-Water-Energy nexus. This idea was taken

Urban greening snakes and ladders

> ZMW, developed by Source (www.zeromasswater.com), are hydropanels (12 m x 4 m) that utilise solar photovoltaic cells and fans to draw in ambient air. Vapour within the air is directed onto a hygroscopic material. Solar thermal heat then converts the vapour, via a process of condensation, into liquid water, which is stored in a 30 litre reservoir where it is mineralised, and sensors monitor water quality. On cloudy days or at night, the system reverts to battery operation. In terms of energy usage, ZMW is self-sustaining and off-grid. The systems, depending on conditions, produce between 180 and 300 litres of drinking quality water a month and can be mounted on roofs or on the ground. ZMW is being piloted in Australia to provide drinking water for a school, office complex, sports centre and public beach. A ground-mounted public drinking water system is also being piloted in a park in Abu Dhabi, United Arab Emirates. To support the proposal to use the water for irrigation for edibles, the Cool Towns team were able to use the example of the Denver Botanical gardens (Colorado, USA), who selected a ground-mounted installation that is dual purpose, providing drinking water for visitors and to water herbs in planters that are used by a local pizzeria.
> https://www.source.co/resources/case-studies/denver-botanic-gardens/

Figure 3.1: Technical summary of Zero Mass Water technology

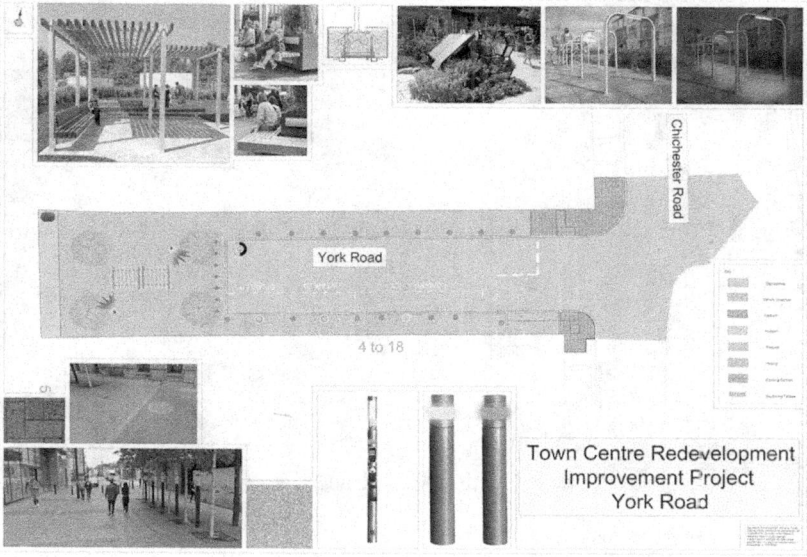

Figure 3.2: York Road Cool Towns plans incorporating ZMW panels
Source: Southend Borough Council

on-board by Cool Towns, and the potential to add a third ZMW system to the High Street area was scoped, specifically on York Road. The proposal for an above-ground ZMW installation, mounted onto a pergola frame which would also provide shading to a seating area beneath, was developed with the planning team based on a proof of concept from the Denver Botanical gardens pilot (see Figure 3.1). The council approved the proposal in autumn 2019.

Installation of the ZME pilots at the pier and York Road was planned for the first quarter of 2020, which was later than planned because the pier is a listed building which required additional planning permission for installation of the ZMW pilot. By April 2020, all civil and groundworks had been completed prior to the nationwide Covid lockdown on 23 March 2020 (refer to Figure 3.3). The Cool Towns Manager was "quite positive" the project would be completed in the third or fourth quarter of 2020, and felt the pilots represented a "low risk". Sadly, this optimism was short-lived. The pergola structure that was delivered was broken and remained in this state throughout lockdown. The CRUNCH team were informed in early August that the decision had been made to abandon the York Road pilot because of health and safety concerns over the seating area under

Figure 3.3: Groundworks at York Road site
Source: Southend Borough Council.

the pergola, upon which the ZMW system was mounted. The issue had been raised by a member of the public and was escalated to the director, under whose remit the Energy and Sustainability team falls. Criticism also came from a member of the business community, who had previously approved the plans but now raised concerns over the design of the pilot. Clearly frustrated that the range of benefits of the pilot were being discounted, the Cool Towns Manger, ever the pragmatist, has "not given up hope and is looking for a better location" for the York Road ZMW pilot. The Acting Manager for the Energy and Sustainability team is still excited about the prospect of piloting the ZMW for irrigation. Meanwhile, for York Road, there will be planters with the potential for a herb garden. A charitable community group will be in charge of watering. The installation of the ZMW pilots at the pier are proving less controversial (so far!)

The development of the internal green wall within the council-owned civic building has also been subject to snakes and ladders. After the lessons of the ZMW on the pier, and a desire to circumvent the need for planning permission on a permanent structure, the decision was taken to investigate a temporary green wall, and again advice over the choice of edibles was sought from the CRUNCH team, with an idea that herbs and spices for local restaurants could be grown. In August 2020, the CRUNCH team were informed that the plans for the internal green wall would not now be progressed under the Cool Towns project, because it was felt it would not fulfil the remit of the funding, which was to pilot projects that reduced heat stress outdoors.

6. Contextualising the experiences of Southend-on-Sea

The case study outlined presents a situation in which a number of barriers were in place to prevent or slow down the implementation of UG and nexus approaches within SoS, despite funding being available for infrastructure. Project-piggybacking was a necessity to achieve the deliverables set out within the obtained funding schemes, and while some UG is now being piloted within SoS, it is less ambitious than originally planned. We wanted to understand whether this is a typical situation or an outlier, so we carried out a number of semi-structured interviews with SoS employees as well as other industry experts in the UK, Netherlands, and Germany. Common themes emerged across our interviews, some of which seem to be systemic barriers to greening seen in the themes outlined in section 3.

6.1 Sustainable funding

The Energy and Sustainability team at SoS, which is the main team responsible for urban greening projects, is a self-funded team. While one member of staff is a permanent employee of the council, the rest of the team's employment was linked to externally funded projects (this structure is currently under review). This has enabled SBC to overcome the challenges posed by decreasing budgets for local councils in the UK; since 2012 councils across the UK have seen dramatic decreases in central government funding; the Local Government Association puts this loss at 60p in every £1 (LGA, 2018), representing an almost ⅔ cut. Often, sustainability projects are the first to suffer in this scenario, viewed as "nice" but not "essential". Indeed, Parks departments across local government have seen dramatic reductions in budget in the last eight years, with cuts of £15m across the UK in the years between 2016/17 and 2018/19 alone, leading to job losses and a lack of investment (R. Ellis, 2018).

As a result of this, many UK councils may feel forced to look outside of their budgets to fund UG projects, but there are significant drawbacks to this approach that are apparent in SBC. Firstly, the message sent externally about an LA's commitment to sustainability is of course questionable if investment is low, and low investment is demonstrated in having very few staff members dedicated to this cause. However, there are a number of significant day-to-day challenges that this funding model also presents at LAs. One issue, which was evident during interviews with SBC employees, is that projects delivered as part of specific externally funded projects tend to be ad-hoc, or reactive, depending on the nature of the funding call. Councils apply for the funding that is available, rather than the specific funding that may be needed. While often it is possible to fit existing projects into these reactive calls, or even occasionally possible to deliver new projects to address a specific need, this can result in projects that are not integrated into the city master plan or that are not appropriately strategically planned for. This has been the case for SBC, where specific projects have had to fit to the obtained funds retrospectively.

In the case of SBC, this was dealt with by piggybacking on other projects (see section 5.2), but this could be extremely challenging for some LAs that have fewer developments already in place. This ad-hoc approach to applying for funding can also result in a mis-match of expertise needed for a project. At SBC, this has manifested in a number of projects taken on by the Energy and Sustainability team that are tangential to their expertise and bordering on being outside of their remit, but they were needed in order to self-fund the team. Not only is this an inefficient use of resources, but it can also result in frustration among team members, which is discussed in greater detail in section 6.7.

A further issue with a self-sustaining team is the risk of loss of institutional memory. Achieving sustainability is still viewed as requiring innovation at SBC (see section 6.3), so there is a great need for expertise in how to deliver sustainability projects. This applies to the technical aspects of UG but also to navigating the silos within government that need to be engaged in order for projects to be successful (see section 6.5). Individuals can play a disproportionately important role in the delivery of UG projects (see section 6.6), so, again, linking these important members of staff to ephemeral funding sources risks losing expertise and enthusiasm for installing UG in cities.

6.2 Maintenance budgets

An emerging lesson from the SoS case study was that the funding available for UG was for the initial infrastructure costs (i.e. capital expenditure) but not necessarily its on-going operational, maintenance or replacement costs. Our Glasgow interviewee confirmed this: "it is really easy to get infrastructure money. Revenue money (for on-going maintenance) is really hard". In relation to SBC, there was no clarification over whose budgets on-going costs would be assigned to. This lack of clarity can hamper the implementation of projects or result in green infrastructure graveyards that receive no maintenance. The resistance of the Parks team over initial plans for Cool Towns is in part related to their already compromised budget, as well as misperceptions that UG is expensive to maintain, a widely held view as reported by Matthews et al. (2015). This led the CRUNCH and Cool Towns team to investigate different options: The York Road ZMW self-watering, Food-Water-Energy nexus pilot "takes the argument away" (SBC employee) about funding the staff time for watering, as does the decision to collaborate with volunteers to tend the planters, a key barrier emerging from our case study. More widely, promoters of UG have started to calculate the life- cycle costs of UG compared with grey infrastructure to try to tackle this problem: the Eindhoven Goes Greener project, initiated by our Netherlands interviewee, helped with justifying the incremental move away from hard paving towards greater use of grasses that are mowed infrequently based on lower maintenance costs over time. For example, the life-cycle cost of hard paving was calculated to be €186/m^2, compared with only €8/m^2 for grassland. The Nature Smart Cities project is also looking at how LAs can access finance for maintenance from both the public and private sector (such as green bonds and green loans) in order to tackle this issue, and it is raising awareness of these funding streams to LAs.

6.3 Urban greening is viewed as an 'innovation'

Almost all of our interviews highlighted that despite the established evidence relating to the benefits of UG, as well as established methods to implement it (see section 2), most kinds of UG beyond the management of parks and already installed trees are considered as 'innovative'. As a result of this, our interview with Eindhoven made it clear that in order to gain support at both a council and public level, projects need to be introduced slowly, starting with simple ideas so that people become used to the unfamiliar. In the case of Eindhoven and Brandenburg, our interviewees made it clear that sustainable, small pots of money are available to do this on an ongoing basis. But as we have discussed, this is not necessarily true in the UK, where the budgets held to do this would typically be within Parks teams, who have seen drastic budget cuts in the last decade, necessitating the need to look externally for funding. While EU funding schemes are mindful that innovation in UG is context specific – i.e. for some LAs, even basic UG will be seen as innovative[6] – there is a temptation to use these large budgets to deliver flagship projects, rather than take the "UG by stealth" approach seen in Eindhoven. This also fits with the financial structure of most successful EU bids, which typically have a single project manager written in as part of the grant structure. This means that although funding is available, it can be diverted to a few, high-risk projects, rather than addressing the problems of long-term funding for smaller projects, which could be deemed as being lower risk (see section 6.4).

6.4 Risk of failure

Sometimes EU and other innovation funding is asking for risks to be taken on as part of implementing new, innovative projects. However, this case study highlights the dangers of this in certain contexts. Failed projects can damage the reputation of the agenda as a whole, as has been demonstrated many times in the case of GI (e.g. London Evening Standard, 2009; Prior, 2013). "When people see botched care as a failure of the installations, they're tempted to think green infrastructure can't improve their town" (Joyce, 2019, in Nemo, 2019). This was also evident in our interviews with SBC employees, who suggested the Parks team were "absolutely against green walls and roofs based on 20 years ago".

Furthermore, the risk of failure varies depending on the expertise and experience of the delivery team. What may be perceived as being low risk on an EU-wide level, where a large pool of expertise and case studies may be drawn upon, could be high risk in a local council where this expertise and experience may be lacking (see section 6.7). It seems that for many councils the learning needed to implement UG does need to occur, to some extent, independently at each location in order to convince stakeholders and build confidence and expertise. This is especially true in smaller or poorly funded councils, where employees are unlikely to have the spare capacity to engage in R&D or visit exemplar cities.

6.5 Silos and communication

Our interviews with SoS, Glasgow, and Eindhoven highlighted that silos are a normal part of local government and can be a significant barrier to implementing UG, agreeing with the literature (Cettner et al., 2013; Roe & Mell, 2013; Winz, Trowsdale, & Brierley, 2014; Matthews, Lo, & Byrne, 2015; Johns, 2019). All three council employees in these teams highlighted that being able to communicate between these silos is an absolute essential skill for enabling UG projects in cities. SBC in particular highlighted that in councils where UG is seen as innovative, this is particularly important, as the implementation of these projects is not seen as "business as usual" and has often been justified on the basis of being cross-cutting. In fact, match-funding for the EU projects obtained at SBC has been on the basis that the benefits of installing UG within SoS benefits a wide variety of teams within SBC.

A theme that was common to both SoS and Glasgow was that the benefits and costs of UG projects need to be realised within each of these silos. An SBC employee pointed out, for example, that the Parks team were a significant barrier to installing UG because they focus on the additional challenges to their workload from having a larger remit, without believing that the benefits to their specific team outweigh these. In other words, it does not matter that UG has cross-cutting benefits across departments if these departments are not contributing to their delivery, upkeep, or finances. A similar frustration was posed by Glasgow; it was noted that financial savings for the National Health Service (NHS) are often posited as a reason to install UG, yet the NHS does not fund these projects. While this was clearly not a criticism of the NHS, it was a voiced frustration that budgets within the departments responsible for delivering UG can be stretched, despite multiple stakeholders supposedly benefiting financially from their implementation. Matthews et al. (2015) also highlight this as an issue, suggesting that the "multiple benefits" often posited as a reason to install UG (see Wright, 2011 and Mell, 2017) can muddy the waters, making economic returns difficult to assess within current planning practises and drawing a picture of added complexity to an already complex process: ". . . the framing of urban greenspace as multifunctional infrastructure can potentially stifle institutional innovation, thus perpetuating a 'business-as usual' model" (Matthews, Lo, & Byrne, 2015, p. 160).

Both Glasgow and SBC have overcome this to a certain extent by engaging in excellent communication between these silos. The SBC Cool Towns Manager said they had to "see from every side – see their aim and goal, see their hurdles and their issues and why they are pushing back", while Glasgow emphasised the importance of finding the right narrative for each silo. This tailoring of messaging also extends to public engagement activities. We hypothesise though, having analysed the snakes and ladders occurring at SBC, that there is a limit to how much can be achieved while these silos have such a strong influence over the success or failure of individual projects.

A further barrier posed by these silos is where to place teams that have cross-cutting agendas. At SBC, the Energy and Sustainability team sits within the Regulatory team, whose day-to-day remit is, for example, to issue permits, and at Glasgow our interviewee sits within the planning team. All these individuals feel that their remit is more cross-cutting than that of the team in which they sit and therefore face barriers in terms of support and expertise from senior management.

6.6 The power of individuals

In our interviews with SBC, Glasgow, and Eindhoven, it was clear that the impetus for UG projects often comes from individuals, who have a disproportionately positive impact within their organisation. There were two skills mentioned as being particularly important; sometimes these were demonstrated by one individual, sometimes they were split between more than one person. Someone is needed to champion the cause, convincing colleagues and councillors of the benefits of these schemes. A second skill required is someone that can navigate the different silos required for the successful implementation of projects; this person needs to understand the barriers that each of these teams face and tailor their message to that particular team. They also need to be *"quite resourceful"* (SBC Cool Towns Manager), tenacious, resilient, and patient. Both of these roles require a certain level of expertise in UG, to enable a clear narrative to be built and adapted depending on the audience; however, it was clear that passion was more important than expertise in UG, while expertise in the internal machinations of the council was absolutely essential. In essence, these people become "brokers" between the various stakeholders, including council colleagues, councillors, and members of the public. This is particularly important in councils where sustainability is seen as being innovative.

In all three cases, it was clear that one or two individuals were essentially driving the UG agenda and that this came proactively from them, rather than reactively from the councils (i.e. it was not necessarily part of their everyday role). In the case of Eindhoven, this had precipitated the formation of a Community of Practice Group, but it was clear that the individual was needed initially to get to this stage.

While individuals are clearly powerful in driving forward the UG agenda, it was also clear from our interviews that individuals can also pose consistent and perhaps insurmountable barriers to UG. We have discussed the reticence towards more innovative UG expressed by the Parks team at SBC (see section 5.2), but it was also discussed that stakeholders viewed by the council as "having influence", such as councillors and successful local business owners, can have a disproportionately large impact on the day-to-day activities of the council. While many councils are reactive to negative feedback from the public, it seems that some voices are louder than others within this context.

6.7 Inappropriate staffing

We have already discussed that in the case of SBC, despite clear commitments to sustainability outlined in, for example, signing up to become net zero carbon by 2030, the majority of the Energy and Sustainability team are funded by external projects. While this was not necessarily common across all those we interviewed, both UK cities we investigated had problems of staff attrition and a lack of expertise.

In section 6.6, we discussed the power of individuals; while this can be seen as a positive, it also highlights that these individuals often do not feel they have the support of a wider team that can drive forward the sustainability agenda. One of the SBC employees noted that in their time working in LAs in the South-East of England (not just SBC) over the last decade, they had observed high attrition of motivated staff, often due to the frustrations experienced in a lack of progress on projects and a lack of much needed institutional change. This was echoed at Glasgow, where our interviewee noted that "young" or "well-trained" staff either left within a few years or "became institutionalized", losing some of the drive and enthusiasm to innovate that they had when they joined the council. Interviewees at SBC and Glasgow also brought up that they faced significant challenges in undertaking their roles and that there was a mismatch in the salary they received for doing so; while this was not necessarily a problem for those individuals interviewed, who both stated that they were not in their roles for the salary, they did both point out that this causes significant challenges when trying to recruit additional staff.

6.8 Urban greening as a statement

We have already noted that LAs in the UK and internationally use the sustainability agenda as a key political issue to garner support, as do the private sector. Almost all UK LAs have now signed up to some sort of sustainability charter or set of targets because the subject is increasing in popularity with the general public. There is, therefore, a strong incentive by both the public and private sector to install GI as a political statement rather than to serve a specific function (Wright, 2011). While this can be viewed cynically, the installation of prominent UG within a city could also be an important statement about the cities' serious intentions to become more sustainable and can be a key factor in convincing the public to support this agenda (ibid.). As such, there is often a temptation to install UG in areas with high footfall, such as the High Street, in the case of SoS, or Sauchiehall Avenue, in the case of Glasgow (Greenspace Scotland, 2019). But there is inherent risk in doing this. As discussed in section 6.3, in the case of Eindhoven, which has been incredibly successful at installing UG, most projects have been small and on the town periphery, filling space as it becomes available. Our interviewee in Eindhoven stressed that this is important in gaining public support, recognising that people "need time to adjust". Another approach used in Eindhoven has been the use of temporary and moveable planters "to show what it will bring". This slow and incremental approach allows councils to gauge which projects have true, rather than abstract, support and to address common complaints that can be ironed out in new projects. The other benefit of this "UG by stealth" approach is that it is easier to convince other silos within the council to support these projects because there is less risk involved. A similar approach was taken at Barking Riverside by academics at the University of East London, where innovative UG projects were installed before residents moved into the area, enabling problems to be resolved and to allow more room for active experimentation before public consultation took place later in the project (Connop, 2014).

In the case of SoS, the CRUNCH Nexus demonstration project was installed on the main High Street, with a footfall of 9,000 people per day. In a reactive council, where a few complaints, particularly from influential people or employees, can halt a project (see section 6.6), this can mean that these prominent projects go through exactly the snakes and ladders issues that we have discussed, due to the perceived importance of the area. This implies that if councils want to make a UG statement, then they either need to ensure that public consultation is extensive and truly representative, with capacity building components, or, potentially more realistically, councils need to decide what the statement will be and manage the criticisms of it; with the assumption people will get used to it eventually. This seems to be the approach in Germany, where our interviewee suggested that complaints are generally not taken seriously unless assessed to have foundation by experts in UG or health and safety – i.e. greater weighting is placed on expert rather than lay opinion.

6.9 Barriers are subjective and time dependent

We often focus on barriers to the implementation of UG as though they are static and equally important. However, the SoS example has highlighted that this is simply not the case. This example highlights that we need to take a more in-depth qualitative approach to the study of barriers to UG implementation; many research papers take a snapshot in time approach to assessing barriers to UG and also rely on asking stakeholders what they perceive barriers to be. While this is useful in itself, there is additional information to be gained with the kind of qualitative longitudinal study presented here, which highlights more clearly pathway dependencies, the messy and complex reality of trying to get things done, the evolution of UG projects in the face of multiple and evolving barriers, and the varying perceptions of the barriers present depending on the positionality of the stakeholder. In this case, it is clear that some barriers may be overcome as the context changes or as other barriers present themselves. A case in point was in the reticence to use voluntary groups to maintain UG installations in SoS in the early stages of the project but the eventual use of volunteers once it was clear that ZMW would not be used.

7. Conclusion

The UG nexus and broader sustainability agenda have a lot in common: both are umbrella and fluid concepts that allow very different stakeholders with conflicting views to find common ground (Wright, 2011). Their woolly nature allows politicians to promote an agenda without having to specifically decide on how this abstract consensus can be translated into practical application: this is a headache for technocrats and council employees. As with sustainability, consensus at the political scale is a veneer: underneath, UG means different things to different people, with some more willing than others to accept trade-offs. To operationalise UG, and optimise its multi-beneficial and scalar potential, LA staff need the training and inclination to work outside their silos and to negotiate with a range of stakeholders with competing agendas and budgets. We agree with Matthews et al. (2015) that in times of austerity the ambiguity surrounding UG promotes prevarication and barrier myth-making within LAs; for example, around maintenance. So how can we promote UG ladders whilst being fully au fait with the organisational realities within councils, where we suggest the main blockages to UG lie? We present some pragmatic suggestions, which we hope will facilitate the transition towards greening. Firstly, if we wait for the multiple benefits arguments to trickle down to construct horizontal ladders across silos, UG in second-tier cities and large towns will not progress. Thus, we advocate working with, not against, silos to identify the UG that is applicable to each sector and where the benefits and life-cycle costs can be internalised.

We must recognise that under austerity, LA staff time is a limited commodity, which does reinforce path dependency and the grey status quo. We must appreciate the precarity of people's positions and acknowledge that UG is still considered a risk-taking innovation within many councils. We know that in many fields, integration across departments makes sense in a vacuum, yet in reality breaking down silos due to defence of organisational turf means the benefits are yet to materialise. Staff will interpret calls for greater integration as a precursor to merger and redundancy: instability is not the way to create space for innovation that promotes cross-departmental working. So, let's make life easier by reducing the need to work across multiple departments. At present, we have units, such as SBC's Energy and Sustainability team, that are trying to promote the UG agenda across councils. Could team members be seconded to implement greening programmes in discrete departments? Our roving UG experts can then build capacity within departments and identify potential champions that can be upskilled and nurtured as well as instructed on the most effective communication mode for their immediate stakeholders.

Another key lesson and suggestion is that where UG is concerned, small is beautiful. "Greening by stealth", as demonstrated in Eindhoven, is our preferred approach because it allows council departments to take people along with them: greening is a journey, and that journey is slow and meandering, but we will get there. Teleporting people to a radical new world is jarring and unsettling: it takes time to see the beauty in unmown verges when the social norm is neatly manicured and paved landscapes. It takes time to appreciate wildflowers when seaside towns enter 'in bloom' competitions for their gardens that to an ecologist are a gaudy biodiversity wasteland. Similarly, we advocate demonstration plots and pilots such as ZMW on the peripheries of town, not flagship locations such as a high street, unless we are also willing to take criticism. Navigating public and business concerns over the form of UG rather than simply capitulating is important. A possible approach would be to follow Eindhoven's lead with the use of a mediator (www.trefpuntgroeneindhoven.nl) to arbitrate between the local authority and affected parties such as residents and businesses with concerns over urban greening.

The benefits of installing UG in cities are well documented, and as a result of the recent lockdowns across the globe in response to the Covid-19 pandemic, building local neighbourhoods that promote happiness and wellbeing through the inclusion of UG has never been in greater focus. By understanding the challenges that LAs face in delivering this in financially strained times and finding pragmatic solutions, which may be piecemeal rather than wholesale, we can ensure that UG transitions from "innovation" to "business as usual" within our cities, creating spaces to live in rather than just exist in.

Acknowledgements

This work was supported by the AHRC, ESRC, and Innovate UK in the framework of the Joint Programming Initiative Urban Europe, with support from the European Union's Horizon 2020 Research and Innovation Program under grant agreement No 730254.

Notes
1. https://www.southend.gov.uk/downloads/file/6148/southend-2050-ambition
2. https://www.centrefortowns.org/our-towns
3. https://civitas-sunrise.eu/wp-content/uploads/2019/08/D4.4_Detailed-Assessment-and-Evaluation-Plan.pdf
4. https://interreg2seas.eu/nl/nsciti2s
5. https://civitas-sunrise.eu/wp-content/uploads/2019/08/D4.4_Detailed-Assessment-and-Evaluation-Plan.pdf

6   See, for example, the 2020 LIFE Awards finalists: https://ec.europa.eu/easme/en/news/2020-life-awards-finalists-announced

References

Akbari, H., Pomerantz, M., & Taha, H. (2001). Cool surfaces and shade trees to reduce energy use and improve air quality in urban areas. *Sol. Energy 70*, 295–310.

Balmford, A., Clegg, L., Coulson, T., & Taylor, J. (2002). Why conservationists should heed Pokemon. *Science, 295*, 2367–2368.

Baró, F., Chaparro, L., Gómez-Baggethun, E. et al. (2014). Contribution of ecosystem services to air quality and climate change mitigation policies: The case of urban forests in Barcelona, Spain. *Ambio, 43*, 466–479.

Brown, R. D., Vanos, J., Kenny, N., & Lenzholzer, S. (2015). Designing urban parks that ameliorate the effects of climate change. *Landsc. Urban Plan, 138*, 118–131.

Byrne, J., & Yang, J. (2009). Can urban greenspace combat climate change? Towards a subtropical cities research agenda. *Australian Planner, 46*, 36–43.

Cettner, A., Ashley, R., Viklander, M., & K. Nilsson. (2013). Stormwater Management and urban planning: Lessons from 40 years of innovation. *Journal of Environmental Management and Planning, 56*(6): 786–801.

Coghlin, P., O'Brien, U. & MacLean, K. (2020). *The report of the independent public inquiry into the non-domestic Renewable Heat Incentive (RHI) scheme.* Northern Ireland Department of Finance: Bangor, NI.

COMEAP. (2010). *The mortality effects of long-term exposure to particulate air pollution in the United Kingdom.* COMEAP: Didcot, UK.

Connop, S. (2014). Barking riverside: TURAS showcase of sustainable and resilient community design. University of East London: London, UK.

Constanza, R., de Groot, R., Sutton, P. et al. (2014). Changes in the global value of ecosystem services. *Global Environmental Change, 26*, 152–158. https://doi.org/10.1016/j.gloenvcha.2014.04.002

Defra. (2013). Climate change adaptation: Information for local authorities. Available at: https://www.gov.uk/guidance/climate-change-adaptation-information-for-local-authorities

Ellis, J. B. (2013). Sustainable surface water management and green infrastructure in UK urban catchment planning. *Journal of Environmental Planning and Management, 56*(1), 24–41. https://doi.org/10.1080/09640568.2011.648752

Ellis, R. (2018, 31 July). The future of our parks is not looking rosy. *Unison.* https://www.unison.org.uk/news/ps-data/2018/07/future-parks-not-looking-rosy/

Evans, B. E., Huizink, A. C., Greaves-Lord, K. et al. (2020). Urbanicity, biological stress system functioning and mental health in adolescents. *PLoS ONE, 15*(3): e0228659. https://doi.org/10.1371/journal.pone.0228659

Greenspace Scotland. (2019). Glasgow's Sauchiehall Street gets greener. Available at: https://www.greenspacescotland.org.uk/news/street-trees-on-sauchiehall-street-avenue

Hoang, L., & Fenner, R. A. (2016). System interactions of stormwater management using sustainable urban drainage systems and green infrastructure. *Urban Water J, 13*, 739–758.

Jaffe, M. (2010). Reflections on green infrastructure economics. *Environ. Pract, 12*, 357–365.

Johns, C. M. (2019). Understanding barriers to green infrastructure policy and stormwater management in the City of Toronto: A shift from grey to green or policy layering and conversion?, *Journal of Environmental Planning and Management, 62*(8), 1377–1401. https://doi.org/10.1080/09640568.2018.1496072

Kaplan, R., & Kaplan, S. (1989). *The experience of nature: A psychological perspective.* Cambridge University Press: Cambridge, UK.

Lee, K. E., Williams, K., Sargent, L. D. et al. (2015). 40-second green roof views sustain attention: The role of micro-breaks in attention restoration. *Journal of Environmental Psychology, 42*, 182–189. https://doi.org/10.1016/j.jenvp.2015.04.003

Lennon, M. (2014). Green infrastructure and planning policy: A critical assessment. *Local Environment International Journal of Justice Sustainability, 20*, 957–980.

LGA. (2018). *Local government funding: Moving the conversation on.* LGA: London, UK.

London Evening Standard. (2009, 21 August). The living wall of Islington is dead. *London Evening Standard.* https://www.standard.co.uk/hp/front/the-living-wall-of-islington-is-dead-6763418.html

Matthews, T., Lo, A. Y., & Byrne, J. A. (2015). Reconceptualizing green infrastructure for climate change adaptation: Barriers to adoption and drivers for uptake by spatial planners. *Landscape and Urban Planning, 138*, 155–163.

Mayor of London/London Assembly. (2016). *London plan chapter two: London's places.* Mayor of London/London Assembly: London, UK.

Mell, I. C. (2017). Green infrastructure: Reflections on past, present and future praxis. *Landscape Research Volume, 42*(2), 135–145. https://doi.org/10.1080/01426397.2016.1250875

Millington, S., & Ntounis, N. (2017). Repositioning the high street: Evidence and reflection from the UK. *Journal of Place Management and Development, 10*(4), 364–379. DOI: 10.1108/JPMD-08-2017-0077

Nemo, L. (2019, 1 November). As cities' interest in green infrastructure grows, so does the need to develop strategies and resources to maintain it. *ensia*. https://ensia.com/features/green-infrastructure-maintenance-flooding-pollution-groundwater/

O'Donnell, E. C., Lamond, J. E., & Thorne, C. R. (2017). Recognising barriers to implementation of blue-green infrastructure: A Newcastle case study. *Urban Water Journal, 14*(9), 964–971.

Ossa-Moreno, J., Smith, K. M., & Mijic, A. (2017). Economic analysis of wider benefits to facilitate SuDS uptake in London, UK. *Sustain. Cities Soc, 28*, 411–419.

Peters, E. B., Hiller, R. V., & McFadden, J. P. (2011). Seasonal contributions of vegetation types to suburban evapotranspiration. *J. Geophys. Res, 116*, G01003.

Portsmouth City Council. (2019). 2018–19 Portsmouth green infrastructure delivery plan. Portsmouth City Council: Portsmouth.

Prior, G. (2013, 8 October). Insects in green roof close Cumbria school. *Construction Enquirer*. https://www.constructionenquirer.com/2013/10/08/insects-in-green-roof-close-cumbria-school/

Roe, M., & Mell, I. 2013. Negotiating value and priorities: Evaluating the demands of green infrastructure development. *Journal of Environmental Planning and Management, 56*(5), 650–673.

Rogers, K., Sacre, K., Goodenough, J., & Doick, K. (2015). *Valuing London's Urban Forest*. https://assets.publishing.service.gov.uk/government/uploads/system/uploads/attachment_data/file/723230/LONDONI-TREEECOREPORT151202.pdf

Roy, A. H., Wenger, S. J., Fletcher, T. D. et al. (2008). Impediments and solutions to sustainable, watershed-scale urban stormwater management: Lessons from Australia and the United States. *Environmental Management, 42*(2): 344–359.

Scalenghe, R., & Ajmone-Marsan, F. (2009). The anthropogenic sealing of soils in urban areas. *Landscape and Urban Planning, 90*, 1–10.

Thompson, C. W., Aspinall, P., & Roe, J. (2014). Access to green space in disadvantaged urban communities: Evidence of salutogenic effects based on biomarker and self-report measures of wellbeing. *Procedia – Social and Behavioral Sciences, 153*, 10–22. https://doi.org/10.1016/j.sbspro.2014.10.036

Tooke, T. R., Coops, N. C., Voogt, J. A., & Meitner, M. J. (2011). Tree structure influences on rooftop-received solar radiation. *Landsc. Urban Plan, 102*, 73–81.

Trees and Design Action Group. (2016). *Using rainwater for tree-based cooling on Garibaldi Street Lyon, France: Reducing weather extremes*. https://www.tdag.org.uk/uploads/4/2/8/0/4280686/garibaldi.pdf

Ulrich, R. S. (1984). View through a window may influence recovery from surgery. *Science, 224*(4647), 420–421. DOI: 10.1126/science.6143402

United Nations Department of Economic and Social Affairs. (2018, 16 May). 68% of the world population projected to live in urban areas by 2050, says UN. *United Nations Department of Economic and Social Affairs.* https://www.un.org/development/desa/en/news/population/2018-revision-of-world-urbanization-prospects.html

Vincent, S., Radhakrishnan, M., Hayde, L., & Pathirana, A. (2017). Enhancing the economic value of large investments in Sustainable Drainage Systems (SuDS) through inclusion of ecosystems services benefits. *Water, 9*, 841.

Wallop, H. (2020, 17 July). How green is your fake lawn? Sales have soared during lockdown but critics say they are bad for the environment and wildlife. *Mail Online.* https://www.dailymail.co.uk/news/article-8535003/How-green-fake-lawn-Sales-soared-lockdown-critics-say-theyre-bad-wildlife.html

Winz, I., Trowsdale, S., & Brierley, G. (2014). Understanding barrier interactions to support the implementation of sustainable urban water management. *Urban Water Journal, 11*(6): 497–505.

Wolf, K. (2005). Business district streetscapes, trees, and consumer response. *Journal of Forestry, 103*(8), 396–400. https://www.fs.usda.gov/treesearch/pubs/34952

Wright, H. (2011). Understanding green infrastructure: The development of a contested concept in England. *Local Environment, 16*(10), 1003–1019. DOI: 10.1080/13549839.2011.631993.

Chapter 4

Capacity

Transforming challenges into opportunities

Joanna Bach-Głowińska, Jacek Łubiński, and Joanna Tobolewicz

The Urban Initiative Laboratory (UIL) aims to upgrade the smart city concept in Gdańsk by introducing the Food-Water-Energy (FWE) nexus to the city. It was agreed in the CRUNCH international consortium that projects on different scales would be implemented in the individual countries to test the Integrated Decision Supportive System platform, which, in principle, would concern urban scale. The regular urban scale was to be researched in Urban Living Labs (ULL) in Uppsala, Eindhoven, Southend-on-Sea, and Taipei. The Miami project developed appropriate tools for an IDSS platform, with maximum use of GIS data on a regional scale. The open test bed of the micro ULL FWE Nexus Square – i.e. a pavilion prototype – was supposed to be opened in Gdańsk in June 2020, in accordance with the CRUNCH action plan. However, the approved functionalities of the pavilion were no longer applicable due to the significant social changes in public spaces caused by the Covid-19 pandemic. Moreover, the ULL's business partner used the prototype pavilion for the purpose of a mobile diagnostic laboratory in a different location. It was absolutely clear that UIL could not continue the micro ULL in Gdańsk in the form previously planned. ULLs focus on, amongst other things, strategic learning to achieve systemic change (van den Bosch, 2010) and better anticipation of constraints on upscaling and inclusion (Dijk et al., 2019). Therefore, UIL began the theoretical research, which emerged from tackling the impacts of the Covid-19 pandemic on city life from the urban perspective.

DOI: 10.4324/9781003112495-13

Joanna Bach-Głowińska, Jacek Łubiński, and Joanna Tobolewicz

The organisational capacity of the city, and the impacts of the Covid-19 epidemic

Cities experiencing the Covid-19 pandemic are facing their greatest challenge in terms of their healthcare systems (WHO, 2020), but they are also encountering hardship in managing the pandemic risk on the streets, in public spaces, in neighbourhoods, and ultimately in the city as a whole. The urban theories on smart cities (Trencher & Karvonen, 2019) and resilient cities (Vale & Campanella, 2005), and guidelines on urban design, such as Climate Sensitive Urban Design (Coutts et al., 2013) or the FWE nexus for self-sustainability (Leibson Hawkins, 2005), should be revised in the light of the pandemic. On the one hand, the self-protective behaviours of social distancing affect the transmission dynamics of influenza (Singh et al., 2019), but on the other, the threat of coronavirus affects human interactions, which are the most basic considerations of living in a city. The built environment can affect health, behaviour, and disease – one can see this in the history of urban planning (Frumkin, Frank, & Jackson, 2004; Schrank & Ekici, 2016). The approach to good health is not only about the absence of disease but a state of complete physical, mental and social wellbeing. Prevention is as important as cure, with long-term solutions (Tsekleves & Cooper, 2017) which need to be smart and resilient in terms of the urban planning response to the massive need for preliminary testing on a daily basis.

The theoretical research was oriented towards examining the consequences of the extensive diagnosis of Covid-19 in a city, providing assumptions for the automation of the Preliminary Diagnostic Module diagnostics (PDM), the guidelines for the distribution of PDMs at locations in the city, and the health procedures. The research proved that the psychological and social effects of a pandemic in a city, and the ways to reduce risk in a public space, can result in positive and significant changes in the health system and policies by improving the city's organisational capacity. The framework of organisational capacity in cities could be built on the FWE Nexus Square network for emergency purposes. The FWE Nexus Square pavilion could become a mobile, diagnostic laboratory to be converted back to its non-pandemic functionality when the threat is over. The theoretical research on the organisational capacity of the city and the impacts of the Covid-19 epidemic demonstrated the FWE Nexus Square's potential for replicability, which resulted in the Co-modal Local Node and Non-invasive Measurement System as innovation patents in the form of open licences.

Extending the model – A city's fragile institutional capacity and the impacts of climate change

What if action is needed to manage the FWE nexus in the case of other disruptions – i.e. in a changing climate? The crisis can occur on various fronts. Floods and droughts may happen regularly in certain parts of the world. However, they are particularly challenging in the Global South, where local authorities and civil society do not have the capacity to cover all of the emerging needs. According to the first State of Environment and Outlook Report (2018) in South Sudan, the impacts of global climate change and natural hazards are conspiring with all of these socio-economic drivers to form a complex dynamic of causes contributing to environmental change in the country. The persistent floods caused by torrential rains have aggravated the living conditions of the South Sudanese people in many parts of the country for the past five years, with the worst reported in June to October 2019. Across the country, authorities and aid organisations have reported that an estimated 234,800 people were affected by the floods in 2019. Polish Humanitarian Action (PAH) is actively working to deliver first assistance and is also looking into much needed sustainable solutions to reoccurring challenges. UIL, with the participation of PAH, conducted preliminary research as part of the development of a JUBA project proposal as follow up to two JPI Urban Europe Sustainable Urbanisation Global Initiative (SUGI) projects – CRUNCH and IFWEN (IFWEN, 2022).

In Juba Central Equatorial State, areas that are constantly affected include Gureyi, Tonping, Joppa, and Block 6. Floods from heavy rains are affecting shelters, water sources, crops, and crucial productive assets in these areas. They have also damaged essential service infrastructure, including electricity, schools, and health facilities, affecting women and children in particular by exposing them to water-, sanitation-, and hygiene- (WASH) related diseases. These floods also rendered many roads impassable, constraining people's access to markets and health facilities, and the ability of humanitarian aid workers to move across the affected area.

The JUBA project proposal aimed to develop a framework of organisational capacity for a co-modal local nodes network, with smart solutions related to risk management in blue and green networks, based on governance analysis of the FWE nexus and its resilience. The embedding of FWE nexus solutions at the microscale was based on the CRUNCH approach to integrating mitigation and adaptation actions. The project's proposal aimed to increase the city's capacity for recovery by providing tangible results based on the PAH simulation model of the impact of disaster risks on the urban infrastructure system, the FWE Nexus Square networks for emergency purposes in the blue and green network, and technical documentation of a replicable, easy-to-build FWE Nexus Square for emergency purposes with guidelines for recovery actions. The JUBA contribution was planned to be based not only on the technical documentation of a replicable, easy-to-build FWE Nexus Square for emergency purposes and recovery actions but the delimitations of nodes in the blue-green network (based on the simulation model of the impacts of disaster risks on the urban infrastructure system). The proposed JUBA solutions could apply at the level of mitigation and in the prevention phase in order to improve resilience to emergencies, with the intent to serve the community to build support for their livelihoods. The project proposal presents an attempt to respond to the critical factors identified for managing the FWE nexus supply upon the impacts of climate change in cities in the Global South with fragile institutional capacity, such as Juba.

The preliminary research for the JUBA project proposal demonstrated a possible framework for how to strengthen fragile institutional capacity in the face of the impacts of climate change by establishing solutions for food, water, and energy, with a component of ICT at the urban and local scale in crisis-affected areas. Whilst in the IFWEN project the blue and green networks served as ecosystem-based solutions for the FWE nexus on the macroscale, the FWE Nexus Square should develop climate change mitigation and adaptation actions which tackle, on the microscale, challenges related to food waste and the re-use of water, and should demonstrate how to ensure that energy resources (incl. solar and wind) combined with water reuse and recovery (i.e. rainwater) are sufficient for running the FWE Nexus Square in situ.

Climate change and the need for resilient neighbourhoods

Considering the impact of the Covid-19 pandemic on cities, the lockdowns implemented in many cities have brought about the need for low-carbon residential neighbourhoods with minimum performance standards for passive design/renewable energy and effective food supply chains, and have strongly emphasised the need for shorter producer-to-consumer models.

What are the main threats of climate change in the case of Gdańsk?

1. **Temperature**: A hotter average temperature (an increase from 7 to 8.5 °C from 1951 to 2010), additional days per year where the maximum temperature exceeds 25°C, a thermophilic blooming of phytoplankton.

2. **Water**: Lower average annual rainfall patterns, more drought conditions, rising salinity in ground water, various forms of pollution (incl. chemical), floods (river, rainfall, storm/strong wind inundation, sea level rise).
3. **More extreme weather events**: (like hot and cold spells, more heavy rainfall, strong winds, coastal storm inundation). Higher storm surges and waves, a shift in the seasons.
4. **Coastline**: Coastal erosion, a change in the coastline (narrowing beaches), current adaptation and response measures, sea level rise 3mm per year over the last 20 years.

What are the responses to the identified risks, and what adaptation measures are already in place in Gdańsk?

1. **Sustainable urban development requirements**: Network connectivity of green and open spaces in the form of OSTAB (reference, or more info needed), storm water infrastructure to be scaled to accommodate extreme weather and flooding events, flood zones, a landscape designed to cope with the potential flooding, a system of retention ponds, accessibility and proximity of green areas and leisure facilities incl. the availability of a safe cycle network.
2. **Designing for a challenging future**: In response to expected sea level rise, much tighter restrictions on coastal development are needed to ensure occupied ground floor space is above the 1.85m projection set by the state government and that landscaping considers potential inundation. Greenfield development must factor in sea level rise for future-proofing in excess of the predicted water level in a 1 in 100 year storm event and targeted performance standards (passive design, renewable energy, the adaptation of infrastructure).

What are the responses to the identified risks around food safety in Gdańsk that are already in place?

A heightened awareness around food safety and a desire for more nutritious food will also increase demand for eating local (Forbes, 2020). As the Ellen MacArthur Foundation's research has highlighted, a circular scenario could lead to a 50 percent reduction of pesticides and synthetic fertilizer use by 2030 in Europe (compared to 2012 levels), while resulting in a 12 percent drop in household expenditure and better products (Ellen MacArthur Foundation, 2020). It therefore appears timely to further explore the potential of large-scale investment in regenerative, peri-urban production, together with digitally enabled precision agriculture.

(Luxembourg, 2020)

Neighbourhood capacity and the impacts of climate change and Covid-19

UIL decided to test the impact of urban scale on the FWE nexus by implementing the ULL FWE Nexus Neighbourhood – a greenfield transit-oriented neighbourhood at Gdańsk Airport Station, located in the hinterland between the city outskirts and the agricultural Kashubian region. The urban design was targeted at adaptation to climate change, the circular economy, and low-emissions at zero waste, with smart solutions aimed at self-sufficiency on the FWE Nexus urban scale. The hypothetical scenarios for the low-carbon residential neighbourhood – green, business as usual, and basic – were calculated using the ELAS calculator (ELAS, 2016). The FWE Nexus Neighbourhood demonstrated the lowest hierarchy unit (with the easiest convenience and accessibility to residents) for interactions/interventions/governance on the urban scale. The research in the ULL FWE Nexus Neighbourhood equipped stakeholders with data input on an IDSS platform and provided three relevant scenarios describing the role of neighbourhood capacity upon the impacts of climate change and food supply.

It is expected that the prolonged nature of the experiment will also have a positive benefit for the educational activities undertaken by various local authorities and scientific teams, in terms of raising social awareness on the issues of averting the negative effects of human civilisation on the Earth's biosphere. The benefit of the location of the FWE nexus facilities within the actual urban/sub-urban tissue of the city will serve as a disseminating factor among the inhabitants of the Tri-City agglomeration (of which Gdańsk is a key part) and visitors transferring through the transport hub associated with Gdańsk Airport.

Conclusions

UIL in Gdańsk represents the ULL model at the city scale. UIL was set as part of the CRUNCH project in agreement between the Mayor of Gdańsk and the Rector of Gdańsk University of Technology (GUT). The third sector was represented by a business partner – Olivia Business Centre (OBC) – which joined the City-University partnership. Therefore, all three pillars of a good ULL (business, municipality, and academic research) were included in this part of the CRUNCH project.

ULL governance flexibility/durability

The flexibility and durability of governance in the ULL proved its strength while facing traumatic challenges, such as the murder of the Mayor of Gdańsk, Paweł Adamowicz, and the Covid-19 pandemic, which both happened during the lifetime of the CRUNCH project. The tragedies were extremely traumatic for both city life and for business. Despite the above- described situations, the ULL managed to continue as part of the CRUNCH project because its governance relied on three pillars.

The university and business partner were engaged most in the progress of the CRUNCH project during the hardest time for the city (the murder of Mayor Adamowicz and the triple local government elections). The first test bed location at the OBC business park entrance was decided upon as a central business district FWE NEXUS Multimodal Node, undertaken on the metropolitan scale of the Tri-City, focusing on economic prosperity in Greater Gdańsk.

Identifying the connections between the living labs and other projects and established policies

The city and university partners together took the lead during the Covid-19 lockdown. It was also the time for testing the ULL's durability and when radical decisions had to be taken. The scope of the project was moved from the test bed laboratory in the city to theoretical studies on the FWE Nexus Square concept and functionalities, which led to a focus on city capacity on the one hand and innovation patents on the other. The ULL has the ability to conquer challenges by identifying the connections across different projects, scales, and stakeholders. The results can take the form of any combinations in order to gain maximum support from residents and communities. The summing up of the efforts of other projects and established policies on different scales was expressed in the JUBA proposal, which considered combining the micro- (Comodal Local Node) and macroscale for crisis management purposes.

The capacity of the ULL formula

The UIL approach improved the learning agenda of the ULL experiments, expanded the learning community across the scales of the ULLs undertaken in Gdańsk, and increased capacity across urban policymakers, business partners, and academia. The capacity of the ULL formula allowed us on several occasions to convert challenges into opportunities during the CRUNCH project.

Acknowledgements

This project has received funding from the European Union's Horizon 2020 research and innovation program (GA No 730254) under the JPI Urban Europe's call "SUGI – FWE Nexus". This project has received funding from the National Science Centre, Poland (2017/25/Z/HS6/03050).

References

Coutts, A. M., Tapper, N. J., Beringer, J. et al. (2013). Watering our cities: The capacity for water sensitive urban design to support urban cooling and improve human thermal comfort in the Australian context. *Progress in Physical Geography*, *37*(1), 2–28.

Dijk, M., da Schio, N. Diethart, M., Hoflehner, T. et al. (2019). How to anticipate constraints on upscaling inclusive Living Lab experiments, SmarterLabs project, JPI Urban Europe.

ELAS. (2016). http://www.elas-calculator.eu/?lang=en

Fineberg, H. V. (2014). Pandemic preparedness and response – Lessons from the H1N1 influenza of 2009. *New England Journal of Medicine*, *370*(14), 1335–1342.

Frumkin, H., Frank, L., & Jackson, R. J. (2004). *Urban sprawl and public health: Designing, planning, and building for healthy communities.* Island Press.

IFWEN. (2022). http://ifwen.org/.

Leibson Hawkins, R. (2005). From self-sufficiency to personal and family sustainability: A new paradigm for social policy. *J. Soc. & Soc. Welfare*, *32*(4), 77.

Pinter-Wollman, N., Penn, A., Theraulaz, G., & Fiore, S. M. (2018). Interdisciplinary approaches for uncovering the impacts of architecture on collective behaviour. *Philosophical Transactions of the Royal Society B*, *373*. https://doi.org/10.1098/rstb.2017.0232.

Renne, J. L. (2016). *Transit oriented development: Making it happen.* Routledge.

Schrank, S., & Ekici, D. (2016). *Healing spaces, modern architecture, and the body.* Routledge.

Singh, M., Sarkhel, P., Kang, G. et al. (2019). Impact of demographic disparities in social distancing and vaccination on influenza epidemics in urban and rural regions of the United States. *BMC Infect Dis 19*(221). DOI: 10.1186/s12879-019-3703-2

State of Environment and Outlook Report (Sudan, 2018). https://www.unep.org/resources/report/south-sudan-first-state-environment-and-outlook-report-2018

Trencher, G., & Karvonen, A. (2019). Stretching "smart": Advancing health and well-being through the smart city agenda. *Local Environment*, *24*(7), 610–627.

Tsekleves, E., & Cooper, R. (Eds.) (2017). *Design for health*. Taylor & Francis.

Vale, L. J., & Campanella, T. J. (2005). *The resilient city: How modern cities recover from disaster*. Oxford University Press.

Van den Bosch, S. (2010). *Transition experiments: Exploring Societal Changes towards Sustainability*. Erasmus University Rotterdam.

WHO. (2020). A coordinated global research roadmap: 2019 novel coronavirus. *World Health Organization*. https://www.who.int/blueprint/priority-diseases/key-action/Coronavirus_Roadmap_V9.pdf?ua=1

Yang, G. Z., Nelson, B. J., Murphy, R. R., Choset, H. et al. (2020). Combating COVID-19 – The role of robotics in managing public health and infectious diseases. *Science Robotics*, *5*(40). DOI: 10.1126/scirobotics.abb5589

Chapter 5

Data and knowledge supporting decision-making for the urban Food-Water-Energy nexus

Mei-Hua Yuan, Joanna Bach-Głowińska, Pei-Te Chiueh, Yu-Sen Chang, Hsin-hsin Tung, Chang-Ping Yu, Hwong-wen Ma, Jacek Łubiński, and Shang-Lien Lo

A. Introduction

Since food, energy and water are basic human needs essential for human welfare and living standards worldwide, the Food–Water–Energy nexus has become a research focus. Following the Bonn 2011 conference and papers highlighting the FWE knowledge gap (Hoff, 2011), international organisations and research institutes are addressing the FWE nexus in publications and forums. The World Economic Forum published *Water security: The water-food-energy-climate security nexus*, which addresses challenges and possible solutions for future water demand from the perspectives of governments, researchers, NGOs, and enterprises (Waughray, 2010). The World Energy Outlook 2012, by the International Energy Agency (IEA), discusses linkages between water and energy. It emphasises the relationship between water supply and demand across national boundaries, which requires more advanced technology and a more comprehensive perspective. *Thirsty energy* by (the World Bank (2013) suggests solutions for technology development and governance strategies to ensure water and energy security (Rodriguez et al., 2013). The United Nations' "World water development report" (2014) discusses the importance of linking energy, water, and agriculture, proposing a hierarchical structure for public

DOI: 10.4324/9781003112495-14

affairs management by exploring possible frameworks and developing reliable data and innovative technologies.

In 2018, more than 55% of the world's population lived in cities, a proportion that is expected to increase to 68% by 2050 (UN, 2018). With this rapid growth, sustainable development depends on the successful management of urban growth. Many countries will face challenges meeting the needs of growing urbanisation, which increases the requirements for housing, transportation, and other infrastructure, as well as for the basic services such as food, energy, and water. Integrated policies to improve the lives of the urban population are needed while building on their existing economic, social and environmental ties. Thus, there is an increasing need for robust science to inform strategic urban policy, combining the efforts of different scientific disciplines but also including an active dialogue between stakeholders from policy and society.

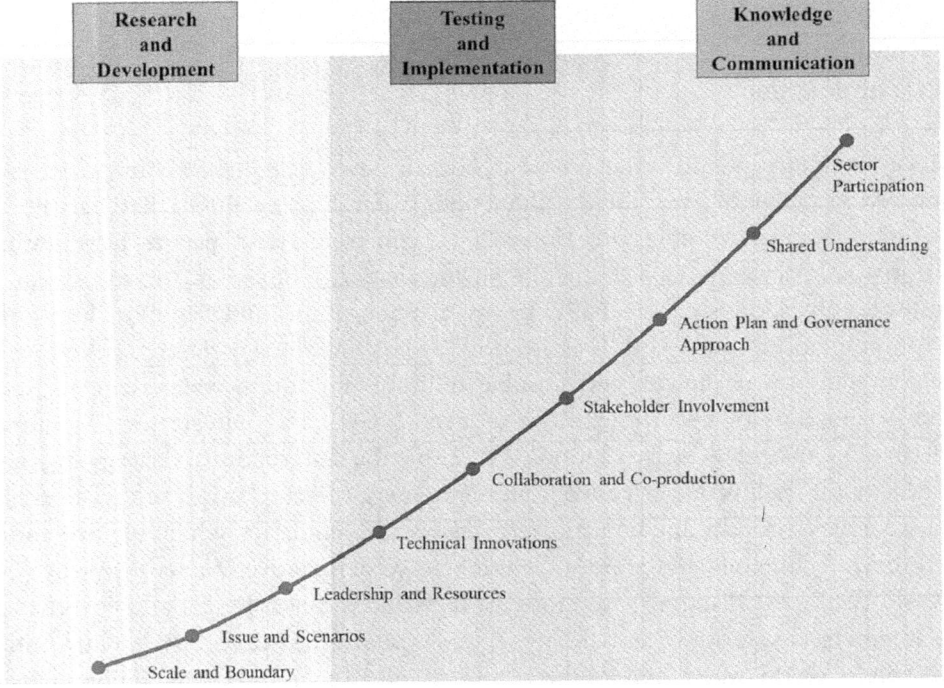

Figure 5.1: Key features of a possible path for implementing recommendations applicable to organisations across sectors

Since the Bonn 2011 Nexus Conference, FWE research and framework development has grown exponentially, but there is still no systematic or agreed-upon framework of existing initiatives – in particular, at the urban scale. This chapter is premised on the notion that to manage food, energy, and water resources in urban areas, it is necessary to bring FWE sustainability into the mainstream of stakeholder decision-making. It also supports dialogue between stakeholders who contribute to building more sustainable food-water-energy cities globally. This chapter provides recommendations for determining appropriate steps to embed the key concept of the urban living lab into Food-Water-Energy nexus management. This includes the identification of a framework underpinning the programmes, its structure, and the resources required, and using the framework to analyse a case study within the CRUNCH project so as to better understand the choice of methodologies developed.

B. Urban living labs and food-water-energy issues

1. Reasons to use urban living labs for the Food-Water-Energy nexus

Food, energy, and water are the most basic human needs and are essential for human welfare and raising living standards worldwide. According to the United Nations, by 2030, people will need 30% more water, 45% more energy, and 50% more food. One of the biggest challenges facing the world is the increasing scarcity of these vital resources. The work of Granit et al. (2012), Yuan et al. (2018) and Yuan and Lo (2020) confirm that food, energy, and water security are interdependent and not easily disentangled. The Food-Water-Energy nexus recognises these linkages and has become a focus of governance and research, with numerous reports on an integrated approach to resource management (Waughray, 2010; Hoff, 2011; Rodriguez et al., 2013). However, integrated policies to improve the sustainability of FWE resources are still needed, building on existing economic, social, and environmental ties. These multiple and interconnected challenges are expected to increasingly intensify the need for robust science in the remainder of this century.

Since the Bonn 2011 Nexus Conference (Hoff, 2011), there has been exponential growth in FWE framework development (Bizikova et al., 2013). ARUP (2014) and Stringer et al. (2014) point out that a novel framework combining nexus thinking will enable more equitable and just access to resources and resilience outcomes. Applying such a framework will help in understanding how the food-water-energy systems affect multiple spatial scales. Mayor et al. (2015) propose a framework for the Food-Water-Energy nexus at a river basin scale and addresses the important conflicts derived from the interdependencies between these three elements. Karnib (2017) presents a coupled framework of FWE nexus simulation and optimisation at national scale that allows the modelling and analysing of interactions across and between FWE sectors to find the best performance options. The work of Shannak, Mabrey, and Vittorio (2018) reviews existing models and frameworks in the FWE nexus literature, highlighting the need to develop innovative frameworks for different geographic levels and different purposes to support resource management planning. The framework of McGrane et al. (2019) focuses on data availability and articulates the steps required to develop nexus thinking to engage multiple stakeholders. This range of frameworks from nexus thinking highlights the complexity of different scales and that the need for a hierarchical framework relies on the perspectives of different stakeholders. Such a key conceptual nexus framework, combining the efforts of political and social stakeholders, does not yet exist.

Voytenko et al. (2016) show how the implementation of urban nexuses for urban living labs is emerging as a form of collective urban governance to address the challenges and opportunities created by urbanisation. ULLs are defined as stakeholder-centred, open innovation ecosystems based on an approach of systematic co-creation, co-design, and co-delivery (ENOLL, 2020). They consequently fit the need for integrating innovation processes in real-life communities and settings (Nesti, 2018). The components of a living lab include aim, infrastructure, activities, management, participants, research, testing, and implementation (Voytenko et al., 2016; Steen & van Bueren, 2017; Chronéer et al., 2019). Furthermore, Juujärvi and Pesso (2013) have identified three main levels of engagement in the plan procedures and vision planning of ULLs. However, given the early stages of the urban living labs as an approach for the FWE nexus context, key elements, characteristics, and features remain unexplored.

Living labs are a way to manage innovation processes in an inclusive and collaborative context, where the innovations are developed by engaging various stakeholders. The urban living lab approach expands its activities to an urban area, which also affects the ways that key stakeholders, including public organisations, private sectors, universities, and citizens, engage and jointly test, develop, and create metropolitan solutions. These environments are a safe place for collaboration and a test bed for innovation-based co-design, co-production, and co-delivery. There are three reasons why urban living labs can help a government assess potential solutions for Food–Water–Energy nexus challenges.

(1) Urban living labs can help a government frame and assess potential impacts from climate change and the Food–Water–Energy nexus. They can enhance the government's strategic conversations by considering issues in a more structured manner.
(2) Urban living labs can assist a government in evaluating the robustness of strategies and plans across sectors. They help to identify indicators to monitor the current status and, accordingly, to reassess strategies and plans along a path, along with associated management actions that may need to be considered in strategic plans.
(3) Urban living labs can help a government consider possible outcomes for physical responses to the Food–Water–Energy nexus, outcomes that will play out over the medium to longer term. Importantly, they broaden decision makers' thinking across a range of considerations and processes where Food–Water–Energy nexus-related impacts can be significant.

2. The process of developing a framework

A qualitative literature review has identified relative contributions and mapped main characteristics through a keyword search of two scientific literature databases (Scopus and Web of Science) without restriction of the time period. The search terms were formed to capture an explicit concern for the main working method of CRUNCH, as well as the nexus concept ('urban living lab' OR 'urban living labs' AND food; energy; water). This narrow filter was necessary to effectively distinguish the field of interest here from the abundant literature on urban living labs while also tracing distinct notions of 'water', 'food', and 'energy' as discussed below. This review investigates candidate characteristics within a framework rather than attempting to exhaustively review the state of research over this vast field.

Finally, a total of 127 references were retained for analysis, using a bottom-up classification based on key words which then resulted in several categories for differentiation. Broadly, three perspectives emerged: research and development, testing and implementation, and knowledge and communication. Together they form a complex framework that provides complementary highlights that have not been explored adequately. Taken individually, these three perspectives reflect certain insufficiencies for addressing the complex subject of cities as living labs.

The research and development phase identified the scale and boundaries in order to identify the multiple layers and variables of the problem of the urban living lab site. It is important to first examine the existing knowledge across different actors and subjects in order to identify the current scientific knowledge relevant for the urban issues in each city. To do so, issues that enjoy policy attention and the areas (places) have been identified by planners.

The testing and implementation phase identified mismatches between urban policy planning and social demands. This step shares understandings of place identity characteristics and experiences by engaging with community, policy officers, and planners from different departments, and with different roles within the local administration. Open dialogue in workshops or small-group forums facilitate this process.

The knowledge and communication phase looks forwards to creating a shared vision and strategic pathways for action and solutions, using outputs from the previous two steps with quantitative assessments of the cities. The expected formats include scientific presentations and publications, videos, and policy briefs for policy officers and planners, as well as simple presentations or social media.

3. Urban Food-Water-Energy nexus frameworks

To reach a better understanding of the focus of these characteristics, we further regrouped the key words under the three distinct categories of the goals to be developed. These reflect different concepts for what the core is at different phases and for possible initiatives, practices, policies, and models that address urban challenges.

Since each city is unique, the challenges and the means of finding solutions plays out differently in each city. This urban Food-Water-Energy nexus framework provides a guideline through which the solutions that contribute to a city's Food-Water-Energy nexus can be explored through nine key goals that comprise the complex outcomes of a Food-Water-Energy nexus city.

(1) Comprehensive scale and boundary
   Exploring the system boundaries and scale from different viewpoints gives a wide overview and helps us to concentrate on the identified scope of action and disregarding extraneous factors within the system in order to focus on the boundaries of interdisciplinary interactions.

Specific indicators that underpin this goal include: ecosystems mapping, protective infrastructure, city monitoring, and data management.

(2) Identified issues and scenarios

Detecting challenges, priorities, synergies, and trade-offs between the three aspects of the Food-Water-Energy nexus by interacting with nexus issues in a variety of ways to address any issues identified in the scenarios.

Specific indicators that underpin this goal include: integration with regional planning, clear baselines, targets, and strategies, and mapping spatial scales.

(3) Effective leadership and resources invested

Leadership that elicits positive change, manages risks, informs investment and infrastructure, implements short-term actions, and develops a long-term vision. This is facilitated by access to sound financial management and the ability to attract adequate investment and emergency funds.

Specific indicators that underpin this goal include: financing mechanisms, public finances, and strong leadership.

(4) Sustainable technical innovations

Diverse and affordable multimodal technological innovations, information networks and skill support i.e. a Non Invasive Measurement System that on a micro scale supports cities to proactively secure that which is necessary to meet basic needs within cities.

Specific indicators that underpin this goal include: skills and training, development and innovation, and technology networks.

(5) Collective collaboration and co-production

The potential and challenges within collaboration and co-production, requiring explanation, negotiation, and mutual integration in order to form a functional, distributed environment for collective action.

Specific indicators that underpin this goal include: multi-stakeholder collaboration, co-ordinated policy sectors and social goals, and partnerships for multi-stakeholder initiatives.

(6) Empowered stakeholder involvement

Stakeholder identification, engagement, empowerment and access to up-to-date information and knowledge to enable stakeholders to make effective choices and decisions, and organisations to take appropriate action, by using multi-functional nodes i.e. Co modal Local Node.

Specific indicators that underpin this goal include: community support, community cohesion, and engaged citizens.

(7) Integrated action plan and governance approach

A vision and an integrated development strategy that provide elements to highlight how and where to improve necessary development, updated by cross-departmental working groups and evidence-based decision-making.

Specific indicators that underpin this goal include: policy mechanisms, enforcement of planning and standards, and the planning approval process.

(8) Increased shared understanding

Education that is broadly accessible and that enables people and organisations to take appropriate action, including environmental stewardship, building appropriate infrastructure, effective land use management, and the enforcement of planning regulations.

Specific indicators that underpin this goal include: broadly available education, community awareness and preparedness, and mechanisms for communities to engage with government.

(9) Diverse sector participation

Participation in the diverse sectors that involve citizens and/or third sector participation in policymaking, which allows them to access diverse perspectives and benefit from various actors in the public and private sectors.

Specific indicators that underpin this goal include: government decision-making, co-ordination with other government bodies, and government emergency management.

Non Invasive Measurement System: Non-invasive measurement system for recording selected physical parameters related to the functioning of a public utility facility. The purpose of the measurements is to record the flows of energy, water and people depending on the time of day, weather conditions, tasks carried out in the measured facility and other factors affecting the movements, flow and other activities of people using the building.

Co modal Local Node: Multi-functional neighbourhood node with variable functionality dedicated to residents, strengthening neighbourly bonds in the locality and constituting a basic unit of the city structure, which ensures efficient communication and governance, including crisis management, from the city level, simultaneously implementing social innovations using smart solutions.

Data and knowledge supporting decision-making

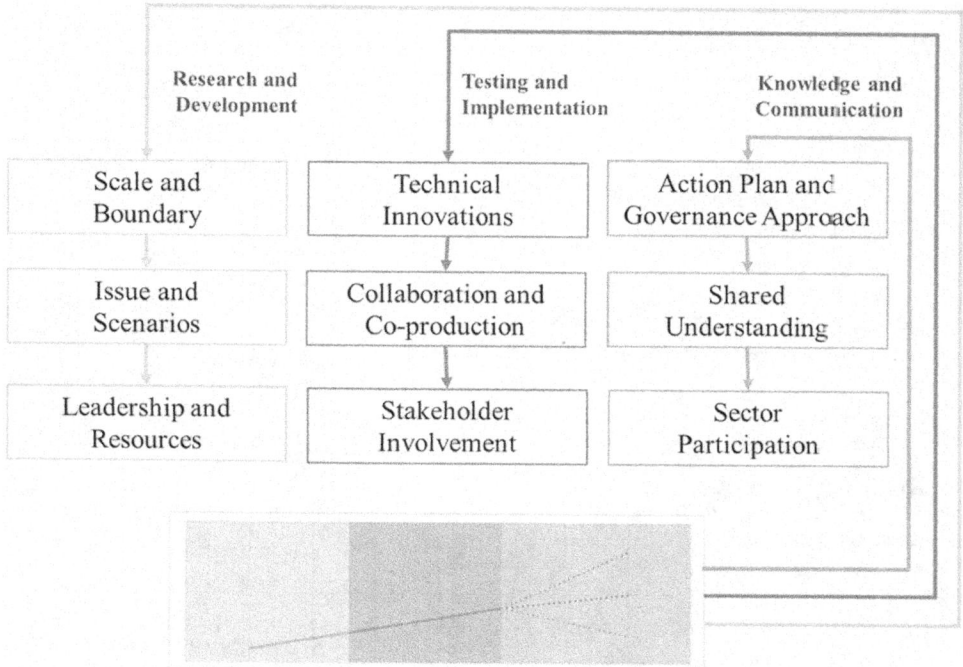

Figure 5.2: Nine goals related to: research and development, testing and implementation, and knowledge and communication

4. Overview of recommendations and guidance

The nine goals can be grouped into three categories: research and development, testing and implementation, and knowledge and communication. The relative importance of the nine goals depends on the urban context and the challenges of the Food-Water-Energy nexus that a city faces. This provides preparers with additional context and suggestions for implementing the recommendations (Figure 5.2).

5. Implementing the recommendations and guidance for all sectors

Despite a substantial focus on urban living labs as a means for providing economic prosperity, social cohesion, and achieving environmental sustainability in both science and governance, there is currently no systematic recommendation or guidance for their use in Food-Water-Energy nexus contexts. The recommendations

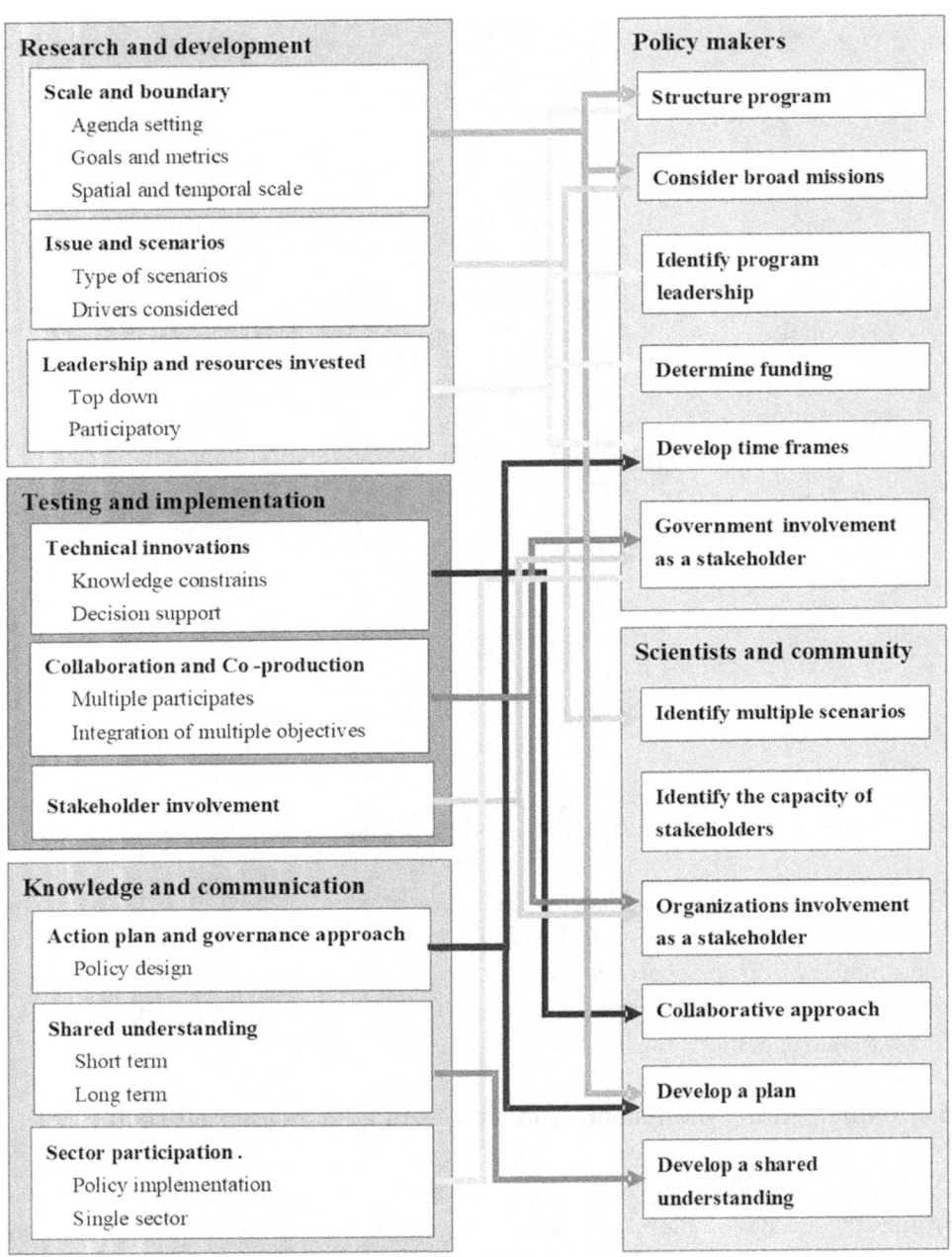

Figure 5.3: Implementing recommendations and guidance for all sectors

here are presented from the perspectives of policymakers, scientists, and community-oriented individuals. Recommendations for an appropriate model to enable food-water-energy sustainability are provided in Figure 5.3. Twelve widely adoptable recommendations for FWE-related measures applicable to governments across sectors were developed. The context covers the sectors potentially most affected by climate change and the transition to food-water-energy sustainability.

Governments, within the context of environmental problems, should design and apply co-production operating spaces for urban environmental governance to inform both scientists and communities. Organisations with more significant exposure to food-water-energy-related issues should consider disclosing the key assumptions and pathways that they use to allow users to understand the analytical process and its limitations.

(1) Structure the programme

When developing a framework for multiple purposes, a carefully structured programme is necessary to ensure that contributors understand their roles and responsibilities. Consideration must be given to the wide range of contexts, including the scales and boundaries under which different stakeholders operate. When developing a programme structure, the wide range of contexts (including scales, boundaries, and stakeholders) must be considered.

(2) Consider broad missions

For a framework to have relevance to multiple stakeholders and be useful for different purposes, a broad range of organisational missions and mandates must be considered. This can be addressed either by applying a collaborative approach to develop the framework, or by a coordinating organisation that manages a broad spectrum of issues and environmental programmes. A wide range of stakeholders work in different contexts, including geographic and jurisdictional scales (e.g. property, city, catchment region, state, national, global).

(3) Identify programme leadership

The most important qualities of a successful programme leader are scientific credibility, experience with projects, and coordination skills. Co-leadership by individuals with complementary and non-substitutable skills and experience should be considered. Leaders and co-leaders with strong, independent, scientific perspectives are required.

(4) Determine funding

The amount of financial support and restrictions on its use are critical factors that will influence the information and tools developed and the purchasing of skills and expertise. The amount of funding provided to programmes should be discussed, along with other resource features such as the time and skills required. Flexibility in funding is desirable, since adequate funding and restrictions on its use will influence the ability to collect data, develop information and tools, and acquire necessary expertise.

(5) Develop time frames

Because the timing of impacts on government will vary, specifying time frames across sectors for the short, medium, and long term could hinder a government's consideration of challenges and opportunities. This chapter, therefore, encourages governments to define their own time frames according to the life of their assets, the profile of the challenges they face, and the sectors and geographies in which they operate.

(6) Government involvement as a stakeholder

Local stakeholder concerns for top-down regulatory enforcement can be a barrier to the government conducting the programme. Thus, it is important to bring the Food-Water-Energy nexus into the mainstream for decision-making by government stakeholders (i.e. local, regional, national and international decision makers).

(7) Identify multiple scenarios

Scenarios can enable people to collectively deal with problems involving high uncertainty and complexity and provide new information, as well as help to develop a shared understanding across sectors and disciplines. These can be supported by broadly accepted methodologies, datasets, and tools for scenario-based evaluation by organisations. Given that these approaches are more complex than conventional sectoral management, there is a need to address, reduce, and communicate this complexity, without compartmentalised thinking and vested interests.

(8) Identify the capacity of stakeholders

The capacity of stakeholders to understand and apply information and tools is an important consideration in view of stakeholders' time, money, and ability. Considering the capacity of stakeholders to access information and tools after the programme ceases, and for the coordinating organisation, is necessary when designing and developing tools to communicate the programme.

(9) Organisations' involvement as stakeholders

Since contextual factors can influence methodological differences, primary consideration should be given to organisations with existing networks and those with representation from different stakeholders as part of their management structure. When reviewing collaborations and expert input, there should be consideration

Data and knowledge supporting decision-making

for the potential use and users of the framework – i.e. business, industry, indigenous groups, agricultural groups, NGOs, natural resource managers, and communities within and across scales. There should be a multi-sector approach to stakeholder engagement and multi-scale technical design of the programme.

(10) Collaborative approach

Stakeholders working across single organisations or initiatives recognise the need for a unified approach to support collaboration with the target audience of their outcomes, and those most likely to be impacted by the application of any actions. The multi-disciplinary nature of this issue requires a wide range of expertise (e.g. economists, planners, cartographers, and natural and social scientists). Various stakeholders (e.g. business, industry, community, government, non-government, and researchers) from different disciplines and cultures allow for collaboration at different scales to be interlinked for both bottom-up and top-down outcomes.

(11) Develop a plan

A plan or blueprint to actively work toward a greater alignment of frameworks and to support their adoption should be developed collaboratively with stakeholders and consider political and market forces in the form of subsidies, profit seeking, and state agendas. This allows the concept to be more detailed and useful for stakeholders for formulating strategies, plans, and policies. Social-environmental planning should be developed with input from local stakeholders in multi-scale technical design. Local and state governments and other stakeholders should review and amend plans and policies, ensuring that their activities continue to reflect regional interests as defined in the plan.

(12) Develop a shared understanding

A shared understanding across stakeholders and disciplines of the food-water-energy system is necessary to ensure a shared vision between stakeholders for further analysis and measurement. This can increase stakeholders' understanding of challenges and opportunities, as well as their ability to access, understand and apply information and tools. Providing information, guidelines and tools can help create awareness and new management strategies that provide a basic structure to address complex issues.

C. Learning from cities

To ensure the framework is widely applicable and grounded in the experiences of cities, we considered six urban case studies: Southend-on-Sea (UK), Eindhoven (Netherlands), Gdańsk (Poland), Uppsala (Sweden), Miami (USA), and

Taipei (Taiwan). These cities were selected since they are part of the CRUNCH programme and had either recently experienced a major shock or are suffering chronic stresses in their Food-Water-Energy nexus. The primary purpose of the fieldwork was to understand what affects the Food-Water-Energy nexus in cities, and how the Food-Water-Energy nexus is understood from the perspective of different cities.

(1) Minimising vulnerabilities under challenging conditions – Southend-on-Sea

A holiday destination in the 1960s, Southend-on-Sea suffers from the disposal of commercial cooking oil into combined sewers, which has led to a demand for a greener environment. The local government of Southend-on-Sea secured £7 million of government funding for various projects, including blue and green infrastructure and plastic recycling.

The level of stakeholder enhancement and its link to biodiversity/ecological suitability was a key learning point for the city. Two possible nexus projects –

Figure 5.4: Minimising vulnerabilities under challenging conditions, Southend-on-Sea

Fatbergs (chip shop food waste recycling) and Smart baskets – high street ornamental planting into high-tech, bio-diverse green street infrastructure – could lead this city to better find projects that bring together food, energy, and water.

(2) Nexus thinking for urban planning and leadership – Eindhoven

Eindhoven is the 5th largest city in the Netherlands, located in the Dommel valley. It has experienced several shocks in recent decades, including floods, droughts, heat island conditions, and energy imbalance. There was a recognised need for improved infrastructure, such as resources from wastewater, energy transition, connecting isolated water bodies, water retention and treatment, and developing more green areas and less pavement to reduce the chances of recurring floods.

The local government enacted measures to conduct hydrological calculations, check the groundwater table, and reduce maintenance costs in most areas, in anticipation of development demands.

Figure 5.5: Nexus-thinking for urban planning and leadership, Eindhoven

(3) Developing cross-sectoral leadership for building, Gdańsk

As one of the fastest growing cities in Poland, and despite its economic prosperity, Gdańsk struggles to keep up with demands placed on its infrastructure and services. The Nexus Square is a co-modal node in Gdańsk. Sensors are used to collect data on water, food, energy consumption, climate quality, ambient air quality, energy, waste, and wastewater production.

The local government and stakeholder groups have developed parallel and complementary approaches, along with a design contest that serves as an example of creating a more sustainable environment. The food flow, water flow, energy flow, and human flow have been estimated to find solutions for the square.

Figure 5.6: Developing cross-sectoral leadership for building, Gdańsk

(4) Enhancing the nexus through community-led actions, Uppsala

Uppsala's citizens live in residential areas which typically contain about 500 homes. A large number of new houses and apartments have been planned in recent years due to rapid population growth in the city. The city faces challenges surrounding air, water, and sound pollution, as well as traffic congestion due to the rapid increase in population and a shortage of housing and public services. Uppsalahem plans to build 7,000 new residential apartments in the area. Within these areas, the city government and stakeholder partners are working to increase community cohesion. Goals include the reduction in greenhouse gas emissions, doubling the capacity of the urban infrastructure, and a new tram service system. It aims to bring about an ecologically conscious smart city.

Figure 5.7: Enhancing nexus through community-led actions, Uppsala

(5) Addressing risk for disaster, Miami

Miami is the centre and leader in finance, commerce, culture, arts, and international trade for South Florida in the United States. As a major tourism hub for international visitors, especially near the coast, Miami Beach and South Miami suffer from climate change, sea level rise, and hurricanes. These issues are exacerbated by urban growth and will have a substantial impact on many of the residents. To improve these vulnerable areas, the local government and local groups have developed a platform for integrated nexus solutions and green infrastructure. To secure safety and increase resilience along the coastal area, the city government, supported by national and international partners, is implementing a number of interventions. They have provided information about the risks associated with the flood defence and how it works, in order to address community vulnerabilities that have been challenging for the city government and that have threatened social breakdown. The city government also struggles to secure and maintain security in these areas.

Figure 5.8: Balancing natural resources through multiple approaches, Taipei

(6) Balancing natural resources through multiple approaches, Taipei

The first household waste landfill site in Taipei was built around 35 years ago and has been a restoration park for 15 years. The city government is conducting a number of interventions. To make this an environmental education park, they took an integrated and inclusive approach that specifically targets the needs identified from the perspectives of the Food-Water-Energy nexus.

In this process, they built a more cohesive nexus system that has become a key point of support and guidance for families and schools. The municipality has recognised that ensuring the robustness of the infrastructure over the long term requires the engagement of stakeholders. Several workshops were held for local authorities, managers, and planners to explain the advantages of environmentally sustainable planning. An innovative system is also being developed with co-design by scientists and planners to give greater space and access for understanding how the Food-Water-Energy nexus responds to climate change.

D. Conclusion

Cities worldwide are currently facing the critical challenge of an increasing scarcity of vital resources. In response, new collaborations are emerging in the form of urban living labs – sites devised to produce, design, and deliver with social and technical innovation in real time.

This chapter examines the governance of food-water-energy sustainability transitions through urban living labs. It brings together research within a systematic comparative framework to evaluate practices related to the integration of food-water-energy concerns that enables the analysis of their potential and their limits. Six study cases have been presented to show applications within the policy cycle to food-water-energy issues, as urban living labs. This framework provides a more systematic, cohesive view of the diverse research related to urban living labs based on FWE sustainability. It provides new insights into the available practices and processes in several ways, so as to help the public sector quickly understand and identify possible pathways to improve the design and implementation of urban living labs considering the Food-Water-Energy nexus.

This chapter can be interpreted broadly in order to include a wide a range of potential practices and processes that could be used to integrate the food-water-energy considerations of sustainable development into urban planning.

Acknowledgements

This study is financially supported by the National Taiwan University (NTUCCP-110L901003, NTU-110L8807), and the NTU Research Center for Future Earth from The Featured Areas Research Center Program within the framework of the Higher Education Sprout Project of the Ministry of Education (MOE) in Taiwan, and the Ministry of Science and Technology of the Republic of China (MOST110-2621-M-002-011, MOST110-2625-M-001-002-MY3). This project has received funding from the European Union's Horizon 2020 research and innovation programme (GA No 730254) under the JPI Urban Europe's call "SUGI – FWE Nexus". This project has received funding from the National Science Centre, Poland (2017/25/Z/HS6/03050).

References

ARUP. (2014). City resilience framework.

Bizikova, L., Roy, D., Swanson, D. et al. (2013). The water–energy–food security nexus: Towards a practical planning and decision-support framework for landscape investment and risk management. International Institute for Sustainable Development Winnipeg, Manitoba, Canada.

Chronéer, D., Ståhlbröst, A., & Habibipour, A. (2019). Urban living labs: Towards an integrated understanding of their key components. *Technology Innovation Management Review*, 9(3), 50–62.

ENOLL. (2020). Living labs. www.openlivinglabs.eu/. (Accessed 27 March 2020).

Granit, J., Jägerskog, A., Lindström, A. et al. (2012). Regional options for addressing the water, energy and food nexus in Central Asia and the Aral Sea Basin. *International Journal of Water Resources Development*, 28(3), 419–432.

Hoff, H. (2011). Understanding the nexus: Background paper for the Bonn 2011 conference: The Water, Energy and Food Security Nexus. Stockholm Environment Institute (SEI), Stockholm, Sweden.

Juujärvi, S., & Pesso, K. (2013). Actor roles in an urban living lab: What can we learn from Suurpelto, Finland? *Technology Innovation Management Review*, 3(11), 22–27.

Karnib, A. (2017). A Quantitative Assessment Framework for Water, Energy and Food Nexus. *Computational Water, Energy, and Environmental Engineering*, 6(1), 11–23.

Mayor, B., López-Gunn, E., Villarroya, F. I., & Montero, E. (2015). Application of a water-energy-food nexus framework for the Duero river basin in Spain. *Water International*, 40(5–6), 791–808.

McGrane, S. J., Acuto, M., Artioli, F. et al. (2019). Scaling the nexus: Towards integrated frameworks for analysing water, energy and food. *Geographical Journal*, *185*(4), 419–431.

Nesti, G. J. P. (2018). Co-production for innovation: The urban living lab experience. *Policy and Society*, *37*(3), 310–325.

Rodriguez, D. J., Delgado, A., DeLaquil, P., & Sohns, A. (2013). *Thirsty energy*. World Bank, Washington, DC.

Shannak, S. d., Mabrey, D., & Vittorio, M. (2018). Moving from theory to practice in the water-energy-food nexus: An evaluation of existing models and frameworks. *Water-Energy Nexus 1*(1), 17–25.

Steen, K., & Van Bueren, E. (2017). The defining characteristics of urban living labs. *Technology Innovation Management Review*, 7(7), 21–33.

Stringer, L., Quinn, C., Berman, R. et al. (2014). Combining nexus and resilience thinking in a novel framework to enable more equitable and just outcomes. Sustainability Research Institute School of Earth and Environment. University of Leeds (Paper No. 73).

UN. (2018). *World urbanization prospects: The 2018 revision*. United Nations Department of Economic and Social Affairs.

Voytenko, Y., McCormick, K., Evans, J., & Schliwa, G. (2016). Urban living labs for sustainability and low carbon cities in Europe: Towards a research agenda. *Journal of Cleaner Production*, *123*, 45–54.

Waughray, D. (2010). *Water security: The water-food-energy-climate nexus*. World Economic Forum (WEF), Island Press, Washington, USA.

Yuan, K.-Y., Lin, Y.-C., Chiueh, P.-T., & Lo, S.-L. (2018). Spatial optimization of the food, energy, and water nexus: A life cycle assessment-based approach. *Energy Policy*, *119*, 502–514.

Yuan, M.-H., & Lo, S.-L. (2019). Developing indicators for the monitoring of the sustainability of food, energy, and water. *Renewable and Sustainable Energy Reviews*, *119*, 109565.

Chapter 6

Development of an integrated decision support system (IDSS)

Vera van Zoest, Edith Ngai, Shashank Shekher Tripathi, and Archit Suryawanshi

1. Background

1.1 Decision support systems (DSS)

The concept of decision support systems (DSS) has been around for many decades. It was first described, albeit under the different term 'management decision systems', at the beginning of the 1970s (Scott Morton, 1971). Ralph H. Sprague Jr (1980) followed up with a description of a framework for the development of decision support systems. He described the reactions towards DSS as twofold: ranging from just another buzzword to an important breakthrough. Now, forty years later, we can safely state that decision support systems still play an important role in our daily lives and contribute to decision-making processes in a wide range of fields. The definition coined in 1980 is still valid: "interactive computer based systems, which help decision makers utilise data and models to solve unstructured problems" or more broadly "any system that makes some contribution to decision making" (Sprague Jr 1980, pp. 1–2). While decision-making processes cover a wide range of topics, it is clear that even in the field of environmental and urban planning these programs and tools can provide a useful way to evaluate criteria and compare planning scenarios.

Decision support systems consist of three main elements: the model base, database, and user interface. The database serves as a repository to store the data needed to run models. The model base provides the main link between the data

DOI: 10.4324/9781003112495-15

and the user interface. The model base can take various shapes depending on the goal of the DSS. Its basic functionalities are the identification and exploration of data in the database, as well as the exploration of relations between variables. Over the years, and with the increasing availability of computational power, models have become increasingly complex and allow for more sophisticated algorithms and the implementation of machine learning techniques. The user interface hides some of that complexity and provides more lightweight access to the data for the end-user. The user interface takes input and requests from the user and visualises the results of the models in a clear and understandable way – at least when designed correctly.

1.2 DSS for food, water, and energy

Within the field of environmental science, many decision support systems have been developed for different purposes, covering a range from local to global case study areas. Some decision support systems are based on geographical information systems (GIS) to organise and store thematic layers of information and link information from different sources through their spatial location (Maina, Amin, & Yazid 2014). An example of a GIS-based DSS for food management is the one developed in the RESTORE project, in which soil and land use maps, as well as production and consumption statistics, are used to predict the spatio-temporal variability in radioactively contaminated ecosystems and risk areas for food contamination (Van der Perk et al., 2001). Other studies have used satellite imagery in combination with GIS data to predict food yield. Satellite imagery is used to estimate the normalised difference vegetation index (NDVI) and land surface temperature (LST). Habibie et al. (2019) used satellite imagery in combination with GIS data, such as distance from roads and rivers, land cover, precipitation, elevation and slope, to identify suitable areas for maize production. In a similar way, GIS data is used to find the most suitable areas for renewable energy production. Voivontas et al. (1998) used spatial data on topography, urban areas, activities and wind for evaluation of the potential of wind park locations. Zambelli et al. (2012) used the morphology of the terrain in combination with road networks to evaluate biomass availability. By far the majority of environmental decision support systems are related to water management, covering water quality, water quantity, and irrigation. GIS-based decision support systems have also been widely applied to water management, e.g. for the prediction of residential water demand based on household size, age, income, and the presence of swimming pools (Jayarathna et al., 2017), but also for water irrigation management, to optimise the allocation of water resources using a GIS based on soil moisture, meteorological changes, and crop characteristics (Chen et al., 2012). Besides the more traditional GIS layers related to land cover, geomorphology, and meteorology, some studies have used spatial point data from sensor networks. For example, Szemes et al. (2011) use a wireless sensor network (WSN) to monitor building energy performance. Khan et al. (2018) use a WSN in a decision support system for the optimisation of irrigation in precision agriculture.

Whereas some decision support systems are based on simple spreadsheets, more recently artificial intelligence and machine learning techniques have also made their way into decision support systems. Li et al. (2013) used Dynamic Linear Discriminant Analysis (D-LDA), an unsupervised clustering technique, in a daily irrigation decision support system. Suntaranont et al. (2020) proposed a decision support system for weir sluice gate level adjustment based on an artificial neural network for water level prediction and a fuzzy logic control algorithm for period estimation of the sluice gate setting. Ali, Mocanu, and Florea (2016) have used machine learning and data mining techniques to predict drinking water quality and suggest decisions on water treatment based on the type and cause of pollution.

Machine learning techniques have also been used to support better management of renewable energy generation. For example, forecasting the output power of solar systems is required for good operation of power grids and optimal management. The energy output of these power plants depends on many environmental factors, such as wind speed and direction, and solar radiation in the region of the power plant. Sharma et al. (2011) explored automatically creating site-specific prediction models for solar power generation from National Weather Service (NWS) weather forecasts using machine learning techniques. Heinermann and Kramer (2016) proposed the use of heterogeneous machine learning ensembles for wind power prediction. Voyant et al. (2017) studied different machine learning methodologies, from neural networks to a support vector machine, regression tree, and random forest, for predicting the energy output of renewable energy generation.

In addition, machine learning has emerged alongside big data and high-performance computing to support decision-making in food production. As discussed by Liakos et al. (2018), the applications of machine learning in agricultural production systems may include crop management, livestock management, water management, and soil management. Boshkoska et al. (2019) used machine learning techniques in a DSS to distinguish knowledge boundaries within agri-food value chains.

1.3 Integrated decision support systems (IDSS)

As we have seen from the examples above, most environmental decision support systems have a very specific objective related to either food, water, or energy. In most cases, they are also very specific to one case study area. In practice, however, the food, water and energy ecosystems are highly interlinked (Tian et al., 2018). Water and energy are required for the production of crops. While most crops are produced for food consumption, part of the crops are used as a source of energy in the form of biofuel. Water is used for energy generation, but in return, energy is needed for water irrigation, drainage, and pumping. Food production may lead to water pollution. The interlinkages make the system complex to comprehend. Decisions made in one of the three sectors will influence the others. To optimise and balance production and consumption in food, water and energy simultaneously, an integrated decision support system (IDSS) is needed.

The idea of an IDSS is to combine decision support for different ecosystems which are strongly connected. The concept of the IDSS is similar to that of an DSS: linking a model base, database, and user interface. However, the models in an IDSS combine interdisciplinary models and the relations between resources and balances of different ecosystems. In the case of an IDSS for the FWE nexus, this means that the model base will translate linkages between the food, water and energy balance into models. The underlying models may range from simple linear relations to sophisticated machine learning models. These models require a large database with underlying data related to the production and consumption of food, water, and energy. Integrating data from different sources comes with its own challenges; for example, challenges related to the incompatibility of geographical units and boundaries used in different datasets (March & Hevner, 2007). Given the large number of inputs in an IDSS, the design of an intuitive user interface may also be challenging. A simple layout with a small number of user-changeable parameters is preferred.

Only a few papers have described decision support systems for the FWE nexus to date. Lin et al. (2019) have combined the food, water and energy subsystems in a GIS-based nexus assessment tool for Taiwan. Combining food, water and energy in a decision support system can also support in tackling other environmental problems such as nitrogen pollution (Tian et al., 2018). A major challenge with FWE nexus integrated decision support systems is the sensitivity of input parameters to climate change (Yuan et al., 2018). Therefore, it is desirable to run different models in parallel to account for different climate change scenarios.

2. IDSS for CRUNCH

2.1 Introduction

Cities all around the world are working hard to improve sustainability and their resilience to climate change. Urban living labs (ULLs) have been set up as innovative playgrounds to test new innovations and their effectiveness in balancing food, water and energy resources. In the CRUNCH project, six ULLs around the world have collaborated. The ULL in Eindhoven, the Netherlands, consists of the Brainport Smart District (BSD). Its innovative design stimulates new ways of using space for living, working, and collaborating. The ULL is designed in such a way that it is carbon neutral and energy neutral. By collecting rainwater and growing vegetables, the district works towards a circular economy and self-sustainable neighbourhood. The ULL in Southend-On-Sea is shaped along Southend High Street, a busy urban street with shops, companies, and exciting nightlife. One of the major challenges in Southend is drought in combination with urban heat island effects. In the ULL, the aim is to develop green infrastructure supported by innovative water panels that use sunlight to capture water from the air. Fudeken, a former landfill site, forms the ULL in Taipei. The large area has now been turned into a landscape park. One of the aims is to grow food in the area, for which polluted water and soil needs to be cleaned first. The landscape park also provides several new innovations to showcase new ways of energy generation, like microbial fuel plants. The ULL in Uppsala is formed of the Rosendal neighbourhood. The unique design of impermeable layers under the neighbourhood allows it to be built on a water conservation and protection area. All rainwater is filtered, cleaned and checked for its quality before it is diverted to a retention pond. To keep the rain water clean, cars are not allowed to enter the neighbourhood. The ULL in Miami Beach covers the Flamingo/Lummus neighbourhood. Flamingo Park forms the green heart of the urban neighbourhood. The main challenges in Miami Beach are the rising sea level and possible flooding of the island due to climate change. When rebuilding Miami Beach to be more resilient against future flooding events, it can simultaneously consider sustainability in other aspects of the FWE nexus. Gdańsk ULL is a proposed greenfield transit-oriented neighbourhood at the Gdańsk Airport Station. Students at the Faculty of Architecture, GUT, developed the master plan of the low-carbon residential neighbourhood. The master plan focused on climate change adaptation, circular economy, and low-emission targeted at zero waste.

Vera van Zoest et al.

The project emphasises public awareness of how to adapt to climate change in Gdańsk, presenting smart solutions aimed at self-sufficiency. Although the ULLs all have their own specific problems, the overall goal is to reach sustainability and resilience. One way to work towards this goal is by balancing the production and consumption of food, water and energy within the ULL, making the ULL self-sustainable and independent of external resources. The IDSS for CRUNCH provides an opportunity to share innovations between ULLs and calculate their impacts on the food/water/energy balance. These will help decision makers to make informed decisions about the implementation of innovative ideas. The IDSS provides calculations for different climate scenarios to improve awareness of, and resilience to, the effects of climate change.

2.2 Model base

In the backend of the IDSS, a simple set of models is used to calculate the self-sufficiency of an urban living lab u in terms of the food, water and energy balance, given a climate scenario c. This self-sufficiency is calculated as a ratio between the production and consumption, maximised at 100 percent. For the food balance, this means:

$$Food\ balance = \min\left(\frac{P_{F,u,c}}{C_{F,u,c}} * 100, 100\right)$$

where $P_{F,u,c}$ is the total daily food production (kcal) in u given climate scenario c, and $C_{F,u,c}$ is the total daily food consumption in u given climate scenario c. Total daily food consumption (kcal) is calculated based on the ULL population Q_u and the per person food consumption $C_{f,u,c}$:

$$C_{F,u,c} = Q_u * C_{f,u,c}$$

Total food production is based on the current area used for food production, the area used for new innovations related to food production, and the yield depending on the type of cultivation, location of the ULL, and the climate scenario:

$$P_{F,u,c} = \left(A_{f,u} + A_{g,u}\right) * Y_{t,u,c} + A_{a,u} * Y_{a,u,c} + A_{r,u} * Y_{r,u,c}$$

where $A_{f,u}, A_{g,u}, A_{a,u}, A_{r,u}$ are the areas (m²) used for current farming, rooftop gardens, aquaponic farming, and rain gardens, respectively. The yield (kcal/day/m²) is equal to $Y_{t,u,c}$ for traditional farming (current farming and rooftop gardens), $Y_{a,u,c}$ for aquaponic farming, and $Y_{r,u,c}$ for rain gardens. Whereas the areas are based on user input, the yields are estimated using machine learning techniques (see section 2.3).

Similar to the food balance, the water balance is calculated by balancing production and consumption:

$$Water\,balance = \min\left(\frac{P_{W,u,c}}{C_{W,u,c}} * 100, 100\right)$$

where $P_{W,u,c}$ is the total daily water production (m³) in u given climate scenario c, and $C_{W,u,c}$ is the total daily water consumption (m³) in u given climate scenario c. Total water consumption is calculated as a multiplication between Q_u and the per person water consumption $C_{w,u,c}$:

$$C_{W,u,c} = Q_u * C_{w,u,c}$$

Total daily water production $P_{W,u,c}$ (m³) is based on the area (m²) used for catchment of rainwater $A_{p,u}$, the daily precipitation $R_{u,c}$ (mm), the area (m²) used for water panels $A_{h,u}$, and the daily production capacity of the water panels $H_{u,c}$ (m³):

$$P_{W,u,c} = A_{p,u} * R_{u,c} * 0.001 + A_{h,u} * H_{u,c}$$

The energy balance is calculated as:

$$Energy\,balance = \min\left(\frac{P_{E,u,c}}{C_{E,u,c}} * 100, 100\right)$$

where $P_{E,u,c}$ is the total daily energy production (kWh) in u given climate scenario c, and $C_{E,u,c}$ is the total daily energy consumption (kWh) in u given climate scenario c. Total energy consumption is calculated as:

$$C_{E,u,c} = Q_u * C_{e,u,c}$$

where $C_{e,u,c}$ is the per person energy consumption (kWh). The per person energy consumption is based on forecasting models (see section 2.3).

The total daily energy production $P_{E,u,c}$ is based on the area used for solar panels $A_{s,u}$ (m²), the daily solar panel production capacity $E_{s,u,c}$ (kWh/m²) at location u, climate scenario c, and the area used for microbial fuel plants $A_{m,u}$ (m²) and their daily production capacity $E_{m,u,c}$ (kWh/m²):

$$P_{E,u,c} = A_{s,u} * E_{s,u,c} + A_{m,u} * E_{m,u,c}$$

The sources and calculations of all parameter values for this IDSS are given in section 2.3.

2.3 Database

The input parameters for the models have been inserted in a database. Fixed parameters are those that are based on the vision or current situation of the ULL; they are not affected by climate scenarios and cannot be changed by the user of the IDSS. These are given in Table 6.1, where $A_{t,u}$ is the total area of the ULL, $A_{b,u}$ is the building area in the ULL, and $A_{w,u}$ is the water body area in the ULL.

The parameters determining the area used for innovations are set by the user. However, they are initialised to the values in the vision or current situation. These values are stored in the database as shown in Table 6.2. A change in user input will affect the calculations of all climate scenarios at the same time; the parameters are therefore independent of the climate scenario. Most values are initialised to zero, because no sharing of innovations between ULLs has taken place in the current situation. This can be changed by the user. Some innovations have no area initialised in any of the ULLs. This holds for the rooftop gardens and aquaponic farming. These innovations were mentioned in the vision document of the Eindhoven ULL but without a specific area. Therefore they have been initialised to zero and can be changed by the user.

Table 6.1: Fixed parameters in the IDSS database

	Eindhoven	Uppsala	Taipei	Southend	Miami	Gdańsk
Q_u	4500	12000	271806	9000	23573	17837
$A_{t,u}$	1550000	443111	830000	183	2362853	1028735
$A_{b,u}$	470000	56800	9608	183	773219	520166
$A_{f,u}$	114000	0	0	0	0	81172
$A_{w,u}$	416592	800	14258	0	0	17389

Table 6.2: Initial user input parameters in the IDSS database

	Eindhoven	Uppsala	Taipei	Southend	Miami	Gdańsk
$A_{s,u}$	140000	0	25212	0	0	0
$A_{m,u}$	0	0	4	0	0	0
$A_{r,u}$	0	0	8	0	0	0
$A_{h,u}$	0	0	0	6	0	0
$A_{a,u}$	0	0	0	0	0	0
$A_{g,u}$	0	0	0	0	0	0
$A_{p,u}$	81400	0	0	0	0	0

The consumption statistics are shown in Table 6.3. For food and water consumption, the input values are the same for each climate scenario. Especially for water consumption, this assumption may not be valid. Based on the available data, we could not make a distinction at this moment. However, a subscript c is used to indicate the possibility in the database to make these parameters climate scenario dependent in the future. For those parameters for which climate scenarios could be calculated, the subscript c is replaced by the specific climate scenario (current, IPCC 2.6, IPCC 4.5, IPCC 8.5). All of the climate scenario values are calculated for the year 2030. Food consumption is based on national data from the FAO database (FAO Statistics Division, 2008). Water consumption for Eindhoven is based on the vision document (Brainport Smart District et al., 2019), for Uppsala based on SCB household statistics data for Uppsala province (SCB, 2015) divided by the number of people per household, for Taipei and Gdańsk based on literature (Stępniewska, 2015; Hung, Chie, & Huang, 2017), and for Southend based on a WWT report using data for England and Wales (WWT, 2019). Current energy consumption for Uppsala has been derived from the SCB database, for which the values were converted to daily per person electricity consumption (SCB, 2018). The climate scenario dependent energy consumption for Uppsala has been predicted using a regression model, for which the input parameters age and salary were forecasted for 2030 using Auto-Regressive Integrated Moving Averages (ARIMA). Other model parameters included county and temperature. Temperature for the IPCC scenarios was derived from the SMHI database (SMHI, 2020) and included in the energy consumption prediction model. For Eindhoven, the current energy consumption was derived from the vision document (Brainport Smart District et al., 2019). For

Southend, this was derived from Statista for UK region East (Statista, 2018). Gdańsk electricity consumption was derived from an EU report on energy consumption and energy efficiency trends (European Commission, 2018). Since no climate effect model was available for residential electricity consumption in Eindhoven, Southend, and Gdańsk, but all are situated in a colder climate region where most energy is used for heating, we assumed the same percentage changes for the IPCC scenarios as compared to those modelled in Uppsala. For Taipei, the values were derived from literature. For the current situation, household electricity consumption was taken from Huang (2015). For the climate scenario calculations, we used the predictions in temperature change for China, adopted from Sun, Miao, and Duan (2015). For each 1 °C in temperature increase, we assume 9.2% increase in electricity consumption, following Li, Pizer, and Wu (2019). For Miami, the electricity consumption was derived from the U.S. Energy Information Administration (EIA, 2017). Since both Miami and Taipei are located in an area where energy is mostly used for cooling rather than for heating purposes, the increase in electricity consumption under the different climate scenarios was considered similar.

Production statistics for the IDSS database are shown in Table 6.4. Precipitation data from Eindhoven is derived from the vision document (Brainport Smart District et al., 2019). Climate projections for Eindhoven were taken from KNMI, predicting an average increase in precipitation of 5% by 2030 (KNMI, 2020). Since no distinction is made between different IPCC scenarios, the value is used for all scenarios. Precipitation for Uppsala was derived from SMHI (SMHI, 2009) as well as its climate scenario predictions (SMHI, 2020). Current precipitation values for Taipei and Southend were provided by their respective ULL project teams. Projected changes for Taipei were made following Sun, Miao, and Duan (2015). For Southend,

Table 6.3: Consumption statistics in the IDSS database, daily consumption per person

	Eindhoven	Uppsala	Taipei	Southend	Miami	Gdańsk
$C_{f,u,c}$	3000	3110	2990	3450	3750	3410
$C_{w,u,c}$	0.074	0.15	0.34	0.141	0.197	0.040
$C_{e,u,current}$	7.306	7.53	13.33	11.32	11.78	3.29
$C_{e,u,IPCC2.6}$	5.941	6.124	18.05	9.206	15.95	2.676
$C_{e,u,IPCC4.5}$	5.85	6.029	17.47	9.064	15.44	2.634
$C_{e,u,IPCC8.5}$	5.625	5.7976	19.80	8.716	17.50	2.533

the changes in precipitation are expected to be negligible for all scenarios (Murphy et al., 2009). For Miami, the effects of climate change on precipitation are taken from the IPCC Statement (Florida Climate Center, 2020). Precipitation data from Gdańsk was retrieved from literature (Szpakowski & Szydłowski, 2018), and changes in precipitation due to climate change were considered of the same magnitude as predicted by the KNMI (KNMI, 2020). The water production of the water panels is based on the average production according to the manufacturer (Zero Mass Water, 2020) but can be adapted to location and climate scenario in the future. Solar panel production was estimated at the location of each ULL using the Global Solar Atlas (2020). In combination with the vision document for the Eindhoven ULL (Brainport Smart District et al., 2019), the actual energy production was estimated at 14.36% of the solar radiation income reported in the Global Solar Atlas. Climate scenario specific solar energy production can be added in the future based on available data. Energy production from the microbial fuel plants and crop yield from rain

Table 6.4: Production statistics in the IDSS database, daily production per m² (except for $R_{u,c}$, in mm)

	Eindhoven	Uppsala	Taipei	Southend	Miami	Gdańsk
$R_{u,current}$	2.13	1.92	4.44	0.48	3.60	1.94
$R_{u,IPCC2.6}$	2.24	1.75	4.52	0.48	3.63	2.04
$R_{u,IPCC4.5}$	2.24	1.73	4.51	0.48	3.63	2.04
$R_{u,IPCC8.5}$	2.24	1.7	4.52	0.48	3.63	2.04
$H_{u,c}$	0.0025	0.0025	0.0025	0.0025	0.0025	0.0025
$E_{s,u,c}$	0.235	0.233	0.262	0.239	0.399	0.241
$E_{m,u,c}$	0.000024	0.000024	0.000024	0.000024	0.000024	0.000024
$Y_{t,u,current}$	4.725	4.725	4.725	4.725	4.725	4.725
$Y_{t,u,IPCC2.6}$	4.491	4.491	4.491	4.491	4.491	4.491
$Y_{t,u,IPCC4.5}$	4.507	4.507	4.507	4.507	4.507	4.507
$Y_{t,u,IPCC8.5}$	4.605	4.605	4.605	4.605	4.605	4.605
$Y_{r,u,current}$	0.51	0.51	0.51	0.51	0.51	0.51
$Y_{r,u,IPCC2.6}$	0.48	0.48	0.48	0.48	0.48	0.48
$Y_{r,u,IPCC4.5}$	0.49	0.49	0.49	0.49	0.49	0.49
$Y_{r,u,IPCC8.5}$	0.5	0.5	0.5	0.5	0.5	0.5
$Y_{a,u,c}$	67.33	67.33	67.33	67.33	67.33	67.33

gardens was based on personal communication with the Taipei ULL. These values were assumed constant for all ULLs, similar to crop yield from traditional farming and aquaponic farming, for which the yield was derived from the Eindhoven ULL vision document (Brainport Smart District et al., 2019). The percentage change in food yield for traditional farming and rain gardens for the different climate scenarios was based on a yield prediction model for Sweden. A random forest model was used to predict yield based on county, precipitation, temperature, energy used in irrigation, water used in irrigation, and sulphur, nitrogen, phosphorus and calcium used as fertilisers. The input variables were forecasted using ARIMA, except for temperature and precipitation, which were derived from the SMHI climate scenario data for the different IPCC scenarios (SMHI, 2020).

2.4 User interface

The user interface is responsible for providing a layer for the user to interact with the model. The user can input the custom values of the aforementioned fields, $A_{f,u}, A_{g,u}, A_{a,u}, A_{r,u}, A_{f,u}$. These values are then sent to the model, which gives a response with the output values signifying the percentage of FWE balance that is fulfilled by the ULL itself. We show the steps of using the IDSS interface in the following.

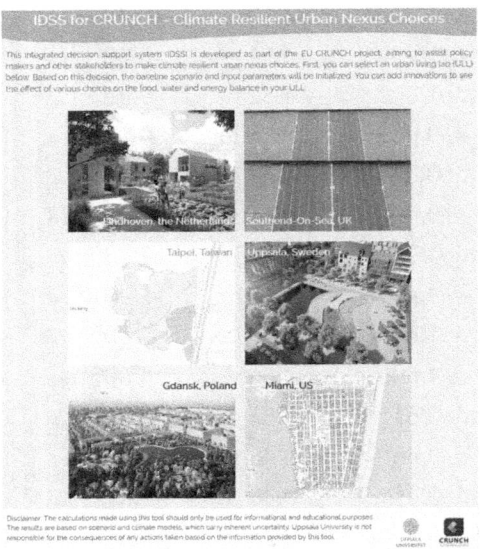

Figure 6.1: Home page of the IDSS displaying available ULLs for the analysis

Development of an Integrated Decision Support System (IDSS)

1. Initially, the user lands on the first page, which shows a short description of the interface itself and clickable ULL pictures as shown in Figure 6.1.
2. The user can click on one of the ULL pictures to enter the specific page of that ULL. The initial values and statistics for the ULL and the IPCC scenario are obtained from the REST API using the GET request in the form of a JSON response (Figure 6.4).
3. On that page, the user can see sliders on the left sidebar as shown in Figure 6.2, and on the right, there is some text briefing the user about the ULL followed by donut charts (Figure 6.3). The sliders are set to the default values for the fields. When the user changes the values, the donut charts will be updated simultaneously. The updated values for the donut charts are calculated by the Food Balance, Energy Balance and Water Balance formulas (section 2.2), which are coded in the REST API. The values for the Food, Water, and Energy Balance are passed to the web application in the form of a JSON response, as shown in Figure 6.4.

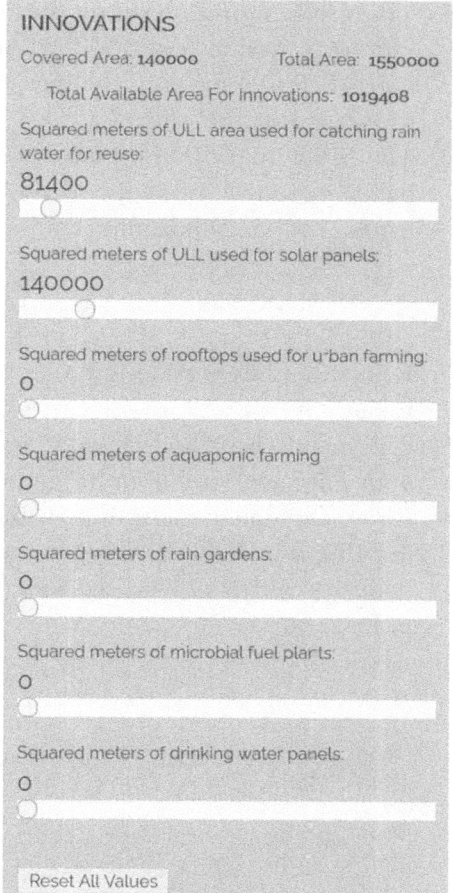

Figure 6.2: Sidebar with sliders to take the values for parameters from the user for calculating the FWE balance

4. The sliders collectively have the constraint that they all sum up to the 'Total Area' $A_{t,u}$, which can be seen written on the top-right of the slider sidebar. The 'Total Area' includes empty areas and building rooftops. Available area ($A_{o,u}$) can be calculated as:

$$A_{o,u} = A_{t,u} - (A_{f,u} + A_{g,u} + A_{a,u} + A_{r,u} + A_{w,u} + A_{s,u} + A_{m,u} + A_{h,u})$$

i.e. 'Total Area' minus 'Covered Area'.

5. The 'Covered Area' shows the area covered by using the slider for various innovations. It maximises at the 'Total Area'. After the covered area is maximised, the sliders will stop moving. The user must decrease the value of one slider in order to increase another slider.
6. The slider 'rooftops used for urban farming' represents rooftop area over the buildings, so they maximise to available building area $A_{B,u}$. It can be represented by the following equation:

$$A_{B,u} = A_{b,u} - A_{g,u}$$

7. Below the sliders, there is a reset button that will set the sliders to the default values.
8. The donut charts update every time a slider is altered or reset. The first donut with the water symbol in the centre represents the value of the water resource. Below the donut chart, there is the percentage indicating how self-sustainable the ULL is with the selected innovations. Similarly, energy sustainability is shown with the electricity icon and food sustainability with the wheat icon, as shown in Figure 6.3.

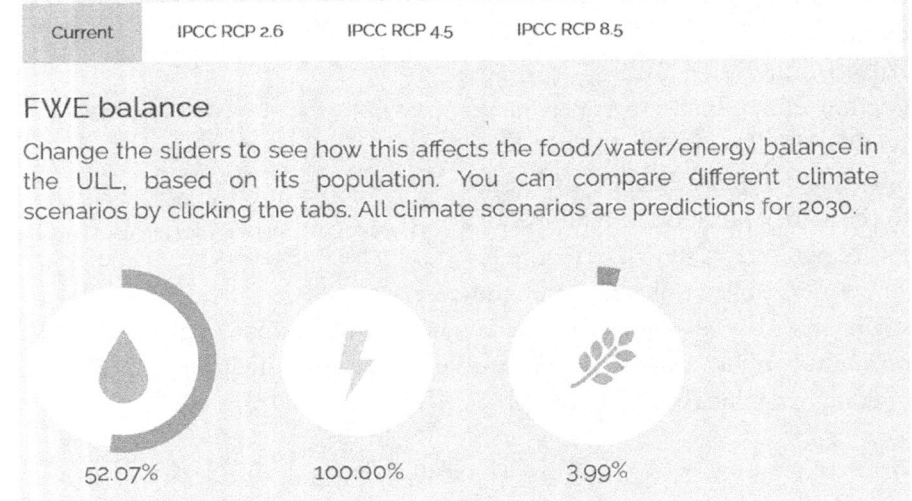

Figure 6.3: Donut charts displaying calculated FWE balance percentage values by considering the current climate scenarios

9. The user can select one of the tabs at the top of the donut chart to choose the desired IPCC scenario. Then, the donut charts will automatically adjust according to this.
10. There is a home icon at the very top of the page. Clicking on it will bring the user back to the home page, where a different ULL can be selected.

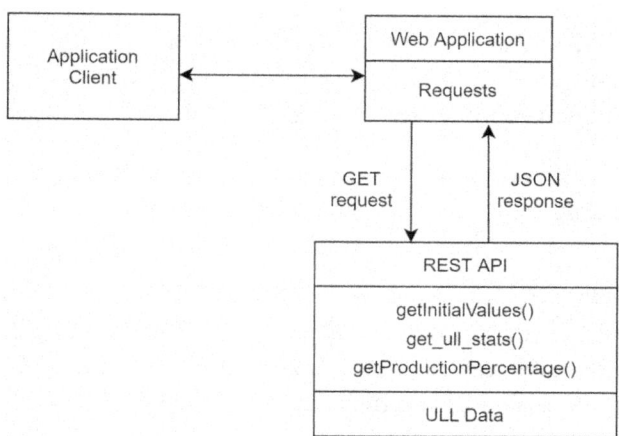

Figure 6.4: Architecture diagram for the IDSS web application
The IDSS can be reached at: http://crunch.research.it.uu.se/.

3. Discussion and conclusion

To the best of our knowledge, this IDSS is a first attempt to cover the FWE nexus in one decision support tool for urban areas. The aim of this tool is to combine knowledge and innovations from different ULLs around the world, so that they can be shared amongst different countries. The IDSS has been built in such a way that it is easy to implement changes. New insights into climate scenarios, local parameters or improved models may lead to changes in parameter values in the database. The IDSS is easy to transfer to new locations: new ULLs can be added in a simple way when enough data is available on all input parameters for the model.

This IDSS has focused on the environmental system around food, water, and energy. A topic for further research may be the inclusion of economic aspects of the innovations to improve decision- making processes. Of course, this tool also comes with its own limitations. Due to data being unavailable for some of the parameters, assumptions had to be made. The tool uses annual average values to calculate daily parameters; for example for temperature, precipitation, solar energy production, and crop yield. In reality, these are affected by seasonal variability. For the UK, where the climate scenario data showed no change in annual average precipitation, it is likely that winters will get wetter and summers drier. Besides this, climate scenarios naturally come with inherent uncertainty. Therefore, this tool is not meant to be used to calculate absolute changes, but rather to create insight into, for example, the impact of climate change on the FWE nexus, the amount of land needed to grow enough crops for the ULL population and new innovations to reduce this. In this way, we provide another step towards cities that are sustainable and resilient to climate change.

Acknowledgements

This work was supported by Formas – The Swedish Research Council for Sustainable Development in the framework of the Joint Programming Initiative Urban Europe, with support from the European Union's Horizon 2020 Research and Innovation Program under grant agreement No 730254.

References

Ali, H., M. Mocanu, & Florea, A. (2016). Development of a real-time web-ecological decision support system to calculate water quality and water pollution (WATERDSS) in the city of Baghdad. *University Politehnica of Bucharest Scientific Bulletin Series C-Electrical Engineering and Computer Science*, 78(2), 53–64.

Boshkoska, B. M., Liu, S. F., Zhao, G. Q. et al. (2019). A decision support system for evaluation of the knowledge sharing crossing boundaries in agri-food value chains. *Computers in Industry*, 110, 64–80. DOI: 10.1016/j.compind.2019.04.012.

Brainport Smart District, UNStudio, Felixx Landscape Architects & Planners et al. (2019). Brainport Smart District: Stedenbouwkundige visie.

Chen, Z. F., Wang, J. L., Sun, J. S. et al. (2012). Water-saving irrigation management and decision support system based on WEBGIS. In D. L. Li & Y. Y. Chen (Eds.), *Computer and computing technologies in agriculture V, Pt I* (pp. 301–312). Springer-Verlag: Berlin.

EIA. (2017, 26 July). Per capita residential electricity sales in the U.S. have fallen since 2010. U.S Energy Information Administration. https://www.eia.gov/todayinenergy/detail.php?id=32212 (accessed 19 November 2020).

European Commission. (2018). Energy consumption and energy efficiency trends in the EU-28 for the period 2000–2016. In S. Tsemekidi-Tzeiranaki, P. Bertoldi, N. Labanca et al. (Eds.), *JRC Science for Policy Report*. JRC: Luxemborg.

FAO Statistics Division. (2008). Food Consumption Nutrients. http://www.fao.org/fileadmin/templates/ess/documents/food_security_statistics/FoodConsumptionNutrients_en.xls#

Florida Climate Center. (2020). Intergovernmental Panel on Climate Change Statement: What does the new IPCC report mean to Florida?

Global Solar Atlas. (2020). https://globalsolaratlas.info/map?c=31.952162,20.566406,2

Habibie, M. I., Noguchi, R., Shusuke, M., & Ahamed, T. (2019). Land suitability analysis for maize production in Indonesia using satellite remote sensing and GIS-based multicriteria decision support system. *Geojournal, 86*, 777–307. DOI: 10.1007/s10708-019-10091-5

Heinermann, J., & Kramer, O. (2016). Machine learning ensembles for wind power prediction. *Renewable Energy, 89*, 671–679. DOI: 10.1016/j.renene.2015.11.073

Huang, W-H. (2015). The determinants of household electricity consumption in Taiwan: Evidence from quantile regression. *Energy, 87*, 120–133.

Hung, M-F., Chie, B-T., & Huang, T-H. (2017). Residential water demand and water waste in Taiwan. *Environmental Economics and Policy Studies, 19*(2), 249–268.

Jayarathna, L., Rajapaksa, D., & Managi, S. et al. (2017). A GIS based spatial decision support system for analysing residential water demand: A case study in Australia. *Sustainable Cities and Society, 32*, 67–77. DOI: 10.1016/j.scs.2017.03.012

Khan, R., Ali, I., Zakarya, M. et al. (2018). Technology-assisted decision support system for efficient water utilization: A real-time testbed for irrigation using wireless sensor networks. *IEEE Access, 6*, 25686–25697. DOI: 10.1109/access.2018.2836185

KNMI. (2020). KNMI'14-klimaatscenario's: Kerncijfers. http://www.klimaatscenarios.nl/kerncijfers/

Li, C., Dutta, R., Kloppers, C. et al. (2013). Mobile application based sustainable irrigation water usage decision support system: An intelligent sensor CLOUD approach. *2013 IEEE Sensors*, 1565–1568. DOI: 10.1109/ICSENS.2013.6688523

Li, Y., Pizer, W. A, & Wu, L. (2019). Climate change and residential electricity consumption in the Yangtze River Delta, China. *Proceedings of the National Academy of Sciences*, *116*(2), 472–477.

Liakos, K. G., Busato, P., Moshou, D. et al. (2018). Machine learning in agriculture: A review. *Sensors*, *18*(8), 2674. DOI: 10.3390/s18082674

Lin, Y. C., Lin, C. C., Lee, M. et al. (2019). Comprehensive assessment of regional food-energy-water nexus with GIS-based tool. *Resources Conservation and Recycling* 151. DOI: 10.1016/j.resconrec.2019.104457.

Maina, M. M., Amin, M. S. M, & Yazid, M. A. (2014). Web geographic information system decision support system for irrigation water management: A review. *Acta Agriculturae Scandinavica Section B-Soil and Plant Science*, *64*(4), 283–293. DOI: 10.1080/09064710.2014.896935

March, S. T., & Hevner, A. R. (2007). Integrated decision support systems: A data warehousing perspective. *Decision Support Systems*, *43*(3), 1031–1043. DOI: 10.1016/j.dss.2005.05.029.

Murphy, J. M., Sexton, D. M. H., Jenkins, G. J. et al. (2009). *UK Climate Projections Science Report: Climate change projections*. Exeter: Met Office Hadley Centre.

SCB. (2015). Hushållens vattenanvändning per typ av vattenförsörjning, efter region. Vart femte år 1995–2015. http://www.statistikdatabasen.scb.se/pxweb/sv/ssd/START__MI__MI0902__MI0902E/VattenAnvHus/

SCB. (2018). Slutanvändning (MWh), efter län och kommun, förbrukarkategori samt bränsletyp. År 2009–2018. https://www.statistikdatabasen.scb.se/pxweb/sv/ssd/START__EN__EN0203/SlutAnvSektor/

Scott Morton, M. S. 1971. *Management decision systems: Computer based support for decision making*. Boston: Harvard University.

Sharma, N., Sharma, P., Irwin, D., & Shenoy, P. (2011). Predicting solar generation from weather forecasts using machine learning. 2011 IEEE International Conference on Smart Grid Communications (SmartGridComm), 17–20 Oct. 2011.

SMHI. (2009). Normal uppskattad årsnederbörd, medelvärde 1961–1990. https://www.smhi.se/data/meteorologi/nederbord/normal-uppskattad-arsnederbord-medelvarde-1961-1990-1.6934

SMHI. (2020). Ladda ner scenariodata. https://www.smhi.se/klimat/framtidens-klimat/ladda-ner-scenariodata/

Sprague Jr, R. H. (1980). A framework for the development of decision support systems. *MIS Quarterly*, *4*(4), 1–26.

Statista. (2018). Average domestic electricity consumption per household in the United Kingdom (UK) in 2018 (in KWh), by region. https://www.statista.com/statistics/517845/average-electricity-consumption-uk/

Stępniewska, M. (2015). Assessing the water footprint of national consumption for Poland. *Geographia Polonica*, *88*(3), 503–514.

Sun, Q., Miao, C., & Duan, Q. (2015). Projected changes in temperature and precipitation in ten river basins over China in 21st century. *International Journal of Climatology*, *35*(6), 1125–1141.

Suntaranont, B., Aramkul, S., Kaewmoracharoen, M., & Champrasert, P. (2020). Water Irrigation Decision Support System for Practical Weir Adjustment Using Artificial Intelligence and Machine Learning Techniques. *Sustainability*, *12*(5). DOI: 10.3390/su12051763.

Szemes, P. T., Baranyai, Z. Hamar, J. et al. (2011). "Energymon": Development of wireless sensor network based decision support system to monitor building energy performance. *2011 IEEE/ASME International Conference on Advanced Intelligent Mechatronics*, 31–36. New York: IEEE.

Szpakowski, W., & Szydłowski, M. (2018). Probable Rainfall in Gdańsk in View of Climate Change. *Acta Scientiarum Polonorum Formatio Circumiectus*, *3*(3), 175–183.

Tian, H. Q., Lu, C. Q., Pan, S. F. et al. (2018). Optimizing resource use efficiencies in the food-energy-water nexus for sustainable agriculture: From conceptual model to decision support system. *Current Opinion in Environmental Sustainability*, *33*, 104–113. DOI: 10.1016/j.cosust.2018.04.003

Van der Perk, M., Burema, J. R., Burrough, P. A. et al. (2001). A GIS-based environmental decision support system to assess the transfer of long-lived radiocaesium through food chains in areas contaminated by the Chernobyl accident. *International Journal of Geographical Information Science*, *15*(1), 43–64. DOI: 10.1080/13658810010005552

Voivontas, D., Assimacopoulos, D., Mourelatos, A., & Corominas, J. (1998). Evaluation of renewable energy potential using a GIS decision support system. *Renewable Energy*, *13*(3), 333–344. DOI: 10.1016/s0960–1481(98)00006–8

Voyant, C., Notton, G., Kalogirou, S. et al. (2017). Machine learning methods for solar radiation forecasting: A review. *Renewable Energy*, 105, 569–582. DOI: 10.1016/j.renene.2016.12.095.

WWT. (2019). Water Consumption: PR19 Challenge Report #5. James Brockett (Ed.).

Yuan, K-Y., Lin, Y-C., Chiueh, P-T., & Lo, S-L. (2018). Spatial optimization of the food, energy, and water nexus: A life cycle assessment-based approach. *Energy Policy, 119*, 502–514. DOI: 10.1016/j.enpol.2018.05.009

Zambelli, P., Lora, C., Spinelli, R. et al. (2012). A GIS decision support system for regional forest management to assess biomass availability for renewable energy production. *Environmental Modelling & Software, 38*, 203–213. DOI: 10.1016/j.envsoft.2012.05.016

Zero Mass Water. (2020). Zero Mass Water. https://www.zeromasswater.com/.

Chapter 7

Genetic Food-Water-Energy nexus design research for Miami's Greater Islands

Climate Resilient Urban Nexus CHoices (CRUNCH) – scripting and coding AI-MLs

Thomas Spiegelhalter, Levente Juhász, and Srikanth Namuduri

1: The development of the Integrated Decision Support System (IDSS)

AI data-driven Geospatial-BIM workflows

Part 1 includes the primary objective of CRUNCH for Miami of the realisation of an Integrated Decision Support System (IDSS) app. It is an nd-digital geo-map-based platform that allows decision makers and citizens with different knowledge levels to provide consistent and coordinated support for multiple users on varied decisions. It includes carbon-neutral city analysis, scenario planning and optimisations (Andia & Spiegelhalter, 2014) (Figure 7.1).

This first test workflow was developed to calculate the Food-Water-Energy nexus and CO_2 emissions at a municipal level using Rapid Energy Modelling (R.E.M.) techniques to create a baseline calculation from which to consider building optimisations, retrofitting, and renewable energy production in design studio experiments to aid in reaching carbon-neutral or net positive energy outcomes on a baseline of iterated existing and newly designed building and city scenarios from 2018 to 2100.

DOI: 10.4324/9781003112495-16

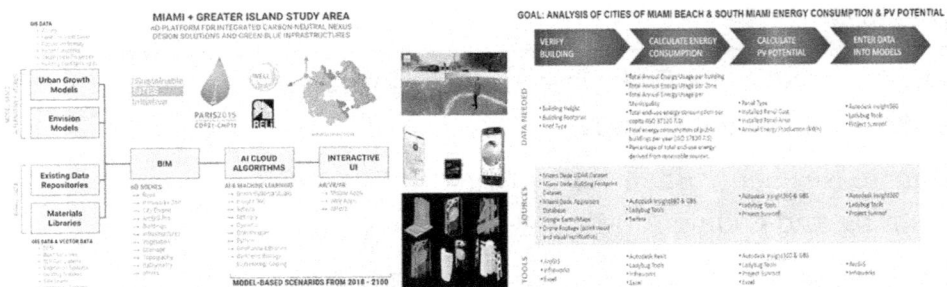

Figure 7.1: Right and left image: Workflow diagram of the general CRUNCH work deliverables (WP) with open source GIS into Autodesk Infraworks, Civil, ESRI ArcGIS Pro, Revit-BIM, Green Building Studio, Insight360, Dynamo, Grasshopper, Python, GeoPanda, etc. for analysing, coding, designing, scripting, and optimisations of cities and buildings. This includes design studio scenarios from 2018 to 2020.

Source: FIU Thomas Spiegelhalter and Darren Ockert.

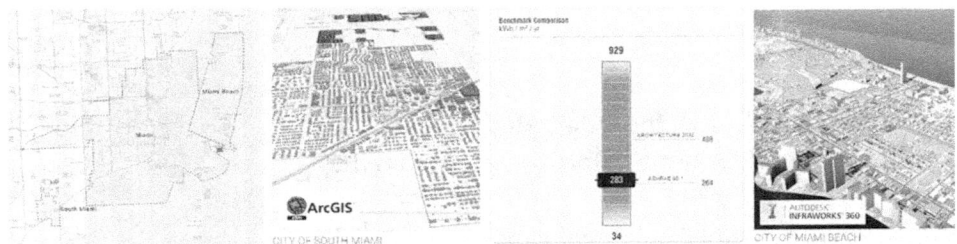

Figure 7.2: Right and left image: Workflow diagram of the open source GIS into Autodesk Infraworks, Civil, ESRI ArcGIS Pro, Revit-BIM, Green Building Studio, Insight360, Dynamo, Grasshopper, Python, GeoPanda, etc. workflows for analysing, coding, designing, and optimisations of cities and buildings. This includes design studio scenarios from 2018 to 2020.

Source: FIU Thomas Spiegelhalter and Darren Ockert.

The R.E.M. method does not require lengthy, in-depth onsite analysis of individual buildings within a municipality; rather it uses verified international industry standards, meaning cloud-based retrieved energy consumption for building typologies, zonings, schedules, materials and systems, and energy supply mix of the municipalities (Figure 7.2).

The second test workflow includes understanding the CRUNCH Food–Water–Energy (FWE) nexus; various parameters such as energy-water-food consumption, population, sea level rise, storm surge, CO_2, etc., were estimated. Also, to assess the opportunities to transition to self-sufficient and carbon-neutral cities, the solar electric and thermal potential was estimated and cross-examined with the first baseline

Genetic Food-Water-Energy nexus design research

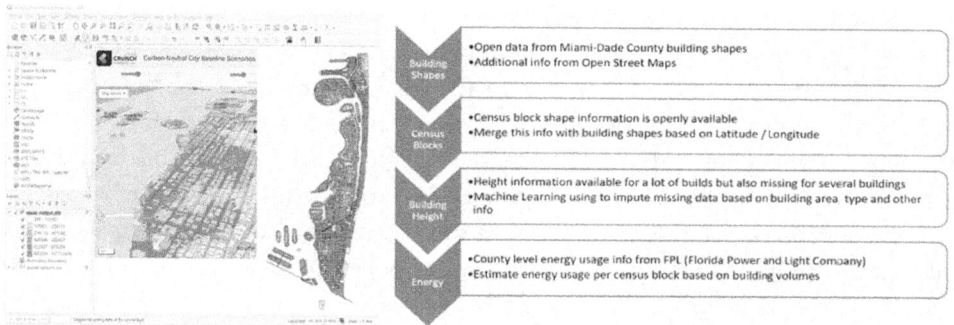

Figure 7.3: Left images: Visualising the energy consumption of South Miami and Miami Eeach on QGIS. Right Image: Excerpt of the Google Solar Building Potential Analysis. Right image: Workflow diagram of the second CRUNCH work deliverable (WP) with open-source Python and QGIS for analysing, geo-coding of cities and building blocks.

Source: Thomas Spiegelhalter, Darren Ockert, Srikanth Namuduri, Damian Ferrer, Perry Gabriel.

workflow. The focus was on two cities, namely South Miami and Miami Beach. The estimates and data processing for the online IDSS were made at the census block level (Figure 7.3).

With the goal of transparency, only open data and free tools were used for the analysis and estimation. The computation was done using Python. QGIS is an open source tool for working with geographical data that also supports Python. Figure 7.3 is a screenshot of visualising the energy consumption of South Miami and Miami Beach on QGIS. Pandas and GeoPandas libraries in Python were used extensively. Pandas is a library for working with tabular data, and GeoPandas is for working with geographical data. Census block shapefiles and population are openly available. Also, Miami Dade County has made 2D building shape information openly available. The building information shared by the county was imported into a platform called OpenStreetMap, which is a volunteer project, similar to Wikipedia but with spatial data and maps. It means that many buildings of the original dataset were updated by volunteers, so it was assumed that it is more detailed and accurate than the county's building data. For example, some demolished buildings have been deleted and newly built ones added. Additionally, in some cases, it also codes the building type. The census block data and building shapes consist of polygonal shapes represented by the latitude and longitude of each vertex. Both these shapefiles were available for different sources and were combined into a single dataset using a 'spatial join' for further analysis. This allowed us to make estimates at a census block level by looking at the building within its boundary.

From the polygonal shapes of each building, the base area can be calculated using existing functions in GeoPandas. The height information was available for about 80% of the buildings and was missing for the rest of them. Since the volume information is required for estimating energy, the missing data needed to be imputed. Machine Learning was applied to estimate the height using the rest of the available parameters as predictors. The python library Sklearn was used for this purpose. For the beta version of the app, a simplifying assumption was made that the energy consumption is proportional to the volume of the building. Also, the city level energy usage was obtained from FPL (Florida Power and Lighting Company). Using this information, the energy usage for each census block was estimated. Water usage was also estimated in a similar fashion, starting with the total usage at the city level. Project Sunroof is an initiative/tool from Google that offers estimates of solar PV potential. Google Earth provides high-resolution imagery of rooftops. Project Sunroof initially used these images to calculate the solar potential of each roof. After the initial estimation phase, Artificial Intelligence was used to predict the solar system's potential. To be specific, the initial estimates were used to train machine learning models that can predict the solar potential based on the information from Maps and Google Earth. This tool can either provide estimates for each building or for a census tract. The latter was leveraged to obtain solar systems potential for South Miami and Miami Beach at a census tract level and was used to make estimates at a census block level.

The weather data is automatically retrieved from National Renewable Energy Laboratory (NREL); utility electricity rates information from Clean Power Research; solar pricing data from NREL's Open PV Project; solar incentives data from relevant Clean Power Research, Federal, State and local authorities, as well as relevant utility websites; Solar Renewable Energy Credit (SREC) data from Bloomberg New Energy Finance, SRECTrade, and relevant state authorities; and aggregated and anonymised solar cost data from Aurora Solar software.

1.a. IDSS app data and methods

The rate of sea level rise (SLR) is not constant across the globe, and it shows great local variations. As a result, adapting to changing water levels and planning has a strong local component, and each coastal area must consider their unique characteristics. For example, Wdowinski et al. (2016) show that the rate of SLR in Southeast Florida is more accelerated than the global average (9 +- 4mm/year vs 3.2 +- 0.4mm/year), which will likely be manifested in larger social and economic impacts compared to some other parts of the world. In addition to the challenges posed by the rising sea levels, anthropogenic climate change also poses a risk to coastal communities by higher storm surges (Bevacqua et al., 2019) and the co-occurrence of sea level rise, storm surge and flooding caused by heavy precipitation (Hall et al., 2019). For this reason, it is crucial that we understand the local impacts of climate change. The following sections detail a web-based application that was developed to support decision-making in the City of South Miami and Miami Beach.

1.b. Modelling inundation levels

A necessary step in modelling inundation levels is to choose a reference surface to which water height or depth is compared to. Tidal datums are locally standardised elevations set to certain phases of the tide for a certain area with the same oceanographic characteristics. Water levels were measured to the Mean Higher High Water (MHHW) surface, which is the average of the higher high water level. A series of SLR inundation scenarios between 1 ft and 8 ft with 1 ft increments was created using a so-called bathtub model. The digital elevation model (DEM) used in the computations was derived from a 2015 LIDAR dataset of Miami-Dade County given in the NAVD88 vertical datum. This surface is 0.1m below the MHHW in South Florida and was adjusted in the calculations. The methodology is described by Zhang et al. (2011). In addition, relevant structures, such as levees and weirs, were also considered to create a hydrologically accurate model. The Sea, Lake and Overland Surges from Hurricanes (SLOSH) model developed by the National Weather Service (NWS) was used to derive storm surge inundations caused by hurricanes category 1 through 5. Due to the uncertainty of modelling, tropical storms are not included in the application. In SLOSH, the Maximum Envelope of High Water (MEOW) shows the maximum likely extent of flooding in a basin for a given storm category with a certain trajectory and forward speed. Our calculations use the MOM (Maximum of MEOWs) output of SLOSH for the Miami basin, which considers multiple combinations of forwarding speed and trajectory for a basin to create a worst-case snapshot for a particular storm category. At a later step, all possible combinations of SLR and storm surge scenarios were created by adding the corresponding inundation layers together (e.g. 2 ft of SLR and storm surge caused by a category 4 hurricane). It is important to point out that this approach likely underestimates the compound effect of SLR and storm surge – that is, storm surges may cause more damage when occurring in addition to already elevated sea levels. However, this compound effect is complex to model and is still an open research question (Hoshino et al., 2016); therefore, our approach uses a simplistic scenario of adding these inundations together.

1.c. Estimating social and economic impacts of SLR and storm surges

Using a GIS based approach, the social and economic impacts of SLR and storm surge inundation scenarios were estimated in the City of South Miami and Miami Beach using US Census blocks as the spatial unit. Census blocks were found to be sufficiently small in size to capture fine urban structures within these cities. Variables were organised into the following categories: demography, property, facilities, land use, and roads. Each category consists of multiple attributes, such as racial breakdown, total assessed property value, total area per land use category, etc. First, inundation scenarios were converted to a binary GIS layer (i.e. area is underwater or not), then these were spatially overlaid with the variable in question. As the last step, the affected supply (e.g. population) within a block was estimated in blocks overlapping the inundation extent. This workflow was automated with Python scripts. At the end of this step, the total and affected values for an attribute (e.g. area of residential land use and area of residential land use underwater for a scenario) were available for each block within the study area for each combination scenario.

1.d. IDSS CRUNCH City of Miami Beach and South Miami web application

Effectively communicating complex environmental issues to a diverse audience is a challenge. This is especially true for presenting potential impacts of future scenarios. Therefore, our goal was to develop a lightweight and user-friendly web application that dynamically and interactively visualises the potential social and economic impacts of coastal inundations and parameters related to the Food-Water-Energy nexus for any given area within the City of South Miami and Miami Beach. Free and open source software has already been used to build interactive web-based GIS applications to model excess waters (Juhász et al., 2016). Our application is built with purely open source software, which allows cost-effective and rapid development. The application implements a flexible design that allows the addition and removal of additional attributes in later phases of the development.

Genetic Food-Water-Energy nexus design research

1.e. IDSS serving data

Two types of data are being visualised in the application: spatial and non-spatial. Non-spatial data consists of the pre-calculated, socio-demographic variables and Food-Water-Energy nexus parameters including infrastructures, sea level rise, storm surge and pandemics for each block within the study cities.

1.f. IDSS API and database

To present these statistics in a web environment, a custom application programming interface (API) was developed for the sole purpose of serving these data over the web. This API connects to a MySQL database that was optimised with multi-column indexes for performance. The API accepts HTTP GET requests through six endpoints that correspond to five socio-economic categories and Food-Water-Energy nexus parameters. The web application makes calls to this API depending on the census block selection. That is, upon request, for any given combination of blocks within the boundaries of study cities, the API returns estimations for energy consumption, water consumption, etc. for those specified areas. For the socio-economic variables, two additional parameters corresponding to SLR and storm values can also be supplied in order to get results for different combinations of SLR and storm scenarios.

1.g. IDSS vector tiles

Serving geographic data can be slow with traditional GIS methods due to the size and complexity of datasets. For this reason, this application utilises a modern concept and serves geospatial data in the form of vector tiles. The tile system divides the Earth into spatially nested tiles of a gradually smaller size and more details and only transfers a subset of the original dataset. For a description, see, e.g., Juhász and Hochmair (2016). Vector tiles transfer geospatial data with vector geometries, which can be exploited for fast and dynamic in-browser visualisation. The application uses two types of tiles: inundation tiles generated from binary inundation layers and background map tiles based on OpenStreetMap (OSM) data. Inundation tiles are built with polygon geometries through the processing framework. Each polygon contains two values, which are the minimum SLR and the storm scenario in which they become inundated. The visual appearance of features stored as vector styles can be modified on the fly in a web map. As a result, inundation scenarios can be quickly changed by filtering these attributes. The same flexibility applies to the background map.

1.h. IDSS user interface

The user interface was written in JavaScript and is running as in a Node.js container. The design of the user interface was aimed at providing an easy-to-use interface for users to instantly see the social and economic impact of SLR and storm surge inundation and properties related to the Food-Water-Energy nexus within the study cities. The interface is divided into a map viewer and a statistics report area. The map viewer provides spatial interactivity, such as selecting custom areas within cities, interactive zooming, etc. The other main component of the user interface is the statistics reporting tool, which is achieved by dynamically created and updated charts.

1.i. IDSS application functionality

The main functionality of the application is to present and visualise details for a user-selected area within the study cities. Figure 7.4 highlights such a selection on the map interface, while areas not selected are greyed out. Users can change the selection interactively. Upon choosing an area, the statistics on the right pane are dynamically updated. The beta version of the application shown in Figure 7.4

Figure 7.4: The user interface of the application shows an interactive selection (highlighted on the map) and related statistics on the left, and on the right estimates for urban food farming.
Source: Prof. Thomas Spiegelhalter, Dr Juhász Levente.

currently displays estimated floor area, energy consumption, CO2 and PV potential for the selected area. Users also have the option to select entire cities at once.

Another main function of the application is the dynamic visualisation of SLR and storm surge inundations. This is done by adjusting the sliders on top of the map panel. Figure 7.5 shows a scenario of 3 ft of SLR in Miami Beach (Wdowinski et al., 2016). Socio-economic variables corresponding to this level of inundation inside the user-selected area are reflected in charts on the right side (i.e. Demography, Property, Facility, Land Use, and Road). Information corresponding to these categories reflects the current settings (SLR and storm surge) inside the selected area, and all statistics groups present information for both totals and affected counts or values (i.e. population, property value) (Wdowinski et al., 2016). Changes in inundation level settings and area selection are instantly reflected in both the map and statistics panes (Zhang et al., 2011). This dynamic relationship empowers users to interactively explore and study the potential impact of climate change and also get information about the Food-Water-Energy nexus. On the application level, each change triggers five API calls to load statistics for each topic category. To improve performance, data caching is also implemented so that previously loaded scenarios can be displayed without loading data through the API again. Several other features have also been implemented to aid the interpretation of results. For example, the size of the selected area is dynamically calculated and reported in the interface. Additional GIS layers, such as land use (Figure 7.5) can also be turned on to be rendered on the map. Furthermore, these polygons are dynamically linked with the corresponding statistics. Upon highlighting a land-use category on the right side, the corresponding category will also be emphasised on the map, such as recreational areas rendered with dark brown colour on both the

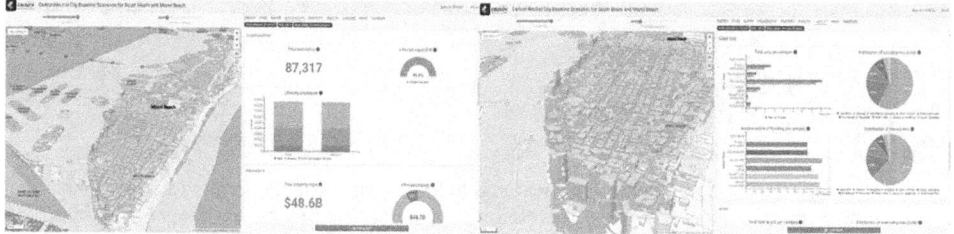

Figure 7.5: Left image: The user interface of the application dynamically visualising 3ft of SLR and reporting potential impacted resident demographics. The right image: User interface in 3D mode showing a perspective view of Miami Beach.
Source: Prof. Thomas Spiegelhalter, Dr Juhász Levente.

map and the charts. The WebGL technology utilised in this application also supports 3D rendering, and the view can be tilted and rotated freely. Currently, buildings are rendered with their correct heights as shown in Figure 7.5. An export functionality was also implemented that dynamically generates and downloads a PDF document for the current settings. This report also features additional data tables and further explanations that help with the interpretation of results, in addition to the map and charts shown in the application.

2: Design studio experiments with carbon-positive building, green-blue infrastructure and city typologies including synthetic biology imaginations, ranging from 2018 to 2020

The CRUNCH research studios have been working on a series of resilient design projects for the City of Miami Beach and South Miami since Fall 2018. Only a small fraction of the entire experimental results can be discussed in this chapter. One specific scenario presents a stage of the flooded City of Miami Beach for the year 2100. All new buildings are 25–30 feet above the current sea level on stilts, totally off-the-grid and self-sufficient, mixed-use skyscrapers and floating structures. They all have been modelled with AI-assisted Revit-BIM-GBS-Insight360-COVE,

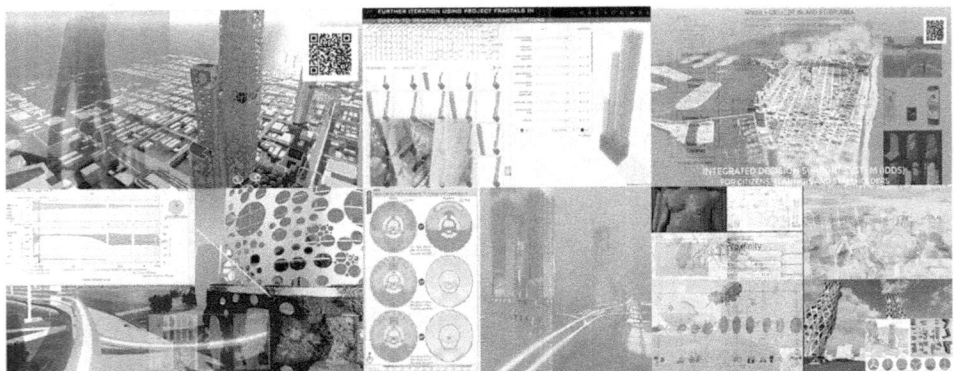

Figure 7.6: Image captions above show the featured hypothetical scenarios for the Miami Beach Dynamo-BIM script and node workflow for a test series of carbon-neutral facade/shape/orientation and blue-green infrastructure contexts. Image captions below show scenarios with WUFI temperature, vapour migration, and humidity simulations, and CFD new hurricane category forces on the facade and overall structures of carbon-neutral facade/shape/orientation and blue-green infrastructure benchmarks that match the Paris Agreement treaty goals.
Source: Master's thesis studio Prof. Thomas Spiegelhalter, Sadiel Ojeda.

Genetic Food-Water-Energy nexus design research

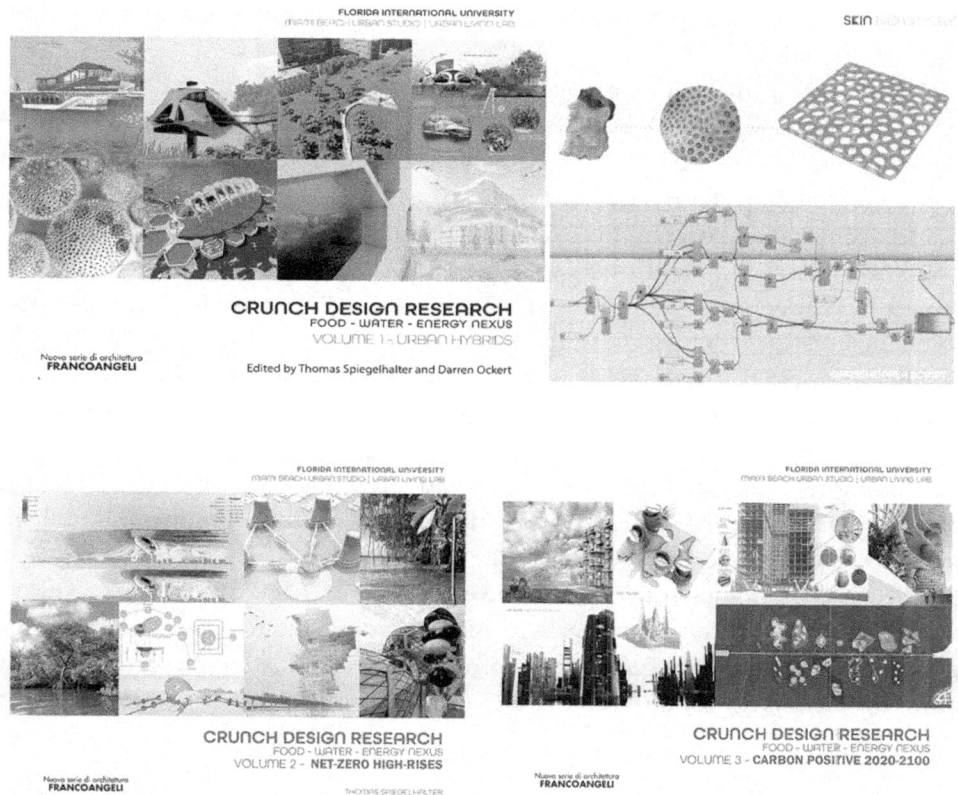

Figure. 7.7: Above image: excerpts of the D8 Studio Design Studio Publication for the Food-Water-Energy nexus Volume 1 – Urban Hybrids in Miami Beach. Below image: Publication cover for Volume 2 and Volume 3, featuring CRUNCH design research results from Spring 2019 to Summer 2020.
Source: Prof. Thomas Spiegelhalter and FrancoAngeli, Milan, http://crunch.fiu.edu/about/research/.

Robotic-Structure, Dynamo-Python, Infraworks360, Computational Fluid Dynamics (CFD), and generative Fusion360 workflows due to their geometric complexity for carbon-neutral operation, hurricane, and tornado-induced resilience impact forces. All the scenarios were modelled during a mixed FIU master research design studio, in order to reflect on a type of parametric resilient geometry with real-world engineering applications, technologies, and features. This includes multi-functional systems and modules, renewable energies from solar/wind/water/kinetic building skins, autonomous transportation, artificial intelligence, deep neural networks, the Internet of Things, robotics, and urban outdoor and indoor farming with self-healing facade tectonics for climate emergencies in 2100 (Figure 7.6 and 7.7).

All of these former and current CRUNCH design research projects are in the process of publication by FrancoAngeli in Milan (http://crunch.fiu.edu/about/research/) and are also included in the new beta IDSS app organised by topics and indicators, based on the FWE nexus (Figure 7.8).

One of the most successful master's thesis studio projects of CRUNCH Miami is the American Institute of Architects (AIA) MIAMI 2020 Design Award-winning project by master's thesis student Amalia Tomey of the Studio Prof Thomas Spiegelhalter in June 2020. This case study is sited in Miami downtown for a high-rise building scenario that addresses dynamic changes in sea level rise, storm surge, adaptive building structures for renewable energy, water and food using the Urban Living Lab (ULL) approach; identifying data and mapping a baseline for the city's needs, developing tools and a framework, testing and analysing data-driven models using different self-sufficiency strategies, and carbon-neutral, carbon-positive and resilient scenarios from now to 2100 (Figure 7.9).

The research design studios extended the topic of Food-Water-Energy nexus to the Miami Bay. It envisions artificial islands, carbon-positive and resilient high-rise building clusters, living shorelines, programmable soils, and infrastructures that grow by themselves using synthetic biology. We are working with processes that

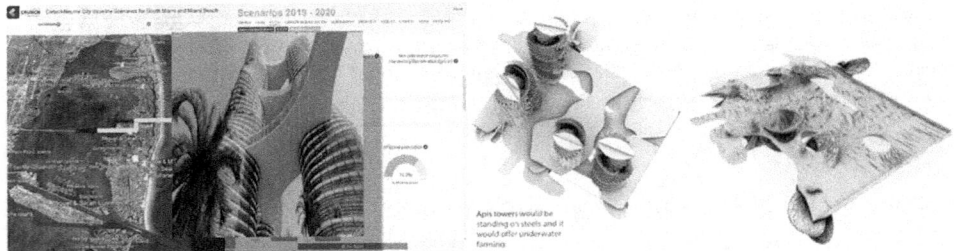

Figure 7.8: Right and left image: Excerpt of the D9 Spring 2020 Design Studio for the Food-Water-Energy nexus for the IDSS app inclusion of scenarios from 2020 to 2100 with projects by Alexander Bahensky and Patrik Osvaldo (left image) and Laura Gomez and Sophia Neves (right image) of Studio Spiegelhalter in the Miami Bay area and new Publication of Volume 2 – Miami Bay Hybrids, publisher FrancoAngeli Milan, 2020.
Source: Prof. Thomas Spiegelhalter and Prof. Alfredo Andia, D9 Design Studios, Spring 2020.

Genetic Food-Water-Energy nexus design research

Figure 7.9: American Institute of Architects (AIA) MIAMI 2020 Design Award project by master's thesis student Amalia Tomey of the CRUNCH Design Studio Prof. Thomas Spiegelhalter in June 2020. Source: Thomas Spiegelhalter and Amalia Tomey.

could produce quick methods and low-energy practices of biomineralisation such as cyanobacteria, synthetic protein, and collagen to produce artificial materials, and other things (Figure 7.10 and 7.11).

2.a. Synthetic biology and a renewable energy abundant society

Parallel to the project described above, we are working with more hypothetical scenarios that look at trends that are outside the main discourse in carbon-neutral design. When we architects look at ways to mitigate climate change, we tend to go back to just slightly improve the methods and construction techniques with which we created the climate emergency. So what is out there that can radically change our imagination? In particular, we have begun to follow the trends in the emerging field of Synthetic Biology (SynBio). In the past decade, SynBio has surfaced as the fastest growing technology in human history. SynBio involves emerging techniques that allow us to design, edit, and engineer all kinds of living organisms. Today we can manufacture, molecule by molecule, lab-grown meat, bio-grown leather, milk, wood, plants that do not need fertiliser, fuels, fragrances, fabrics, novel pharmaceuticals, and even age-reversal techniques, which has already been proven in mice in laboratories at the Salk Institute in California Synthetic Biology that were officially

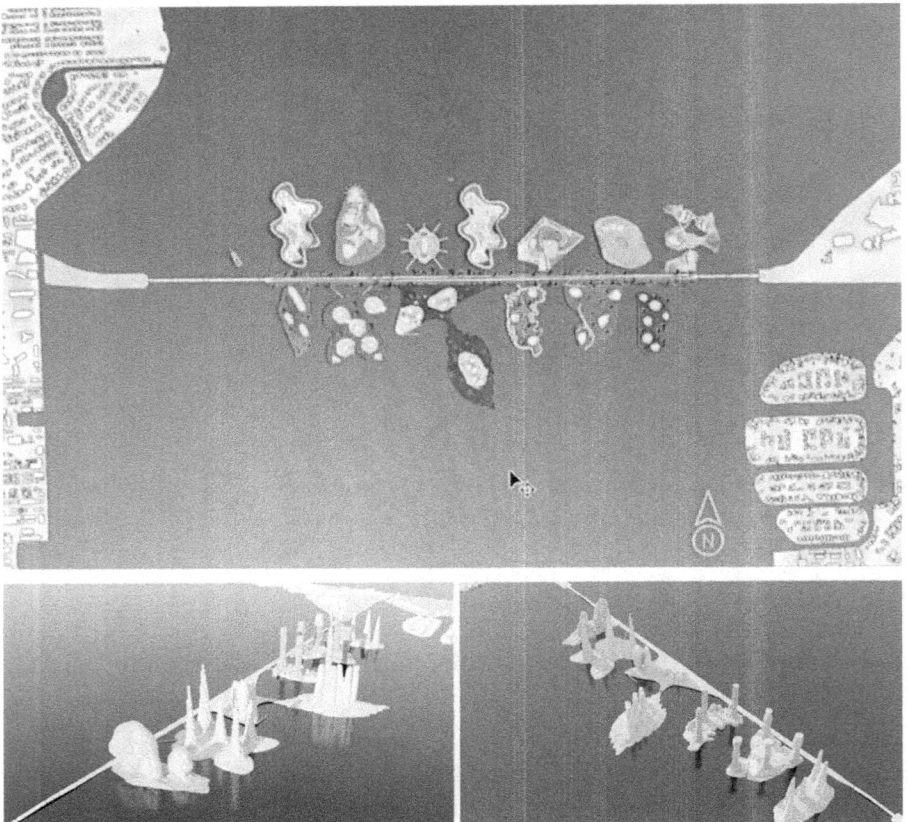

Figure 7.10: Site plan and axonometric images above and below: The images show the current joint FIU Spring 2020 experimental, carbon-neutral high-rise design studio projects of Thomas Spiegelhalter and Alfredo Andia, envisioning a series of islands along the I95 freeway of Biscayne Bay between Miami and Miami Beach.
Images by Alexander Bahensky. Source: Alexander Bahensky, Studio Spiegelhalter-Andia.

Genetic Food-Water-Energy nexus design research

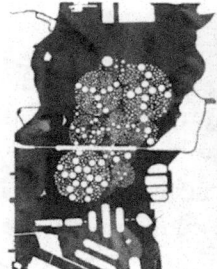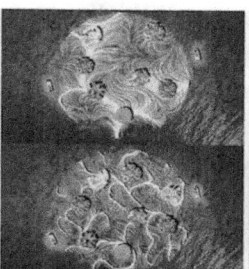

Figure 7.11: Left image: Site plan, 2018. Right image: A project by Daniela Romero & Solange Salinas (Alfredo Andia Design 8 Studio, Fall 2019). Right image shows desalination, absorption, and a retention tower that follows the process of growth via aggregation through a semper's knot weight distribution; a project by Renzo Lopez (Alfredo Andia D8 Studio)

born in 2006 (Salk, 2005). Synthetic technology is growing by a factor of 10 times per year, compared to computer technology, which is rising at a factor of 1.5 times per year (Church & Regis, 2012). But what are the direct surprises SynBio is bringing to us?

One speculative studio project of Prof. Andia envisioned a series of islands that grow in Biscayne Bay by a process of reengineering cyanobacteria. A biological circuitry would allow cyanobacteria to capture carbon dioxide in the water via photosynthesis and transform it into finely layered rock material. The process is similar to the living stromatolites that were abundant in the Precambrian age. Cyanobacteria created the Earth's atmosphere.

2.b. BioNet and the PB (Personal Biosynthesiser)

In the next decade, we will begin to see BioNet. Like the internet, it will allow us to download the DNA code anywhere. Our Personal Bio Synthesiser will let us redesign the DNA and create new organisms and then send them through the BioNet to grow everywhere where there is distributed DNA manufacturing. Today we see the quick rise of formate fermentation, not only in the labs but as a disruptive technology in many industries. In the material innovation front, we are beginning to see Bio-concrete, Bio-Soils, mushroom-based insulation and lab-grown wood (Figure 7.12).

2.c. Towards an abundance of bio-energy civilisation

But perhaps one of the most surprising things about the industrialisation of SynBio is the emergence of fermentation processes which will allow us to quickly generate high quantities of bioenergy, so it will allow us hopefully to move from an energy scarcity society to an renewable energy abundance civilisation. A significant number of the earlier pioneers of SynBio derived from engineering and computer science. They were interested in "making" or "manufacturing" life rather than understanding the principles of life which controlled the ethos of traditional biology (Roosth, 2017). We can begin to change, for example, the total natural freshwater cycle. Architecture buildings design and materials instead of avoiding sunlight can begin to behave more like plants that develop more surfaces to capture the sun.

2.d. Carbon-positive and resilient bio-cities

In this more speculative part of the project, we believe that climate change is telling us that we are in a crisis of imagination! To be more precise, we began to develop a speculative vision/plan for the Biscayne Bay estuary that envisions infrastructures in Biscayne Bay that grow by themselves using synthetic biology. In this project, we visualise a series of islands and buildings in the estuary of Biscayne Bay which grows by using living matter. Based on previous research on a gene circuitry that uses bacteria that can precipitate calcite to solidify sand, we envision the growth of a series of islands over the shallow Biscayne Bay as a way to create a 'living shoreline' for relocating populations from Miami threatened by sea level rise. These growing territories will have increased soil pressure that will self-transform according to the levels of rising seas. The proposed system of islands works like atolls that will create defences from currents and surges.

The infrastructures above the islands are designed for living, entertainment, work, food production, and functions such as water desalination. Synthetic biology has the possibility to make living matter fully programmable. In this project, we try to challenge our imagination and move more deeply into bio-aesthetics. We find the process very difficult to visualise with traditional architectural methods and thinking. One of the main drivers is to observe biological agents that could activate spatial evolution and how our bodies will be augmented in a SynBio age. Each project we work on is developed based on particularly desirable

Genetic Food-Water-Energy nexus design research

Figure 7.12: Images from left to right show the sequence of physarum polycephalum as a grown tower by Martha Morales and a diffusion-limited aggregation project by Van Le, followed by a bioengineered plant tower by Allison Tapia (Alfredo Andia D8 Studio).

conditions; we study particular processes of growth and investigate what makes an organism develop its shape.

2.e. Technology vs Fiction

Fiction can be a taboo in architecture. The method of making in SynBio inhabits a different epistemic space than traditional scientific discovery; it celebrates the fact that synthetic biology has a deeper relationship with seeing, with envisioning. In this project, at first, we tried to find existing SynBio techniques. We studied processes that could produce quick methods and low-energy practices of biomineralisation such as sporosarcina pasteurii bacteria, synthetic protein, and collagen to produce artificial bone, synthetic spider silk, and other materials. However, after conversations with several SynBio researchers, we were convinced that the next plateau of SynBio was envisioning fiction, not just technology. A space in which the next generation of SynBio can begin to reinvent itself.

Conclusion and Future Work

Designers and architects are often unable to adequately explore the impact of design alternatives on the environment, looking upfront at energy, water, and resource consumption with greenhouse gas calculations and benchmarks. This leads to an alarming illiteracy, which represents the dilemma of the architecture, engineering and construction industry and the design culture very much with the well-published climate emergencies worldwide. Any integrated project delivery process for carbon-positive design scenarios must require early on participatory, cloud-based master planning with machine learning and deep neural learning processes to retrieve feedback for all project domains, coding, scripting, interoperability among different expert domains and plug-in platforms for shared cloud modelling, intensive analysis, and fitness test processes.

Our critically discussed analysis and automated cloud-based optimisation workflows, with experimental design research testing, including synthetic biological investigations and the development of the IDSS platform are critical to question our imagination on how we can mitigate the effects of climate change, resource scarcity, sea level rise, salt water intrusion, tropical cyclone genesis, extreme precipitation, and increasing latent heat events. Our research analysis and testing conclusions are not finalised, and we will keep asking and testing what will be a carbon-neutral, AI-powered, smart, green-blue and resilient infrastructure for coastal cities in 10, 30, or 80 years from now on.

For example, we will critically continue to experiment on how synthetic biologically designed and operated urban green-blue buildings and infrastructures will interact with their ecosystems and be much more resourceful. There is no ending, and much exploration, research and testing are needed in the future to identify feasible solutions, as the compound effects are too complex to model and are still an open research question; therefore our approach uses mostly simplistic scenarios of testing all workflows together.

Acknowledgements

We would like to thank Darren Ockert, Sadiel Ojeda, and all D7, 8, 9, 10 and master's students of the FIU CRUNCH research studios; all CRUNCH team members http://crunch.fiu.edu/about/team/, Prof. Alfredo Andia, and Autodesk Elite Expert Karam Baki from Amman in Jordan for their assistance and contributions. The majority of this material for the case studies is based upon work supported through a grant by the EU BELMONT, Intelligent Europe, US National Science Foundation (NSF) under Grant No. 730254. Any opinions, findings, and conclusions or recommendations expressed in this material are those of the authors and do not necessarily reflect the views of NSF or FIU in Miami.

References

Andia, A., & Spiegelhalter, T. (2014). *Post- parametric automation in design and construction*. ARTECH HOUSE.

Bevacqua, E., Maraun, D., Vousdoukas, M. et al. (2019, 18 September). Higher probability of compound flooding from precipitation and storm surge in Europe under anthropogenic climate change. *Science Advances, 5*(9). https://doi.org/10.1126/sciadv.aaw5531

Church, G. M., & Regis, E. (2012). *Regenesis: How synthetic biology will reinvent nature and ourselves*. Basic Books.

Hall, J. A., Weaver, C. P., Obeysekera, J. et al. (2019). Rising sea levels: Helping decision-makers confront the inevitable. *Coastal Management, 47*(2), 127–150. https://doi.org/10.1080/08920753.2019.1551012

Hoshino, S., Esteban, M., Mikami, T. et al. (2016). Estimation of increase in storm surge damage due to climate change and sea level rise in the Greater Tokyo area. *Natural Hazards, 80*, 539–565. https://doi.org/10.1007/s11069-015-1983-4

Juhász, L., Podolcsák, Á., & Doleschall, J. (2016, 12 August). Open source web GIS solutions in disaster management – with special emphasis on inland excess water modeling. *Journal of Environmental Geography, 9*(1–2), 15–21. https://doi.org/10.1515/jengeo-2016-0003

Roosth, S. (2017). *Synthetic: How life got mad*. The University of Chicago Press.

Salk. (2005, December 12). Human embryonic stem cells integrate successfully into mouse brain. *Salk*. https://www.salk.edu/news-release/human-embryonic-stem-cells-integrate-successfully-into-mouse-brain/ (accessed 23 October 2020).

Wdowinski, S., Bray, R., Kirtman, B. P., & Wu, Z. (2016). Increasing flooding hazard in coastal communities due to rising sea level: Case study of Miami Beach, Florida. *Ocean & Coastal Management, 126*, 1–8. https://doi.org/10.1016/j.ocecoaman.2016.03.002

Zhang, K., Dittmar, J., Ross, M., & Bergh, C. (2011). Assessment of sea level rise impacts on human population and real property in the Florida Keys. *Climatic Change, 107*(1), 129–146.

Chapter 8

The role of Digital Twins in the CRUNCH project

Chris Cooper and Claire Coulter

Introduction

The focus of this chapter on Digital Twins, within the content of the CRUNCH project, is to promote the Integrated Decision Support System (IDSS) and Urban Living Labs (ULLs) as a Digital Twin, which has been made easier because of the project's up-front application of common standards and principles. This has ensured a set of behaviours that aligned the IDSS towards being interoperable and sustainable. In this chapter, the reader will learn how the original IDSS evolved from a set of common principles that originated in the Smart City Interoperability Framework, a core tenet of international smart city standards. Through their support for using these principles, the CRUNCH ULLs and the IDSS are strongly aligned with industry standards, including the Gemini Principles, which will be discussed in further detail later.

The success of the CRUNCH IDSS depends on exploiting the data in a sustainable manner. This is looked at from a data life-cycle perspective and using the concept of having an event horizon moment for the data contained in the Digital Twin – a key moment when the data is being accessed and is of most use. It is vital to recognise that Digital Twins are evolving and not static. In light of this, we will explore the Digital Twin maturity matrix and see that the IDSS is currently situated in the lower to mid-table zone, driving scope for future improvement and growth in capability.

Digital Twins are entering common parlance as things which places and communities want, and which they should have (National Infrastructure Commission, 2017). This chapter argues that the CRUNCH ULLs and IDSS are ahead of the game, since the six project cities now have the genesis of a Digital Twin. However, with the

CRUNCH ULLs varying in their needs, being dispersed across the globe, and each having its own outcomes and data inputs, it proved difficult to compare and contrast them in the IDSS. Learning from our peers, we will explore a possible fix that we have identified, a data broker component, which has successfully been implemented in similar projects (see DUET, 2021). Looking to the future, and how Digital Twins in the urban environment can seek to evolve our understanding of the Food-Water-Energy (FWE) nexus, we need to explore where we can find more value from the answers that our Digital Twins provide. Namely, can our current Digital Twins be improved, and if we were going to do it all again, what would be done differently?

What is a Digital Twin?

The concept of a Digital Twin is a relatively recent one, and as Jones and colleagues (2020) note, there are still varying definitions used across different fields in both industry and academia. For our purposes, we found it helpful to take the description provided by Greaves and Vickers (2017) as a starting point:

> It is based on the idea that a digital informational construct about a physical system could be created as an entity on its own. This digital information would be a "twin" of the information that was embedded within the physical system itself and be linked with that physical system through the entire lifecycle of the system.

Alternatively, Barricelli, Casiraghi and Fogli (2019) provide the following, more concise, suggestion: "The concept of Digital Twin posits that the flow of data, process and decision is captured in a software avatar that mimics the operation or offers, at the least, a digital proxy."

The CRUNCH IDSS is a Digital Twin in so far as that for each of the six ULLs the IDSS is a digital representative. It draws upon source information from embedded systems from each of the different sites, and the realisation of the decision is a software avatar. The CRUNCH Digital Twins are focused on an outcome and a purpose, delivered in an open and interoperable manner with citizen engagement at the forefront. The purpose of the IDSS is to better inform city decision makers as to the opportunities and challenges related to the FWE nexus. The purpose is to be a decision support service – it is a what-if storyteller that allows the user to test different scenarios.

The CRUNCH IDSS does not offer a real-time dashboard; it is disconnected and relies on previously collected datasets. It is no less of a Digital Twin for this, instead it rightly has a place and purpose. The CRUNCH Digital Twins are categorised as both 'Offline' and 'Deeper Insights' Digital Twins by Jackson (2018), who reflects on the different types of Digital Twins and their relative merits. Just because a system is not 'real time' does not make it any less effective in terms of outcomes it seeks to impact, but realistic expectations need to be set as to the limit of their capabilities. The IDSS, as part of its intended research scope, is intended to be a powerful tool for assisting decision makers and community leaders. It is also a vehicle to inform and shape citizen-led debates, as it can help articulate and visualise complex outcomes and to 'sell' difficult choices. This is highly relevant in places where the impact of climate change is expected to be especially extreme.

The IDSS consequently can become a location's what-if scenario planner and storyteller. We can liken the outcomes being modelled by the IDSS as like a semi-inflated balloon being squeezed in different places. The same amount of air is in the balloon irrespective of the squeeze point, yet depending on the force involved and where the squeeze occurs, the balloon becomes misshapen, and different parts of the balloon structure come under stress. Comparing this to the FWE nexus, the 'balloon' is in constant flux, and at different times any one of the elements may cause more stress than normal. Drawing upon this analogy, the IDSS is where the nexus can be modelled and the stress points identified. Once known, corrective and predictive actions can be implemented, reducing the stress overhead and allowing the nexus to find equilibrium with greater ease.

The different scenarios that can be forecasted range from planning an emergency response to extreme events driven by climate change, through to finding the optimum allocation of scarce FWE resources that will derive the best possible set of outcomes for a given place. The IDSS recognises that due both to geography and local requirements each place will have its own view of what 'good' looks like when it comes to managing the best outcome for the particular FWE nexus dilemma which that place is facing.

The CRUNCH IDSS is a Digital Twin

From the outset, the IDSS was not conceived of, or tagged as, a 'Digital Twin'. As a transdisciplinary project, through working across academic disciplines and with the involvement of key partners from industry, the relevance of the IDSS as a potential

Digital Twin emerged over the course of the project's first team meeting. The concept of Digital Twins was unfamiliar to many of the partners working on the project, despite the fact that the concept of a Digital Twin was out in the public domain; as per the Michael Greaves explanation. This unfamiliarity may possibly have been because Digital Twins to date have very much focused on actual buildings or product life-cycle management/manufacturing sectors; for example, in the oil and gas industry the use of data to deliver digital representations goes back decades (Cameron, Waaler & Komulainen, 2018).

As mentioned above, the realisation that the IDSS was a candidate Digital Twin came during the first discussions surrounding the IDSS and how it would be built. This coincided neatly with the publication of new industry reference points and standards (such as the Gemini Principles in December 2018), enabling the CRUNCH IDSS to be in a much stronger position with reference to how it would align itself. Having a digital model of a real place is all well and good, but for the Digital Twin to be more than a vanity or a marketing project, it has to be useful. We have aimed from the start for the CRUNCH ULLs to demonstrate their worth, and to collect useful data to feed into the IDSS. The answers and outcomes which the IDSS generates are intended not only to aid in policy planning but also to boost citizen engagement. By allowing communities to 'play' with modelling different scenarios, the IDSS can show what alternative outcomes might look like.

Ultimately, the primary role of the IDSS is focused on providing what-if scenario analysis. This allows both civic and community leaders to make better informed decisions when it comes to managing the FWE nexus. Every location faces its own unique FWE nexus challenges, yet how nexus outcomes can be predicted, modelled and interpreted can be common and repeatable across different places and scenarios. It was quickly acknowledged that the six CRUNCH ULLs are all vastly different, not only in size and scope but also in the challenges that they are facing. Although this was a daunting prospect, there was nothing to be gained by reducing the six sites to smaller-scale projects with more characteristics in common – this would have been easier, but the results would have had little real-world relevance. Instead, we chose to retain the initial sites, in all of their complexity, and attempted to build a decision support system that could handle a greater variety of inputs and variance. The key problem here was that several of the sites were ongoing projects, with existing data, and the lack of a common standard in terms of data collection and storage had not fully been appreciated. This would be an ongoing issue throughout the project, and we will return to this later in the chapter.

As a transdisciplinary partnership, CRUNCH relied heavily on involvement from partners outside of traditional academia. From the outset of the project, the purpose of KnowNow Information's involvement was to help the rest of the team to appreciate and better understand the significance of aligning with smart city best practice and standards. A core standard that the CRUNCH IDSS principles are grounded in is ISO 37106: Sustainable Smart Communities standard (International Organization for Standardization [ISO], 2018). This provides a blueprint on how to create a sustainable smart city operating model from a people and process perspective, as well as a set of principles that support this new data-centric operating model. The IDSS, with its close alignment to the ISO 37106 foundational principles, is also designed to become a core element of any 'smart community' operating model.

One of the key findings is that embracing open data, privacy, interoperability and outcomes forms the critical foundation for realising a successful Digital Twin. This link will be explored in the next two sections, firstly by looking at the core principles that were established from day one of the CRUNCH project, and secondly through the project's serendipitous alignment with the Gemini Principles.

Where the journey began: the IDSS principles

From a CRUNCH perspective, it was clear that if data was to be used by city decision makers, those individuals had to have a high degree of trust in the data. To that end, the starting point in the CRUNCH journey was to establish some data principles, which were discussed and vigorously debated during the first consortium meeting following the project's kick-off in Gdańsk in September 2018. Five core principles were agreed upon, and these are described in detail below.

Open data

The first principle is about making sure the data created by the ULLs is open data. Open data has certain specific criteria which is explained in the Open Data Handbook (Open Knowledge Foundation, 2021): "Open data is data that can be freely used, re-used and redistributed by anyone – subject only, at most, to the requirement to attribute and sharealike."

Open data has to be curated data in order to ensure that it is both machine and human readable, which in turn motivates data owners to apply an active data management policy. This is important, as the open data may potentially be used by multiple actors across multiple use cases, all of whom need to know that the data which they consume and process can be trusted.

Looking at the CRUNCH ULLs, there was the potential for vast quantities of data to be considered as being 'within scope'. This was a particularly difficult issue to resolve at such an early stage of the project, when the individual ULLs hadn't all been finalised, and when different members of the interdisciplinary team argued for the inclusion of data related to their particular discipline. Ultimately, it was decided that regardless of the volume and type of data collected by each individual site, only data that had an immediate use for the IDSS or which had been identified for future use by a data stakeholder would be processed.

By forcing the ULLs to consider how their data would be used, not only by themselves but also in the context of the wider project, this ensured from the start not only that any data collected had a purpose but also that key issues surrounding data management were addressed. The establishment of an active data policy, which asked from the outset what data will be archived, in which datasets and formats, and where, how and to what extent the data would be made available, helped both to contain scope and to manage data processing overheads, as well as ensure that funder-related mandates were adhered to.

Collaboration

Collaboration underpins all aspects of the CRUNCH project, both during its lifetime and beyond. To make smart decisions, a collaborative approach is a necessity. In a project such as CRUNCH, collaboration starts with considering where to place sensors and data collectors and asking how often that data is then processed. By default, we would like to ensure that different FWE nexus datasets come from the same locations and are sampled at a similar (ideally the same) time. Ultimately, the principle behind this collaboration and cooperation goes back to ensuring that the data from all the nexus elements is fit for purpose and is open. These principles drive the subproject teams in each of the ULLs to be responsible data stakeholders, meaning that data owners from one element (e.g. water) need to collaborate with other project members (e.g. food) to ensure that data from the ULL meets the key criteria of being trusted, useful, and outcome centric.

For the benefits at a local level to be fully realised, the local stakeholders also need to ensure that they collaborate in order to make integrated decisions. There is the assumption that by employing an IDSS a community is going to obtain better outcomes when handling the dilemma of managing FWE nexus-related challenges. However, to maximise the gain that using an IDSS enables, a collaborative approach is required. This is because by default the nexus brings together different elements and stakeholders that may not previously have been part of a common discussion. Furthermore, as this is only a decision-support service, any outcome based on a decision provided can only be realised through cooperation.

Interoperability

Interoperability is the third principle. It is not sufficient that data is open and made available if it is unable to be used. For datasets to be usable across the FWE nexus, it is imperative that an interoperable approach is adopted from the start. The interoperability between the six CRUNCH ULLs was an area that caused particular concern, and which was conceptually difficult for some of the academic partners to move beyond. The idea of six sites collecting similar but non-identical datasets was challenging; however, we realised that for the teams on the ground the best option was not to worry about other places but concentrate only on their own ULL.

The focus here was on making sure the ULLs' datasets were not necessarily identical but were interoperable. Similar to collaboration (which is more focused on the people and process collaboration requires), interoperability is focused on the machine readability and processing of diverse datasets to get a consolidated sensical outcome. This means that any provider (vendor/supplier) of a data processing service can work across multiple IDSSs and also accept working with project actors outside CRUNCH.

A Digital Twin, because it brings together multiple different types of data and is seeking a common understanding, has to embrace interoperability, and this is enshrined in both the Open Data definition (Open Knowledge Foundation, 2021) as well as being a core tenet of ISO 37106 (ISO, 2018).

Standards

Standards enable interoperability. This is not limited to the ISO 37106 standard but any standard that will better safeguard interoperability and collaboration. Standards codify how something should work. Where a third party or another internal agency wishes to work with a particular ULL, it is the standards regime that ensures that the data flows seamlessly to that other entity. Standards are everywhere in the world of IT, from managing network connections through to ensuring that the colours used on a web page are consistent across any device. Put simply, standards are both the glue and the oil that ensure that the data engineering for a ULL works as expected.

Standards evolve over time, and part of the complexity surrounding the CRUNCH project is using the best available standards for the ULLs and the IDSS, covering not only data accessibility but also security, GIS, data management, and systems design. Going forwards, we expect to see progress in the development of standards supporting the role of ULLs and other Digital Twins in supporting smarter community development. A new standard from the British Standards Institute (BSI) PAS 186:2020 *Smart cities – Supplying data products and services for smart communities – Code of practice* (BSI, 2020) is an example of a standard that will support the data interoperability between data sources within a ULL. Another set of relevant standards which have emerged since the start of CRUNCH are the Gemini Principles, which will be discussed in further detail shortly.

Outcomes

An outcome by its very nature needs to be measurable, which creates opportunities for governance and tracking of whether expectations are being met. This final principle, therefore, is the most important, since it aims to ensure that a ULL project sticks to its objectives and scope. By using the outcome as the reason for processing, this immediately means that interesting datasets which are out of scope will not be processed unless required by an actor. This helps to keep costs down, but also allows for the benefit of this data to be less abstract and more easily understood. Adopting an outcome-centric focus also facilitates the adoption of standards and interoperability and supports the end goal of a sharable and freely available IDSS.

The Gemini Principles

The Gemini Principles (Bolton et al., 2018) were created by the UK's Centre for Digital Built Britain (CDBB) and published in late 2018. As the CRUNCH project started prior to this, it was not until later that the applicability of the Gemini Principles to CRUNCH was identified, almost halfway through the project.

The role of Digital Twins in the CRUNCH project

The Gemini Principles

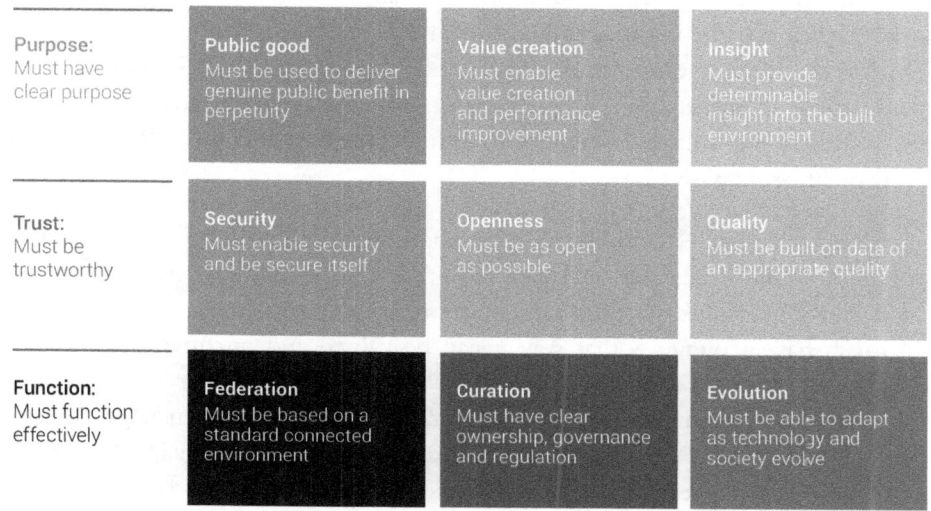

Figure 8.1: CDBB – Gemini Principles
This work is licensed under the Creative Commons Attribution 3.0

    The ULLs (as described in Part I of this book) map very well against the Gemini Principles. They all have a purpose and are focused on improving outcomes for the public good: their outcomes enable the improved allocation of scarce resources, and they are all anchored in the urban environment and are improving awareness and insight about their own particular site. Each ULL is locally designed and governed too, so has a strong alignment to the Gemini Principles right from day one.

    Through the IDSS, the ULLs drive trusted data to inform an outcome. This data is secure, it is open, and the quality of data is key. Each ULL is secure in itself, independent, and yet embraces a federated model, feeding into the overarching CRUNCH IDSS. This is important, for although the ULLs need to share certain components, the idea underpinning the different sites is that each place has its own unique FWE nexus demands.

    Looking to the future, the alignment of the IDSS to the Gemini Principles is a really positive outlook, as it will likely increase the ongoing chances of continued use of the IDSS. This means that the IDSS can evolve over time without hindrance, as it will not have vendor lock-in or a proprietary approach. In terms of the future direction of the IDSS, there are opportunities to see the IDSS increase its scope in terms of location coverage (it has already expanded from the initial four core sites to include our more experimental ULLs in Gdańsk and Miami), as well as further relevant indicators (for instance linked to health).

Within the lifetime of the project, we tried to learn from the Gemini Principles and use these to inform our data collection and management strategies. The list below outlines the links between the Gemini Principles and the CRUNCH data management principles:

- Privacy by design – including GDPR compliance – The key is to have a good understanding of any personal data required and the lawful basis for processing that data. This aligns with the *Gemini Principle Trust via Security*.
- All data has an owner – that way it can be valued and nurtured. Open data is loved and nurtured. As per *Gemini Principle Function via Curation*.
- It is necessary to throttle exponential data growth. This is to manage costs and reduce risk. There is a strong correlation with the open data principle as well, as it will force all data elements to have owners that care. From a practical perspective, this means redundant data can be deleted or moved to a cheaper media (the use of tape versus disk, making use of available funded repositories). As per *Gemini Principle Trust via Quality*.
- All data is clearly labelled using the standard agreed naming conventions. As per *Gemini Principle Trust via Quality*.
- Any integration has to be interoperable. As per *Gemini Principle Trust via Quality and Purpose via Value Creation*.
- Any extraction or manipulation of the data has to meet both standards for this task and outcomes. As per *Gemini Principle Purpose via Value Creation*.
- Data should be generated to create discernible insight. As per *Gemini Principle Purpose via Insight*.
- Each of the ULLs have their own section of the IDSS. This aligns with the *Gemini Principle of Function via Federation*.
- The data contained in the IDSS for each ULL is intended to be open and transparent. This aids and builds trust with citizens interacting with the IDSS. As per the *Gemini Principle of Trust via Openness*.
- Overall, the intention of the IDSS is to derive public good, and to help make smarter decisions with what are scarce resources. This is as per the *Gemini Principle Purpose via Public Good*.

The missing data broker – a lesson learnt

One of the challenges of the different ULLs is that they have different focus areas, as well as different types of data. For example, Gdańsk has a focus on using water for energy, whereas Miami is worried about water from a flooding perspective. How is it possible to compare and contrast this?

Additionally, when looking at the 'Vs' of data (velocity, volume, veracity, variety, and variability), the ULLs have markedly different requirements and data outputs. Velocities (as in the data refresh rate) can range from once daily, through to updates every minute or second. There are also different levels of variability and variety, which can be from a few square metres between data points to multiple kilometres. The different data volumes depend on what is being collected and processed (which is made up of data types and size of the data payload), as well as the scope of geographical coverage, the number of data points in that area, and the refresh rate. Trusting the IDSS data is key when making big decisions on what could or should happen, or what situation is to be avoided by acting now versus later. The veracity will therefore only be proven over time, and based on trends and ongoing success.

Within the current scope of the CRUNCH project, it is very difficult to compare and contrast the different ULLs and the associated IDSS. This is because each ULL has many differences across the types, volume, variety and variability of its data. An energy sensor in Taipei is recording at a different volume to an energy sensor in Southend-on-Sea, which means that the portability of outcomes across ULLs becomes difficult.

One of the ways to fix this situation is to implement a data broker component that can act as middleware to smooth over the differences in the volume, values and variety of data used in the IDSS. The data broker has a dual role. It becomes the translator and data normaliser. A number of designs have been proposed for this function. The first is from the Digital Urban European Twins (DUET) project, an EU Horizon 2020 project that is creating three new Digital Twins in Flanders, Athens, and Pilsen (DUET, 2021). An alternative option, released in 2018, is from an Innovate UK-funded project, Tombolo (2018). The Tombolo digital connector has an open licence, meaning that it can be exploited by any Digital Twin project. It focused on urban modelling, which has a good synergy with the CRUNCH ULLs and IDSS, and was instigated to fix a gap in the marketplace:

> The Tombolo Digital Connector is a new piece of open-source software designed to interconnect datasets and urban models. Urban specialists can now

create models based on a much wider range of data sources. Because of its modular structure, the software can be expanded by users to cater for a diverse range of datasets.

Currently, the CRUNCH IDSS relies upon data that has already been collected. If the next generation of IDSS seeks to evolve into a real-time Digital Twin, then the scaling of the IT infrastructure to handle vast amounts of data will require further investment in design, development, and deployment. This will likely lead to a data broker component being required and be a valid reason to implement it. To support this new data processing overhead, the overall IDSS solution can take advantage of another trend in the IT landscape – the rapid rise in cloud-hosted data processing. This has proved revolutionary in a number of ways: firstly by collapsing the price of computing, both in terms of raw cost per gigabyte processed and the speed of preparing a server on the cloud to be ready to accept workload (now measured in seconds to be ready, versus weeks just a decade ago), to the point that if managed well a low end server is virtually free to use; secondly by reducing the barriers to entry and enabling anyone to build a server, this has unleashed innovation in new products and services provided by cloud-hosted data processing, which is attracting further investment and new clusters of expertise (Koomey et al., 2011).

A Digital Twin that wants real-time data injection, and publish and subscription capability, would be advised to invest in a Digital Twin Data Broker. This component is at the heart of the Data Aggregation/Access layer, and the bonus is that it serves two purposes:

a) It can aggregate and transform data from various external data sources to create a single standard that is harmonised;
b) It can expose a unified data API for all open linked data in the repository, which makes subscribing to the various different federated Digital Twins easier as only the API data link is required.

One candidate solution that is already available for re-use is the Digital Twin Data Broker from the DUET project (Raes et al., 2021). The data broker can solve the discrepancies of data that originate from federated Digital Twins to create a normalised set for all parties to use for a comparison perspective. The following diagram is taken from the DUET project:

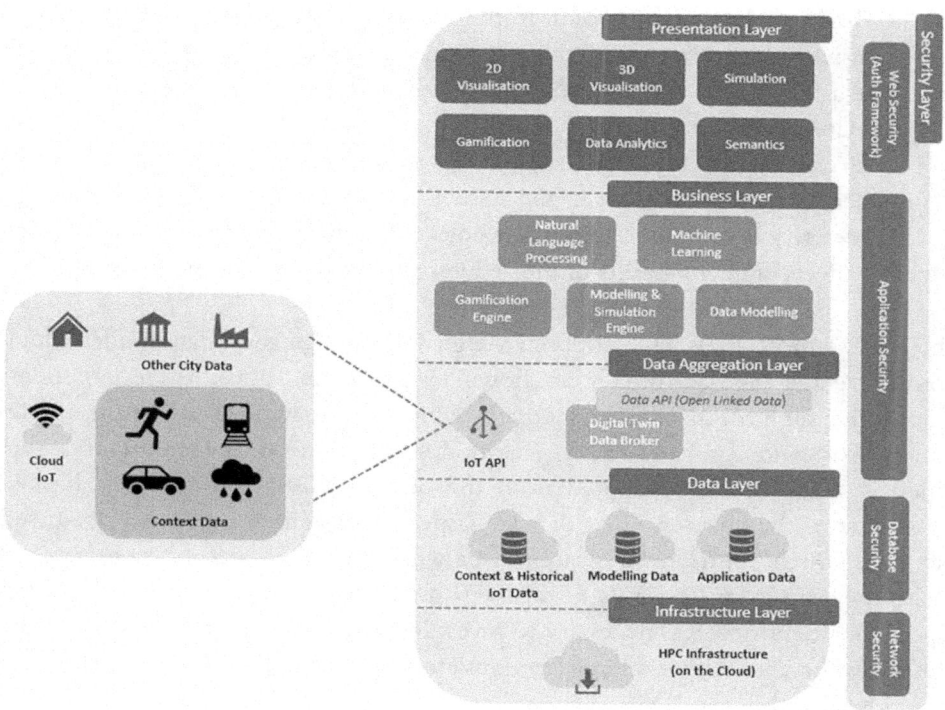

Figure 8.2: Layer Overview (DUET, 2021 component 8.3)

1. The **Infrastructure layer** corresponds to a cloud-based infrastructure with support for the High Performance Computing (HPC) workloads of the platform. The platform will be designed to be agnostic of the backed cloud provider.
2. The **Data Layer** refers to the repositories/databases of the platform, where each database is deployed in a distributed mode that spans multiple nodes in the cloud cluster for enhanced scalability, availability, and performance.
3. The **Digital Twin Data Broker** is at the heart of the Data Aggregation/ Access layer, which serves two purposes: it is responsible not only for aggregating data from the various external data sources but also for exposing a unified data API for all open linked data in the repository. The Internet of Things (IoT) API component facilitates the ingestion of new data pipelines from sensors and other sources.

4. The **Business layer** corresponds to the processing components that implement the business requirements of the platform. All components in that layer will expose a REST API to be consumed by the visualisation/UI components of the presentation layer.
5. The **Presentation layer** relies on a service-oriented architecture. This layer provides the interfaces between the systems and the user.
6. The **Security layer** is applied to the whole architecture as a cross-cutting concept, and it affects different aspects of the architecture (web, database, network etc).

The DUET project has also proposed a high-level design for a data model which would leverage the data broker, as shown in the figure above. Key components include the application of data standards, which also drives the adoption of data management and data governance methodologies. This is an important aspect which is reinforced and adopted from the original IDSS principles established at the start of the chapter. The other key aspect is to embrace an ontology-based mapping, which comes from awareness of what the different data types are and where they are from (those Vs of data!). To fix one of the gaps which the IDSS experience identified, it is necessary to invest in an agreed taxonomy and notation. This gives the data broker a target to translate to, so as to allow normalisation and comparison within the IDSS.

The data management story does not stop with engineering the data to flow to a server and be analysed. Projects are encouraged to invest time in a semantic notation for tagging and categorising their data. This will cover elements such as location, date, and time, as well as information on the data source, quality (truthfulness/veracity of the data), service level and licence, and then bring this all together into the Digital Twin semantic inventory – i.e. a catalogue of the data for that IDSS. This then makes the data taxonomy machine readable and easily searchable.

Digital Twin maturity

Looking to the future, there are plenty of opportunities to grow and evolve the CRUNCH Digital Twins. Evans and colleagues (2019), building on research provided by the private firm Atkins, drew up a hierarchy of maturity for Digital Twins. Although the maturity matrix has a distinctly built environment and civil engineering bent, it remains relevant for urban planning Digital Twins, such as the CRUNCH ULL models in the IDSS. The maturity matrix looks at both the inputs and outcomes of a Digital Twin and is looking to drive smarter decisions that look at time and cost (those 4D and 5D elements). To that end, the CRUNCH IDSS Digital Twins are already at a Maturity Element of 2 in the logarithmic scale (see Figure 8.3 below). Looking forward to future levels of maturity, the IDSS has a clear evolutionary path towards becoming a real-time Digital Twin (level 3). Eventually, assuming the data quality is good enough, the IDSS could even theoretically become a level 5 autonomous decision-making entity.

Ultimately, in the case of citizen-focused decision support tools such as the CRUNCH IDSS, the determination of desirable outcomes will require constant validation from the local communities who are using the tool. This may even vary year on year, as taking the I nexus into consideration, seasonal variability may mean that viable solutions for food and water challenges may need to be tweaked as the weather and climate changes.

Even where the variability of the season is diminished – for example, by growing in a closed-loop system in an urban farm hosted in a warehouse – there will still be the opportunity to micromanage the different elements of the nexus: the use of energy (derived from solar and waste); the recycling of water and the subsequent choice of crops for food production. Although potentially less complex to manage

Maturity element (logarithmic scale of complexity and connectedness)	Defining principle	Outline usage
0	– Reality capture (e.g. point cloud, drones, photogrammetry, or drawings/sketches)	– Brownfield (existing) as-built survey
1	– 2D map/system or 3D model (e.g. object-based, with no metadata or BIM)	– Design/asset optimisation and coordination
2	– Connect model to persistent (static) data, metadata and BIM Stage 2 (e.g. documents, drawings, asset management systems)	– 4D/5D simulation – Design/asset management – BIM Stage 2
3	– Enrich with real-time data (e.g. from IoT, sensors)	– Operational efficiency
4	– Two-way data integration and interaction	– Remote and immersive operations – Control the physical from the digital
5	– Autonomous operations and maintenance	– Complete self-governance with total oversight and transparency

Figure 8.3: The Maturity Index, Evans et al. (2019)

in the long term, this will still require data inputs of high fidelity and trust, which due to the nature of the setting (a controlled and closed environment), have a greater chance of moving up the maturity index.

Security is paramount, and the Gemini Principles support this by taking a multi-faceted view of security. For the design and development phases of the CRUNCH IDSS, there were various aspects of security that did not present major stumbling blocks. This is because, firstly, no personal data were ever in scope to be processed (i.e. there were no GDPR concerns); secondly, the IDSS was not connected in a bi-directional fashion to the physical world, so a cyber security hack would not have had a material impact in real time (e.g. opening a floodgate erroneously); finally, the ULL models within the IDSS are federated – they share common building blocks but are distinctly separate IT landscapes.

Going forward, and as the IDSS matures, security will become ever more relevant and require further design thinking. Various authors have suggested that operationalising security and privacy-by-design security becomes a critical enabler of trust (Gunes et al., 2014; Rasheed, San, & Kvamsdal, 2020). This is important as the veracity of data from the Digital Twin has a considerable influence on whether citizens will buy in to the predicted outcome that the IDSS will suggest to them.

Continuous service improvement

No one can predict the future. During the lifetime of the CRUNCH project, we watched as the Covid-19 pandemic developed, and we saw how it affected the different projects in our six ULL sites spread across the globe. As part of the evolving maturity of the IDSS, influenced by the global pandemic, there has been a discussion over whether there is the need to include two additional data perspectives: resilience, and health indicators. These measures are already captured as elements in the UN sustainable development goals (UN General Assembly, 2015), and they align neatly with the aforementioned ISO 37106 standard for sustainable communities (ISO, 2018).

The FWE nexus is merely one model for exploring the interconnectedness of resources, and possible extensions have been suggested, including adding waste (Lehmann, 2018). In the future, as the IDSS matures and grows its historical back catalogue of input data, the range of nexus options available and the actual decisions made will open up new opportunities. These opportunities fall into two distinct arenas.

The role of Digital Twins in the CRUNCH project

The first is the improved accuracy that will be possible as more data is fed into the IDSS. As the nuances of the place and the nexus choices that take place there become known, the IDSS will be able to more easily move up the maturity index.

The second is recognising the value of data, which is linked to the sustainability of data in terms of value over time. Data sustainability seeks to unearth fresh value from historical data, beyond just the immediate value that is accrued at the point when it is initially used to make a decision (the aforementioned event horizon). Instead, over time, the answers previously recorded flow through into the historical record, and as this historical record grows, the data takes on new value as part of a broader dataset.

This data can be used by other agencies and partners outside the primary user communities within the six original ULL sites. Additionally, from an IDSS perspective, this new value exploitation can give rise to new use cases (e.g. a time machine view) and potential new users (for example, in education and training), helping to avoid a repeat of mistakes made when a previous nexus decision does not lead to the outcome expected.

The graphic below, taken from a new Data Canvas Paper (Gomer, Cooper, & Verma, 2021), explains this new value opportunity from historical data. The use case being exposed here is maximising energy use versus the choice of storing, selling or consuming that energy.

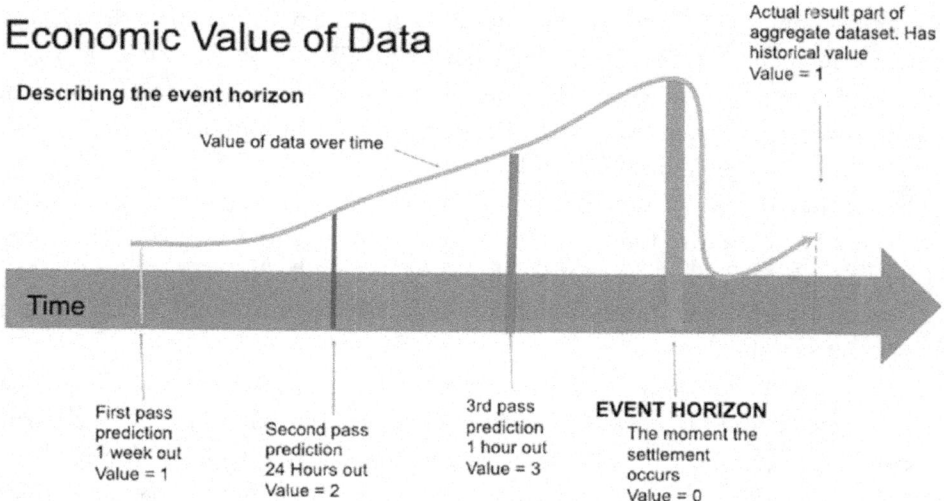

Figure 8.4: The Economic Value of Data (Gomer, Cooper & Verma, 2021)
This work is licensed under the Creative Commons Attribution 3.0

The model shows over time that the data points that influence a nexus decision have a relatively low value to start with. As the data points start to increase nearer to the point where a decision is being made, two things are happening. The first is that the demand for a more accurate prediction is increasing. Second, the available trend data that drives that prediction is becoming ever more nuanced and accurate, to the extent that at the point of the decision (the event horizon) the percentage of deviation between the prediction and the actual becomes tiny. Then just as rapidly once the event horizon passes, the data that made that decision loses its value, and does so very rapidly.

And yet all is not lost. The residue of the decision data, its metadata, the predicted outcome it pushed, and the aggregate results, do have an ongoing forever value, which when added to all the other decision points made that day, month and year have a historical purpose. They provide the learnings for the next trend analysis and prediction, and the more history that passes, the better the future predictions. Although the project itself is now complete, the CRUNCH IDSS remains available for public use. Through continued use and data input it will only get better with age.

Conclusion

The six CRUNCH ULLs and their respective IDSS are categorically Digital Twins, and through the nature of the outcomes which they seek to help inform, as well as the core principles they follow, they stand in alignment with the exemplar Digital Twin, as referenced by the Gemini Principles. The CRUNCH principles of open data, transparency, interoperability, citizen centricity, and being outcomes-focused, are part of a broader strand of standard adherence that is grounded in ISO 37106 and reinforced by the Gemini Principles.

The journey of the CRUNCH Digital Twins need not stop at the IDSS stage. They could feasibly move further up the maturity index and evolve over time into autonomous decision-making entities; however, this will also require investment in citizen and leader education, as well as more granular and robust data at higher velocity and volume.

The key dilemma for any Digital Twin is how to ensure that they are sustainable in the longer term. One answer is to recognise that data which the Digital Twin processes has ongoing value that accrues as time moves forward. The trick is exploiting this value at the right time, as well as assembling a community that can extract this value. One aspect of ensuring ongoing value is for community decision makers to trust the insights which the IDSS provides. This will create new stories to engage local citizens with, which in turn, assuming that the outcomes the IDSS predicts are accepted, will inform policy and action on the ground. Exactly how these policies and actions actually resolve to improve citizens' lives will be something that can only be observed in the fullness of time.

Yet the IDSS has already demonstrated value, simply by proving that capturing food-water-energy data about a place leads to new conversations, new analysis and new questions and answers to be tested. This in turn leads to new actions that by definition are leading to more positive outcomes than simply doing nothing. Likewise in the rare case in which the status quo remains the optimum solution, the IDSS can prove via its demonstration that the old way is still best.

Ultimately, the CRUNCH IDSS is one aspect of the wider project, and one tool amongst many for the communities in the ULLs. Each ULL has a unique set of FWE nexus challenges, and each of the ULLs will identify an independent path and future for their new Digital Twin. Our CRUNCH IDSS Digital Twins remain a work in progress. When they do grow and evolve, the inclusion of a data broker will be an important development. This will enable users to compare and contrast across the different locations within the IDSS platform and gain added value from the suggestions which the IDSS provides. We look forward to seeing how the IDSS develops over time, and hope that it continues to help communities to tackle their own climate-related challenges.

Acknowledgements

This work was supported by the AHRC, ESRC and Innovate UK in the framework of the Joint Programming Initiative Urban Europe, with support from the European Union's Horizon 2020 Research and Innovation Program under grant agreement No 730254.

We thank the DUET project for granting us permission to reuse their image. DUET has received funding from the EU Horizon 2020 research and innovation programme under grant agreement No 870697.

References

Barricelli, B. R., Casiraghi, E., & Fogli, D. (2019). A Survey on digital twin: Definitions, characteristics, applications, and design implications. *IEEE Access*, 7, 167653–167671. DOI: 10.1109/ACCESS.2019.2953499.

Bolton, A., Butler, L., Dabson, I., et al. (2018). Gemini Principles. (CDBB_REP_006) https://doi.org/10.17863/CAM.32260

British Standards Institute. (2020). Smart cities: Supplying data products and services for smart communities. Code of practice (PAS 186:2020).

Cameron, D. B., Waaler, A., & Komulainen, T. M. (2018). Oil and gas digital twins after twenty years. How can they be made sustainable, maintainable and useful? In Proceedings of The 59th Conference on Simulation and Modelling (SIMS 59), Sep 26–28 2018, Oslo Metropolitan University, Norway, Linköping University Electronic Press, pp. 9–16. https://doi.org/10.3384/ecp181539

Digital Urban European Twins (DUET). (2021). https://www.digitalurbantwins.com

Evans, S., Savian, C., Burns, A., & Cooper, C. (2019). *Digital Twins for the built environment*. The Institution of Engineering and Technology: London. https://www.theiet.org/media/4719/digital-twins-for-the-built-environment.pdf

Gomer, R., Cooper C., & Verma, J. (2021). *Energy Data Management Canvas – A tool and process to help you to define and document the use and governance of data in your project*. Energy Systems Catapult: Birmingham. Available at: https://es.catapult.org.uk/brochures/energy-data-management-canvas/

Grieves, M., & Vickers, J. (2017). Digital Twin: Mitigating unpredictable, undesirable emergent behavior in complex systems. In F. J. Kahlen, S. Flumerfelt, & A. Alves (Eds.), *Transdisciplinary Perspectives on Complex Systems*. Springer, Cham. https://doi.org/10.1007/978-3-319-38756-7_4

Gunes, V., Peter, S., Givargis, T., & Vahid, F. (2014). A survey on concepts applications and challenges in cyber-physical systems. *KSII Trans. Internet Inf. Syst.*, 8(12), 4242–4268.

International Organization for Standardization. (2018). Sustainable cities and communities — Guidance on establishing smart city operating models for sustainable communities (ISO Standard No. 37106).

Jackson, C. (2018, December 14). What is a Digital Twin. *Lifecycle Insights*. https://www.lifecycleinsights.com/tech-guide/digital-twins/.

Jones, D., Snider, C., Nassehi, A. et al. (2020). Characterising the Digital Twin: A systematic literature review. *CIRP Journal of Manufacturing Science and Technology*, 29, Part A, 36–52. https://doi.org/10.1016/j.cirpj.2020.02.002

Koomey, J., Berard, S., Sanchez, M., & Wong, H. (2011). Implications of historical trends in the electrical efficiency of computing, *IEEE Annals of the History of Computing*, 33(3), pp. 46–54. DOI: 10.1109/MAHC.2010.28.

Lehmann, S. (2018). Implementing the urban nexus approach for improved resource-efficiency of developing cities in Southeast-Asia. *City Cult Soc*, *13*, 46–56. https://doi.org/10.1016/j.ccs.2017.10.003

National Infrastructure Commission. (2017). *Data for the public good.* https://nic.org.uk/app/uploads/Data-for-the-Public-Good-NIC-Report.pdf

Open Knowledge Foundation. (2021). Opendata Handbook, "What is open data". https://opendatahandbook.org/guide/en/what-is-open-data/

Raes, L., Michiels, P., Adolphi, T. et al. (2021). DUET: A framework for building secure and trusted Digital Twins of smart cities. *IEEE Internet Computing*. DOI: 10.1109/MIC.2021.3060962

Rasheed, A., San, O., & Kvamsdal, T. (2020). Digital Twin: Values, challenges and enablers from a modeling perspective. IEEE Access, *8*, 21980–22012. DOI: 10.1109/ACCESS.2020.2970143

Tombolo. (2018). Tombolo Digital Connector. https://github.com/FutureCitiesCatapult/TomboloDigitalConnector

UN General Assembly. (2015). Transforming our world: The 2030 Agenda for Sustainable Development, 21 October 2015, A/RES/70/1. https://sustainabledevelopment.un.org/post2015/transformingourworld/publication

Conclusion

Julia Brown, Claire Coulter, and Alessandro Melis

The Climate Resilient Urban Nexus CHoices (CRUNCH) project focused on six different sized cities (ranging from 170,000 to 2.7 million inhabitants), spread around the world, each with its own distinct climate-related challenges. The heart of the CRUNCH project was to demonstrate how the Food-Water-Energy nexus could be implemented at different levels, from building design scale, to urban design scale, to neighbourhood and precinct planning scale, to highlight the opportunities for fundamental new urban design strategies. Thus, as well as directly identifying and tackling the issues within these six cities, the wider aim of the project was to gain transferable knowledge and strategies for boosting community resilience in any urban neighbourhood, regardless of its size or location. This was to be achieved through a fuller appreciation of how, on a variety of scales, urban design and citizen engagement can influence the integration of food, water and energy systems. Urban Living Labs (ULLs) were the primary approach for testing the FWE nexus. These physical urban spaces were designed to facilitate engagement with stakeholders and to test and to yield quantitative and qualitative data on the appropriateness of design options.

In this conclusion, we evaluate how far we were able to meet the ambitious aims of CRUNCH, as well as practical lessons learnt along the way that may have wider applicability to other cities planning on exploring nexus approaches as a vehicle to realise resilience. In reviewing the CRUNCH project, we first discuss what we have learnt about improving community resilience through targeted actions in our ULLs. It is apparent from Part I (ULL descriptions) and discussed more fully in the associated ULL chapters in Part II, that each ULL worked on different aspects of the CRUNCH project, and operated at different scales, and thus had its own challenges and trajectory. Mature projects, such as the Taipei Fudeken urban farming development is progressing as before (ULL 1.5 and Chapter 5), but with a renewed FWE nexus focus. In large-scale council-led projects like the Uppsala Rosendal housing development (ULL 1.6), they are pushing through cutting-edge innovation and new ideas. However, small-scale, match-funded, council-led projects, like Southend-on-Sea (ULL 1.4 and Chapter 3), face institutional barriers due to the level of innovation and the level of coordination required between departments with no budget for on-going maintenance. Whilst cities like Southend-on-Sea agree on the broader policy direction, the implementation identified the gap between policy aspiration and commitment by different stakeholders to new approaches. Community-led projects, like Eindhoven (ULL 1.1 and Chapter 2), saw learning through co-design. The participants were also likeminded people with a shared vision. The micro ULL in Gdańsk (see 1.2 and Chapter 4) highlights the challenges of working on private land, as well as how projects can be at the mercy of external events. The Gdańsk team did collect data on what forms of urban design have the greatest impact on the integration of FWE systems within a city, which was useful more broadly in the development of the CRUNCH IDSS. The Miami virtual ULL (1.3 and Chapter 7), with its use of computational modelling to present different sea level-rise scenarios, is working with rich sources of existing data, which may not always be readily available in other contexts. The challenge for this project is how to engage policymakers with climate scenarios that do not align with the current, more optimistic, sustainability master plan. Ultimately, there is not a one-size-fits-all ULL approach because each context is unique and requires a bespoke, and politically and culturally aligned, approach. Several of the projects also stressed the importance of co-creation and the challenge of meaningful public engagement.

Lessons about developing the Integrated Decision Support System

City planners are faced with an enormous challenge when trying to plan for more resilient futures that incorporate food, water and energy systems. The CRUNCH project wanted to reduce the level of complexity and to integrate FWE considerations into their planning.

The starting point in the development of the CRUNCH IDSS – a main output of the project – was the recognition that integrating a city's food, water and energy systems is a daunting mission. There is a need to develop an on-line digital platform system that reduces complexity and assists policymakers and planners to make choices that are based on quantifiable data for more climate-resilient futures. This can be realised by better understanding the interconnectedness of the systems and how a change in one system affects others, and where there are opportunities to maximise multiple benefits.

The Uppsala team in Sweden took the lead in developing the IDSS tool, the initial version of which is already accessible online (see Chapter 6). Other CRUNCH teams provided data to assist with the development of the IDSS: the Eindhoven team, through their ULL survey, provided relevant stakeholder data. The Gdańsk team provided data and insights into what form of urban design impacts FWE systems in cities. The different CRUNCH case study city locations and climate challenges fed into the IDSS, which will allow cities in other parts of the world to potentially find FWE nexus solutions which are applicable to their contexts.

If the IDSS was to be a useful tool for policymakers, it needed to balance usability with accuracy. We believe that the advantage of the CRUNCH IDSS is its simplicity. The IDSS relies on machine learning models, which means that users do not need to undertake extensive training to use the system. Users can investigate the potential of different innovations to their context, knowing the model has been built using data from a broad range of different cities and climates. For example, city planners can determine the amount of energy that could be generated from solar panels for a particular building design in a given climatic zone and determine the optimal urban design. In some locations, solar panels alone would not provide enough energy: batteries may also be needed, or if designed with rainwater harvesting capabilities, a building can be modified so that stored rainwater can power a dynamo to supplement the solar panels. The IDSS would allow users to determine the volume of rainfall required to be feasible in their context.

The CRUNCH IDSS continues to be refined, but it is already garnering interest: the Uppsala team report: "The IDSS shows so much promise that the municipality of Uppsala are planning on using it for the development of new neighbourhoods responding to their local population growth."

In terms of lessons learnt from the development of the IDSS, it is clear that agreeing on a shared taxonomy and a shared vision of the ultimate purpose of an IDSS is essential. Ensuring that the end-user is at the heart of the design and all attendant decisions is key. Without care, an IDSS can become input-focused, losing sight of the end-user. We had to recognise that ultimately CRUNCH was not about celebrating what our ULLs had achieved, rather how the data that we collected could be used for a global audience of potential IDSS users.

With hindsight, the balance of the transdisciplinary teams was uneven: those with IDSS expertise were in the minority. The IDSS development needed to drive the CRUNCH agenda and should have been more central to work packages 1 and 2: if a key project output was designing an IDSS, then we needed the involvement of the system designers from the outset. Debates about standards and interoperability are useful but only when decisions have been made over what data can be collected. Amongst the urban planning academics, there was often little understanding of how an IDSS functions, and many of us probably commenced the project with very preconceived ideas over what data was needed without necessarily having a strong decision science background or considering how this would fit into the system architecture, and without considering the uniqueness of the ULLs. An innovative system that incorporates and creates space for difference proved very conceptually challenging for all members of the team to appreciate. Ultimately, however, CRUNCH delivered on an IDSS that is simple to use by end-users.

FWE nexus project management conclusions

The research funding landscape strongly supports multi-country consortiums, and we wanted to provide some reflections on the experiences of managing a large and ambitious project. When the CRUNCH project commenced in the spring of 2018, optimism prevailed: the topic of the FWE nexus for urban resilience was under researched and in its infancy in academic circles and in terms of evaluating its potential. We were linked with funded projects in an interesting range of countries with a spread of city sizes and different climate change challenges. We were testing the potential of Urban Living Labs (ULLs) as a methodology to generate data needed to build a user-friendly IDSS that would help decision makers navigate complexity.

With hindsight, CRUNCH was possibly over ambitious with regards to what could be achieved in the three years of its funding. The successful bid committed the team to an edited book with project outcomes before the end of the project, and a functional IDSS. The reality was that ULLs had to be designed, implemented, tested, and evaluated from scratch within three years, and yield data to be fed into IDSS: this was extremely challenging. A proposal that expected outcomes and evidence of impact, within a three-year timescale, given the requirements of funding cycles, was unrealistic: for an inherently complex and integrated approach, we feel it is still too early to see evidence of sustained impact to assess whether nexus thinking can yield resilient urban outcomes.

The rationale behind the project was well founded. There is abundant academic evidence of the value of integrated and nexus approaches and urban greening that underpins SUGI funding (as specifically discussed in the Southend-on-Sea chapter). Nexus thinking tries to overcome silos within city technical departments and budgets: climate change problems have multiple sources and require cross-departmental support. Whilst integration and nexus approaches in the abstract make sense, and merging expertise appears to be novel, crucially the evidence that it has multiple benefits is still in its infancy. A lot of nexus work is theoretical: in a context of underfunding, there is still a massive need for practical evidence of implementation. Nexus thinking for the CRUNCH project was based upon the assumption that the infrastructure was funded and in place; instead, what was needed was better coordination and cooperation between actors, but this has a high cost in terms of human resources, particularly in a time of budget cut-backs, the legacy of the 2008 world financial crisis, and coupled more recently with Covid-19, which dominates the final third of this project.

The practicalities of nexus thinking necessitate closing organisational gaps: integrating food, water and energy requires different departments to work together. In addition, technical staff and politicians need to collaborate because public support for interventions is needed. The chapters in this book demonstrate the potential fragility of political support for innovations that challenge aesthetic norms, and where the results may not be immediately apparent. CRUNCH had to consider how to make the nexus agenda both publicly and politically palatable. The reality is that many projects assumed that these approaches would automatically have broad support.

As academics, we tend to collaborate or interact with the evangelical early adopters of nexus thinking (funding bodies, and with our city partners, who are outward-facing council employees who have a personal and professional commitment to sustainability): this may give a false impression over how widespread support is for nexus approaches. Was CRUNCH an echo chamber of enthusiasm? Our early excitement was dampened in some projects, such as Southend-on-Sea, when we began to see the challenges that many council pioneers faced with progressing the projects.

Overall, the success stories from CRUNCH fall into two categories, those with committed funding which was on-going and external to CRUNCH (e.g. Uppsala and Taipei); or with the example of Eindhoven, a very small and self-selecting community of like-minded people, where the wider applicability may be limited unless those conditions can be met. For a project like Southend-on-Sea, which relied on being matched to other funded projects that were subject to delays, this was a risky strategy: it proved a challenge to overlap the timescales of the potentially funded projects with the three-year CRUNCH funding window. In addition, trying to fit into a pre-existing project meant that the team had to coordinate with other partners and departments, with their own agendas, for whom CRUNCH and the FWE nexus was not a priority. Having a committed CRUNCH point of contact and project champion was crucial for the progress that was made, as they were flexible and able to work well with other teams. However, these personal attributes cannot be manufactured and are never guaranteed in a project team. Southend-on-Sea is also an example of how easy these projects are to derail: once again a key lesson is how to translate the importance of the FWE and resilience agenda in non-technical language to garner widespread support at all levels of local government and with the public.

Some of the resistance to nexus innovations came from a justifiable critique of the funded projects, which may have had finance for new technologies but not their on-going operation and maintenance. Life-cycle costing needs to be better accounted for in the post-project period, notably out of whose budget the on-going maintenance is coming from. Again, within a context of austerity, and on-going with Covid-19, this resistance is understandable. Research project designers and funders need to work more closely with the implementers of projects they intend on partnering with to ensure not only long-term viability but also that projects are not blocked in the short term due to future funding concerns.

The various projects had differing levels of success with public participation in the ULLs. Eindhoven, again because of its small scale and homogeneity of participants, and because it piggy-backed onto an existing project, proved the most successful. With Southend-on-Sea, CRUNCH was at the mercy of project matching, which, as the chapter outlines, took considerable time, meaning participation was not feasible. Gdańsk proved that even initial strong support, from the business community in this case, is at the mercy of external events beyond the project's control. Sustaining momentum with public involvement is also challenging, especially when timescales for research projects mean a kick-off meeting and seeing change resulting from engagement can take up a year. The dissipation of interest is understandable.

Our experience is that the food component of the FWE nexus was the most challenging element to integrate. Food for many projects was not a focus, and for those that did try to incorporate it, such as Southend-On-Sea, it tended to be a bit gimmicky or an add-on. While there is value in a demonstration plot – using water to irrigate herbs – it is not a viable route for food self-sufficiency. There is a need for more research into the food component of the nexus.

Nexus thinking does not require just technically strong staff; there is a need to make politically astute collaborations, and successful projects cannot afford to alienate politicians. The art of communication and compromise is fundamental, otherwise nexus projects run the danger of being purely academic exercises; they must work with the practical and political realities they find themselves in. Finding ways to 'to take people with you' emerges as being important. Eindhoven Council's advice, discussed in the Southend-On-Sea chapter, over the value of incremental greening was very useful, as was their use of an environmental arbitrator to mediate complaints, rather than simply ceding to a vocal minority. We argue that academics also need to learn to compromise and accept incremental change. Ultimately, CRUNCH was never going to be as radical as first envisaged.

What is the legacy of CRUNCH going forwards?

CRUNCH Principal Investigator Professor Alessandro Melis was appointed the curator of the Italian Pavilion for the 2020 (postponed to 2021) Venice Biennale of Architecture (https://www.comunitaresilienti.com). Over 300,000 people visited the postponed Biennale, with those under 26 years accounting for 32% of visitors (Biennale di Venezia, 2021). As well as providing impact and dissemination for the CRUNCH project, this opportunity allowed us to reach as many people as possible, in particular the general public, students, and interested non-experts. Identifying how to engage politicians and the general public to appreciate the resilience benefits of the FWE nexus led Professor Melis to develop installations to entice visitors and to spark discussion, which is vital for growing public support for nexus approaches and, importantly, for upscaling – see Figure 9.1 below.

A recent development has been the role of CRUNCH in providing the underpinning research behind the *Peccioli Charter for Resilient Communities* in Italy, which provides a practical action plan to support municipal initiatives towards building resilient communities. Peccioli municipality is well known for its innovative approach to landfill and its commitment towards building sustainable communities. Elements of the project have also been adopted by the state of Campeche in Mexico for a research study which they are currently conducting.

There is a desire to continue to develop the reach and impact of nexus approaches by the CRUNCH team, taking into consideration the following reflections:

o There is a need to work more in the Global South, which is highly vulnerable to climate change and has some of the fastest growing urban areas.

Figure 9.1: Genoma FWE curatorial installation, part of the Italian Pavilion, Architecture Venice Biennale
Source: La Biennale, Venezia.

o We encourage greater sector discussion around barriers and causes of failure. We argue strongly there is immense value in not only celebrating project successes but also in highlighting failures. This may help others not to make the same mistakes.
o The CRUNCH ULLs indicate that it is often difficult to activate the full FWE nexus within a single project. Proposals may prove more effective with a willingness to make small changes; for example, it may be easier to develop projects that target food-water, or energy-water or food-energy initiatives than all three.
o For nexus project resilience, we need long-term financing, political and stakeholder commitment, and independent arbitration to help overcome the temptation to cede to a vocal minority.
o Green financing has the potential to assist with the long-term financing of projects. Project developers and funders need a clearer understanding of the full costs and benefits of making FWE nexus changes.
o There is a need to be realistic about project scales and time frames, and finally we recommend that project developers are not too radical in their designs; as the

Eindhoven case demonstrates, there is value in giving stakeholders time to get used to new initiatives, and for projects to develop.

A coda on Covid

The Covid-19 pandemic stalled some parts of the CRUNCH project (e.g. Southend-on-Sea and Gdańsk) but also provided some momentum for the green agenda; for example, widespread adoption of pedestrian zones and pop-up cycle lanes in the UK. In many regions, the growing recognition of the therapeutic value of green spaces on mental health in dense urban areas grew during lockdown (Douglas & Douglas, 2021).

An important research agenda is how the initial greening momentum can be sustained. There is a danger that this urban greening agenda is seen as a luxury: in times of crisis or when funds run out, green commitments tend to be reneged upon. In the UK, there is some optimism that the strategy of a 'green industrial revolution' or so-called 'green recovery' (Kraus, 2021), with potential for job creation, may yet see wider adoption and uptake of the agenda this research project seeks to contribute towards: making our cities resilient and healthy places to work and live in, to better meet the challenges of the future.

References

Biennale di Venezia. (2021). The Biennale Architettura 2021 closes with over 300,000 visitors. https://www.labiennale.org/en/news/biennale-architettura-2021-closes-over-300000-visitors

Douglas, K, & Douglas, J. (2021, 24 March). Green spaces aren't just for nature – they boost our mental health too. *New Scientist*. https://www.newscientist.com/article/mg24933270-800-green-spaces-arent-just-for-nature-they-boost-our-mental-health-too/

Kraus, J. (2021). Green shoots and deep roots: Towards sustainable recovery. *RICS World Build Environment Forum*. https://www.rics.org/uk/wbef/megatrends/markets-geopolitics/green-shoots-and-deep-roots-towards-sustainable-recovery/

Index

Note: Page numbers in *italics* indicate figures and page numbers in **bold** indicate tables in the text

Adamowicz, P. 93
adaptive capacity 29, 30
age-reversal techniques 153
AI-ML-GIS-BIM-Python-Green-Blue-Infraworks data-driven planning and scenario tools 17
AIA MIAMI 2020 Design Award-winning project 150, *151*
AI data-driven geospatial-BIM workflows 139; CRUNCH FWE nexus 140–141, *141*; for FWE nexus and CO_2 emissions calculation 139; general CRUNCH WP 139, *140*; open source GIS *140*; R.E.M. techniques 139, *140*; visualising energy consumption of South Miami *141*
Ali, H. 121
American Institute of Architects (AIA) 150
Andia, A. *152*, 153
application programming interface (API) 145
artificial intelligence 121, 142, 150
Attention Restoration Theory 62
Auto-Regressive Integrated Moving Averages (ARIMA) 127, 130
automated cloud-based optimisation workflows 156

Bach-Glowinska, J. 4
background map tiles 145
Balmford, A. 62
Barricelli, B. R. 160
bathtub model 143
Belmont Forum 2
BioNet 153
Biscayne Bay 153, 154
Bonn 2011 Nexus Conference 97, 99
Boshkoska, B. M. 121
Brainport Smart District (BSD) 10–11, 34, 39, 123
Brierley, G. 63
British Standards Institute (BSI) 166
Brown, J. 3
Business layer 172
Byrne, J. A. 63

carbon-positive building 148–151; carbon-neutral design studio projects 151, *152*; design scenarios 156; and resilient bio-cities 154–155
carbon circularity 34
carbon neutrality 34, 39
Casiraghi, E. 160

Index

CBD master plan 13
Centre for Digital Built Britain (CDBB) 166, *167*
Chang, Y. -S. 4
Chiueh, P. -T. 4
climate change 9, 13, 105, 114, 122–124, 129, 134, 143, 161; effects of 1; impacts in Gdańsk ULL 89–90, 92; and need for resilient neighbourhoods in Gdańsk 90–92
Climate Resilient Urban Nexus CHoices project (CRUNCH project) 2, 3, 4, 28, 67, 89, 99, 164, 181, 182, 184; Covid-19 pandemic impact in 189; Genoma FWE curatorial installation *188*; in GI project 20; IDSS 5; legacy of 187–189; Nexus demonstration project 78–79; nexus thinking for 185; principles 176; Smart City concept in Gdańsk 12; in SoS ULL 59; UIL in Gdańsk as part of 93; ULLs in 60, 65, 123
climate scenario 127, 129, 134
Climate Sensitive Urban Design 88
co-creation approaches 29–30, 32
CO_2 emissions calculation, IDSS app for 139
collaboration between CRUNCH ULLs 109–110, 164–165
community-led projects 182
Community of Practice Group 77
Co-modal Local Node 14, 88, 93
Complete Disjunctive Table (CDT) 36
Computational Fluid Dynamics (CFD) 150
Cool Towns project 4, 20, 66–68; internal green wall development 71; York Road Cool Towns plans incorporating ZMW panels *69*
cooperative interactions 29; level of openness for 39; sociability to facilitate 44
Cooper, C. 6
Coulter, C. 6

Covid-19 pandemic 81, 87, 93, 189; impacts in Gdańsk ULL 88, 92
Cronbach's alpha 37
CRUNCH Digital Twins 160–161, 172, 176
CRUNCH FWE nexus, test workflow for 140, *141*
CRUNCH Integrated Decision Support System (CRUNCH IDSS) 9, 170, 176, 182–183; Digital Twins 159, 161–163, 173–174, 177
CRUNCH Urban Living Labs (CRUNCH ULLs) 9, 20, 65, 66, 159–160, 162, 176; difficulties to activate full FWE nexus 188; interoperability between 165; models in IDSS 172; quantities of data 164; status in operationalising transdisciplinary FWE nexus 38–42; urban modelling synergy with 169
cyanobacteria 153

Dane, G. 3
Data Aggregation/Access layer 170
database: in DSS 119–120; in IDSS 122, 126–130; *see also* model base; user interface
data broker 169–172
Data Canvas Paper 175
Data Layer 171
de Vries, B. 3
decision support systems (DSS) 119; elements 119–120; for food, water, and energy 120–121; papers for describing for FWE nexus 122; *see also* integrated decision support system (IDSS)
Denver Botanical gardens 69
digital elevation model (DEM) 143
Digital Twin Data Broker 170, 171
Digital Twins 6, 159–160, 165; CRUNCH as 160–161, 172, 176; CRUNCH IDSS as 159, 161–163, 173–174, 177; definitions and types 160–161; dilemma

for 176–177; Gemini Principles 166–168; IDSS principles 163–166; maturity 172–174, *173*; missing data broker 169–172; semantic inventory 172; service improvement 174–176

Digital Urban European Twins project (DUET project) 169; high-level design for data model 172; layers of 170–172, *171*

Dynamic Linear Discriminant Analysis (D-LDA) 121

dynamic neighbourhood 65

efficient resolutions 29, 31; socio-eco-techno integration to introduce 45–46

Eindhoven Goes Greener project 73

Eindhoven ULL 2, 3, 9, 34, 87, 109, 182, 185; BSD in 10–11, 39, 123; climate projections for 128; consumption statistics in IDSS database 127, **128**; FWE nexus in 110; nexus thinking for urban planning and leadership 111, *111*; power of individuals 76–77; production statistics for IDSS database 128, **129**; project range 2–3; silos in 75; success with public participation 186; "UG by stealth" approach in 74

ELAS calculator 92

Energy and Sustainability team 60, 72, 76, 77; funded by external projects 77; Interreg projects 66, 67; at SBC 65–66, 76, 80; at SoS 72

energy balance calculation 125–126

environmental degradation 1

Evans, S. 172, *173*

"FactoMineR" package R 37

Flamingo/Lummus neighbourhood 123

Florea, A. 121

Florida Power and Lighting Company (FPL) 142

Fogli, D. 160

Food-Water-Energy nexus (FWE nexus) 1, 3, 9, 87, 97, 174, 181; actors 28; approaches in UG project designs 60; CBD Multimodal Node 13; ecological dimension of 43; economic value of data 174–175, *175*; experiment in Taipei ULL 21–23; framework development process 101–102; Gdańsk ULL 12, 14; goals *105*; governance of FWE sustainability transitions 115; IDSS app for 139; implementing recommendations and guidance 105–109, *106*; key features of path for implementing recommendations *98*; learning from cities 109–115; Miami CRUNCH ULL 17; Multimodal Node 93; needs of urbanisation in 98; project management conclusions 184–187; reasons to use urban living labs for 99–101; recommendations and guidance 105; research and expertise on 2; research and framework development 99; for self-sustainability 88; stakeholder's requirement 42; strengthening urban metabolism and resilience 2; urban FWE nexus frameworks 102–104; variations on 34; *see also* transdisciplinary FWE nexus ULLs; urban FWE nexus frameworks

food balance calculation 124–125

Fudeken Environmental Restoration Park 21

Futekeng Rehabilitation Park (FRP) 38–39

FWE Nexus Square concept 4, 93, 112; micro ULL 14, 87; networks for emergency purposes 90; pavilion 88

Gdańsk-Gdynia model 13

Gdańsk Development Plan 2016 13

Gdańsk ULL 2, 4, 5, 9, 34, 87, 109, 182, 186; climate change impacts 89–92; consumption statistics in IDSS database

Index

127–128, **128**; Covid-19 epidemic, impacts of 88, 92; data types 169; developing cross-sectoral leadership for building 112, *112*; difference in scale and objectives 2; fragile institutional capacity of 89–90; FWE Nexus Neighbourhood 13; greenfield transit-oriented neighbourhood in 123; identified risks and adaptation measures 91; neighbourhood capacity in 92; organisational capacity of 88; pavilion prototype in 87; production statistics for IDSS database 129, **129**; project range 2–3; resilient neighbourhoods in Gdańsk 90–92; responses to identified risks around food safety in 91–92; UIL in 12–14, 87, 89, 92; ULL FWE Nexus CBD Multimodal Node 13; ULL FWE Nexus Neighbourhood 13–14

Gdańsk University of Technology (GUT) 12, 92, 123

Gemini Principles 166–168, *167*, 174, 176

generative Fusion360 workflows 150

geographical information systems (GIS) 120

GeoPandas library 141, 142

Ghodsvali, M. 3

GIS-based DSS for food management 120–121

Glasgow 64; benefits and costs of UG projects 75; engaging in communication between silos 76; inappropriate staffing 77–78; power of individuals 76–77; silos in 75

Global Solar Atlas 129

Granit, J. 99

Great Wakering 19, 65

Greaves, M. 160, 162

greenfield transit-oriented neighbourhood 123

green financing 188

green industrial revolution 189

green infrastructure (GI) 61, 64; development in ULL 123; paucity of 62–63; project for climate resilience 19–20

"greening by stealth" approach 80–81

green recovery *see* green industrial revolution

ground-mounted public drinking water system 69

Habibie, M. I. 120

Heinermann, J. 121

High Performance Computing (HPC) 171

High Street project in SOS 67–68, 78

IDSS app 139; AI data-driven Geospatial-BIM workflows 139–142; API and database 145; application functionality 146–148; CRUNCH City of Miami Beach and South Miami web application 144; data and methods 142–143; using open data and free tools 141–142; serving data 145; user interface 146, *146*, *147*; vector tiles 145–146; *see also* Integrated Decision Support System (IDSS)

IFWEN project 89, 90

Infinity Loop Model 13

Information and Communication Technologies (ICT) 30; ICT-based participatory modelling methods 43; ICT-supported participatory modelling methods 46

infrastructure layer 171

Integrated Decision Support System (IDSS) 2, 4, 87, 122, 159–160; architecture diagram for web application *133*; for CRUNCH project 13, 123–124; database 122, 126–130; displaying available ULLs for analysis *130*; fixed parameters in IDSS database 126, **126**; FWE balance percentage values *132*; for FWE nexus

122, 133–134; initial user input parameters in IDSS database 126, **127**; lessons about developing 182–184; Miami ULL 17; model base 122, 124–126; principles 163–166; providing what-if scenario analysis 162; as tool for assisting decision makers and community leaders 161; user interface 122, 130–133; *see also* IDSS app
interactive computer based systems 119
International Energy Agency (IEA) 97
Internet of Things (IoT) 171
interoperability between CRUNCH ULLs 165
Interreg projects 66, 67
inundation scenarios 146
inundation tiles 145
iterative stakeholder interactions 43

Jackson, C. 161
Johns, C. M. 63
Joint Programming Initiative Urban Europe 2
Jones, D. 160
JPI Urban Europe SUGI projects 89
Juba Central Equatorial State 89
JUBA project proposal 89–90, 93
Juhász, L. 5, 145
Juujärvi, S. 100

Kaplan, R. 61–62
Kaplan, S. 61–62
Karnib, A. 100
K-J dimensional space 37
knowledge and communication 5, 101, 102, *105*
Köppen Climate Classification 16
Kramer, O. 121

land surface temperature (LST) 120
Liakos, K. G. 121
Li, C. 121
life-cycle costing 186

Lin, Y. C. 122
Lo, A. Y. 63
Local Government Association (LGA) 72
localised interventions 29; based on collaborative knowledge of society 30; knowledge co-production to characterise paradigms of 45
Logical Framework Approach (LFA) 36, 37–38, 40
Logical Framework Matrix (LFM) 38, 41, *42*
Lo, S. -L. 4, 99
Łubiński, J. 4

Ma, H. -W. 4
Mabrey, D. 100
machine learning 121, 125, 142, 156, 183
Macro ULL FWE Nexus CBD Multimodal 13
management decision systems 119
Matthews, T. 63, 76, 80
Maximum Envelope of High Water (MEOW) 143
Maximum of MEOWs (MOM) 143
Mayor, B. 100
McGrane, S. J. 100
Mean Higher High Water surface (MHHW surface) 143
means-ends relationship establishment 41
Melis, A. 187
Miami Beach ULL (MB) 2, 5, 9, 16, 34, 39, 87, 109, 114, 141; addressing risk for disaster 114; AIA MIAMI 2020 Design Award-winning project 150, *151*; consumption statistics in IDSS database 127, **128**; data-driven planning 16–17; design studio experiments with carbon-positive building 148–151; difference in scale and objectives 2; electricity consumption for 128; estimating social and economic impacts of SLR and storm surges 144; excerpt of D9 Spring

Index

2020 Design Studio *150*; excerpts of D8 Studio Design Studio Publication *149*; Flamingo/Lummus neighbourhood in 123; FWE nexus in 110; green-blue infrastructure *148*; hypothetical scenarios for Miami Beach Dynamo-BIM script *148*; IDSS CRUNCH web application 144, 146–148; IDSS serving data in 145; IDSS test workflow in 140, 141; IDSS user interface in 146, *146*, *147*; IDSS vector tiles in 145–146; modelling inundation levels 143–144; production statistics for IDSS database 129, **129**; project range 2–3; scenario tools 16–17; visualising energy consumption of *141*
Miami Dade County 141
Mocanu, M. 121
model base: in DSS 119–120; in IDSS 122, 124–126; *see also* database; user interface
Morales, M. *155*
Multiple Correspondence Analysis (MCA) 36–37, 38; discrimination measures of dimensions **55–56;** in transdisciplinary FWE nexus 4*0*

Namuduri, S. 5
National Health Service (NHS) 75
National Renewable Energy Laboratory (NREL) 142
National Taiwan University 21–23
National Weather Service (NWS) 121, 143
natural attention grabbers 62
nature-based solutions (NBS) *see* green infrastructure (GI)
Nature Smart Cities (NSCiti2S) 20, 66, 73–74
Nexus Square *see* FWE Nexus Square concept
Ngai, E. 5
Non-invasive Measurement System 14, 88
normalised difference vegetation index (NDVI) 120

Olivia Business Centre (OBC) 12, 92; ULL 38–39
Open PV Project 142
OpenStreetMap (OSM) 141, 145
operational commonality 38
outcomes as IDSS principles 166

Pandas library 141
Park Cool Islands 61
participatory modelling in nexus ULL applications 43
pavilion prototype in Gdańsk 87
Peccioli municipality 187
Personal Biosynthesiser (PB) 153
Pesso, K. 100
physarum polycephalum sequence *155*
policymakers 28, 93, 105
Polish Humanitarian Action (PAH) 89–90
Preliminary Diagnostic Module diagnostics (PDM) 88
presentation layer 172
production statistics for IDSS database 128–129, **129**
project-piggybacking 71
project strategies as LFM information item 41
Project Sunroof 142
public-private-people partnership 29
Python 141

QGIS 141

Rapid Energy Modelling techniques (R.E.M. techniques) 139, 140
recommendations and guidance for FWE-related measures 104; collaborative approach 109; considering broad missions 107; developing time frames 108; funding determination 107–108; government involvement as stakeholder 108; identifying capacity of stakeholders

108; identifying multiple scenarios 108; identifying programme leadership 107; implementation for all sectors 105, *106*, 107; organisations' involvement as stakeholders 108–109; plan development 109; shared understanding development 109; structuring programme 107
renewable energy abundant society 151–153
research and development 5, 101–102, *105*
resilient alliance 29, 30
resource scarcity 1
REST APIm 131, 172
RESTORE project 120
Romero, D. *153*
Rosendal neighbourhood 24, 123; groundwater management in 24–25; Talltorget square in Rosendal *25*
Rumble, H. 3

Salinas, S. *153*
Sea, Lake and Overland Surges from Hurricanes model (SLOSH model) 143
sea level rise (SLR) 142, 145; dynamic visualisation of 147; estimating social and economic impacts of 144
Shannak, S. d. 100
Sharma, N. 121
Sklearn library 142
Smart City Interoperability Framework 159
socio-technical system design 30, 33
Södra District ULL (SD ULL) 39
solar panel production 125, 129
Solar Renewable Energy Credit (SREC) 142
Southend-on-Sea ULLs (SoS ULLs) 2, 4, 9, 20, 34, 59, 87, 182, 185–186; benefits of installing UG in cities 81; consumption statistics in IDSS database 127, **128**; contextualising experiences of 71; current energy consumption for 128; difference in scale and objectives 2; FWE nexus in 110; GI project for climate resilience 19–20; High Street 59–60, 65; inappropriate staffing 77–78; maintenance budgets 73–74; minimising vulnerabilities 110–111, *110*; power of individuals 76–77; production statistics for IDSS database 128, **129**; project range 2–3; risk of failure 74–75; SCH ULL in 39; silos and communication 75–76; Southend High Street 123; subjective and time dependent barriers 79; sustainable funding 72–73; UG snakes and ladders 65–71; urban greening 74, 78–79; *see also* urban greening projects (UG projects)
Southend Borough Council (SBC) 19, 59, 60, 66, 72–73; Energy and Sustainability team at 76, 80; engaging in communication between silos 76; inappropriate staffing 77–78; power of individuals 76–77
Southend Central Highstreet ULL (SCH ULL) 39
South Miami, City of 16, 114, 141; city typologies 148; design studio experiments with carbon-positive building 148–150; estimating social and economic impacts of SLR and storm surges 144; green-blue infrastructure *148*; IDSS application functionality in 146–148; IDSS CRUNCH web application 144; IDSS serving data in 145; IDSS test workflow in 140, *141*; IDSS user interface in 146, *146*, *147*; IDSS vector tiles in 145–146; modelling inundation levels 143–144; visualising energy consumption of *141*
Spiegelhalter, T. 5, 150, *151*, *152*
SPONGE2020, 20, 66
Sponge project 67

Index

Sprague Jr, R. H. 119
State of Environment and Outlook Report 89
Stringer, L. 99
SUNRISE project 65, 66, 67
Suntaranont, B. 121
Suryawanshi, A. 5
Sustainable Drainage Systems (SuDS) 61
Sustainable Urbanisation Global Initiative (SUGI) 2, 89, 185
Synthetic Biology (SynBio) 151–153, 154; BioNet 153; carbon-positive and resilient bio-cities 154–155; Personal Biosynthesiser 153; technology *vs.* fiction 155

Taipei ULL 2, 4, 9, 34, 87, 110; balancing natural resources *114*, 115; consumption statistics in IDSS database 127–128, **128**; difference in scale and objectives 2; energy production for 129, 130; energy sensor in 169; FWE nexus in 110; power of local government in 38; production statistics for IDSS database 128, **129**; project range 2–3; sustainable management for wastescapes 21–23; Taipei Fudeken urban farming development 123, 182; water consumption for 127
testing and implementation 5, 101, 102, *105*
Thirsty energy 97
tidal datums 142
Tobolewicz, J. 4
Tombolo digital Connector 169–170
Tomey, A. 150, *151*
transdisciplinary FWE nexus ULLs 29; actors and users participation 32; adaptive capacity 29, 30; assessment framework for defining characteristics *33*, 33–34; case selection and research methods 34, *35*; co-creation approaches 29–30; cooperative interactions 29; data analysis 36–38; data collection 35–36; defining operational characteristics of 38–40; efficient resolution 29, 31; governance structure 30, 32–33; ICT infrastructure 30–31; key peculiarities 29; knowledge requirements for implementing 42–46; likelihood of advancing implementation 40–42; localised interventions 29, 30; operational components for employing 31; problem trees of *57*; resilient alliance 29, 30; social-ecological-technological integration 46; socio-technical system design 30, 33; *see also* Food-Water-Energy nexus (FWE nexus)
Tripathi, S. S. 5
TRIPS project 66–68
Trowsdale, W. 63
Tung, H. -H. 4

"UG by stealth" approach 74, 78
UK National Productivity Infrastructure Fund 66
Ulrich, R. S. 62
University of East London 78
Uppsala Rosendal housing development 182
Uppsala ULL 2, 9, 24, 34, 109; consumption statistics in IDSS database 127–128, **128**; CRUNCH IDSS 5; difference in scale and objectives 2; enhancing nexus through community-led actions 113, *113*; FWE nexus in 110; production statistics for IDSS database 128, **129**; project range 2–3; Rosendal neighbourhood in 24–25, 123; SD ULL in 39
Uppsala University 24
urban FWE nexus frameworks 102; collective collaboration and co-production 103; comprehensive scale

and boundary 102–103; diverse sector participation 104; effective leadership and resources invested 103; empowered stakeholder involvement 103; identified issues and scenarios 103; increased shared understanding 104; integrated action plan and governance approach 104; sustainable technical innovations 103
urban green-blue buildings and infrastructures 156
urban greenery 59, 61
urban greening projects (UG projects): ameliorating impact of 60; barriers to 62–64; benefits city dwellers 62; FWE nexus approaches in 60; "greening by stealth" approach 80–81; installing urban greenery 61–62; Lyon's Rue Garibaldi 61; methods 64; UG nexus and sustainability agenda 79–80; *see also* Southend-on-Sea ULLs (SoS ULLs)
urban heat island (UHI) 61
Urban Initiative Laboratory (UIL) 12–14, 87, 89, 92, 93
urbanisation 1, 27, 98
Urban Living Labs (ULLs) 2, 4–5, 28, 59, 87, 100, 101, 123, 150, 159, 167, 181, 184; capacity of ULL formula 93; CRUNCH 9; development mechanism of 32; governance flexibility/durability 93; identifying connections with other projects and policies 93; Nexus Square 4; online survey questions **52–55**; operational weakness in implementation 28
user interface: in DSS 119–120; in IDSS 122, 130–133; sidebar with sliders *131; see also* database; model base
users participation in nexus ULL's activities 32

van Zoest, V. 5
Vickers, J. 160
Vision 2050, 59
Vittorio, M. 100
Voyant, C. 121
Voytenko, Y. 100
Vs' of data (velocity, volume, veracity, variety, and variability) 169

wastescapes 21
water-, sanitation-, and hygiene-related diseases (WASH-related diseases) 89
water balance calculation 125
Water security: The water-food-energy-climate security nexus 97
Wdowinski, S. 142
WebGL technology 148
what-if scenario analysis 162
wireless sensor network (WSN) 121
work deliverables (WP) *140*
World Economic Forum 97
World Energy Outlook 2012 97
World water development report 97

York Road ZMW self-watering 73
Yu, C. -P. 4
Yuan, K. -Y. 99
Yuan, M. -H. 4, 99

Zambelli, P. 120
Zero Mass Water technology (ZMW technology) 4, 68, *69*, 79; Groundworks at York Road site *70*; to High Street area 68, 70; installation at pier and York Road 70, 71; on peripheries of town 81; York Road Cool Towns plans incorporating *69*, 70–71
Zhang, K. 143

For Product Safety Concerns and Information please contact our EU representative GPSR@taylorandfrancis.com
Taylor & Francis Verlag GmbH, Kaufingerstraße 24, 80331 München, Germany

www.ingramcontent.com/pod-product-compliance
Lightning Source LLC
Chambersburg PA
CBHW081556300426
44116CB00015B/2900